THE NEW MIDDLE AGES

BONNIE WHEELER, *Series Editor*

The New Middle Ages is a series dedicated to transdisciplinary studies of medieval cultures, with particular emphasis on recuperating women's history and on feminist and gender analyses. This peer-reviewed series includes both scholarly monographs and essay collections.

PUBLISHED BY PALGRAVE:

Women in the Medieval Islamic World: Power, Patronage, and Piety
  edited by Gavin R. G. Hambly

The Ethics of Nature in the Middle Ages: On Boccaccio's Poetaphysics
  by Gregory B. Stone

Presence and Presentation: Women in the Chinese Literati Tradition
  by Sherry J. Mou

The Lost Love Letters of Heloise and Abelard: Perceptions of Dialogue in Twelfth-Century France
  by Constant J. Mews

Understanding Scholastic Thought with Foucault
  by Philipp W. Rosemann

For Her Good Estate: The Life of Elizabeth de Burgh
  by Frances A. Underhill

Constructions of Widowhood and Virginity in the Middle Ages
  edited by Cindy L. Carlson and Angela Jane Weisl

Motherhood and Mothering in Anglo-Saxon England
  by Mary Dockray-Miller

Listening to Heloise: The Voice of a Twelfth-Century Woman
  edited by Bonnie Wheeler

The Postcolonial Middle Ages
  edited by Jeffrey Jerome Cohen

Chaucer's Pardoner and Gender Theory: Bodies of Discourse
  by Robert S. Sturges

Crossing the Bridge: Comparative Essays on Medieval European and Heian Japanese Women Writers
  edited by Barbara Stevenson and Cynthia Ho

Engaging Words: The Culture of Reading in the Later Middle Ages
  by Laurel Amtower

Robes and Honor: The Medieval World of Investiture
  edited by Stewart Gordon

Representing Rape in Medieval and Early Modern Literature
  edited by Elizabeth Robertson and Christine M. Rose

Same Sex Love and Desire among Women in the Middle Ages
  edited by Francesca Canadé Sautman and Pamela Sheingorn

Sight and Embodiment in the Middle Ages: Ocular Desires
  by Suzannah Biernoff

Listen, Daughter: The Speculum Virginum *and the Formation of Religious Women in the Middle Ages*
  edited by Constant J. Mews

Science, the Singular, and the Question of Theology
  by Richard A. Lee, Jr.

Gender in Debate from the Early Middle Ages to the Renaissance
  edited by Thelma S. Fenster and Clare A. Lees

Malory's *Morte D'Arthur: Remaking Arthurian Tradition*
  by Catherine Batt

The Vernacular Spirit: Essays on Medieval Religious Literature
  edited by Renate Blumenfeld-Kosinski, Duncan Robertson, and Nancy Warren

Popular Piety and Art in the Late Middle Ages: Image Worship and Idolatry in England 1350–1500
  by Kathleen Kamerick

Absent Narratives, Manuscript Textuality, and Literary Structure in Late Medieval England
  by Elizabeth Scala

Creating Community with Food and Drink in Merovingian Gaul
  by Bonnie Effros

Representations of Early Byzantine Empresses: Image and Empire
  by Anne McClanan

Encountering Medieval Textiles and Dress: Objects, Texts, Images
  edited by Désirée G. Koslin and Janet Snyder

Eleanor of Aquitaine: Lord and Lady
  edited by Bonnie Wheeler and John Carmi Parsons

Isabel La Católica, Queen of Castile: Critical Essays
  edited by David A. Boruchoff

Homoeroticism and Chivalry: Discourses of Male Same-Sex Desire in the Fourteenth Century
  by Richard E. Zeikowitz

Portraits of Medieval Women: Family, Marriage, and Politics in England 1225–1350
  by Linda E. Mitchell

Eloquent Virgins: From Thecla to Joan of Arc
  by Maud Burnett McInerney

The Persistence of Medievalism: Narrative Adventures in Contemporary Culture
  by Angela Jane Weisl

Capetian Women
  edited by Kathleen D. Nolan

Joan of Arc and Spirituality
  edited by Ann W. Astell and Bonnie Wheeler

The Texture of Society: Medieval Women in the Southern Low Countries
  edited by Ellen E. Kittell and Mary A. Suydam

Charlemagne's Mustache: And Other Cultural Clusters of a Dark Age
  by Paul Edward Dutton

Troubled Vision: Gender, Sexuality, and Sight in Medieval Text and Image
  edited by Emma Campbell and Robert Mills

Queering Medieval Genres
  by Tison Pugh

Sacred Place in Early Medieval Neoplatonism
  by L. Michael Harrington

The Middle Ages at Work
  edited by Kellie Robertson and Michael Uebel

Chaucer's Jobs
  by David R. Carlson

Medievalism and Orientalism: Three Essays on Literature, Architecture and Cultural Identity
  by John M. Ganim

Queer Love in the Middle Ages
  by Anna Klosowska

Performing Women in the Middle Ages: Sex, Gender, and the Iberian Lyric
  by Denise K. Filios

Necessary Conjunctions: The Social Self in Medieval England
  by David Gary Shaw

Visual Culture and the German Middle Ages
  edited by Kathryn Starkey and Horst Wenzel

Medieval Paradigms: Essays in Honor of Jeremy duQuesnay Adams, Volumes 1 and 2
    edited by Stephanie Hayes-Healy

False Fables and Exemplary Truth in Later Middle English Literature
    by Elizabeth Allen

Ecstatic Transformation: On the Uses of Alterity in the Middle Ages
    by Michael Uebel

Sacred and Secular in Medieval and Early Modern Cultures: New Essays
    edited by Lawrence Besserman

Tolkien's Modern Middle Ages
    edited by Jane Chance and Alfred K. Siewers

Representing Righteous Heathens in Late Medieval England
    by Frank Grady

Byzantine Dress: Representations of Secular Dress in Eighth-to-Twelfth Century Painting
    by Jennifer L. Ball

The Laborer's Two Bodies: Labor and the "Work" of the Text in Medieval Britain, 1350–1500
    by Kellie Robertson

The Dogaressa of Venice, 1250–1500: Wife and Icon
    by Holly S. Hurlburt

Logic, Theology, and Poetry in Boethius, Abelard, and Alan of Lille: Words in the Absence of Things
    by Eileen C. Sweeney

The Theology of Work: Peter Damian and the Medieval Religious Renewal Movement
    by Patricia Ranft

On the Purification of Women: Churching in Northern France, 1100–1500
    by Paula M. Rieder

Writers of the Reign of Henry II: Twelve Essays
    edited by Ruth Kennedy and Simon Meecham-Jones

Lonesome Words: The Vocal Poetics of the Old English Lament and the African-American Blues Song
    by M.G. McGeachy

Performing Piety: Musical Culture in Medieval English Nunneries
    by Anne Bagnell Yardley

The Flight from Desire: Augustine and Ovid to Chaucer
    by Robert R. Edwards

Mindful Spirit in Late Medieval Literature: Essays in Honor of Elizabeth D. Kirk
    edited by Bonnie Wheeler

Medieval Fabrications: Dress, Textiles, Clothwork, and Other Cultural Imaginings
    edited by E. Jane Burns

Was the Bayeux Tapestry Made in France?: The Case for St. Florent of Saumur
    by George Beech

Women, Power, and Religious Patronage in the Middle Ages
    by Erin L. Jordan

Hybridity, Identity, and Monstrosity in Medieval Britain: On Difficult Middles
    by Jeremy Jerome Cohen

Medieval Go-betweens and Chaucer's Pandarus
    by Gretchen Mieszkowski

The Surgeon in Medieval English Literature
    by Jeremy J. Citrome

Temporal Circumstances: Form and History in the Canterbury Tales
    by Lee Patterson

Erotic Discourse and Early English Religious Writing
    by Lara Farina

Odd Bodies and Visible Ends in Medieval Literature
    by Sachi Shimomura

On Farting: Language and Laughter in the Middle Ages
    by Valerie Allen

Women and Medieval Epic: Gender, Genre, and the Limits of Epic Masculinity
    edited by Sara S. Poor and Jana K. Schulman

Race, Class, and Gender in "Medieval" Cinema
    edited by Lynn T. Ramey and Tison Pugh

Allegory and Sexual Ethics in the High Middle Ages
   by Noah D. Guynn

England and Iberia in the Middle Ages, 12th-15th Century: Cultural, Literary, and Political Exchanges
   edited by María Bullón-Fernández

The Medieval Chastity Belt: A Myth-Making Process
   by Albrecht Classen

Claustrophilia: The Erotics of Enclosure in Medieval Literature
   by Cary Howie

Cannibalism in High Medieval English Literature
   by Heather Blurton

The Drama of Masculinity and Medieval English Guild Culture
   by Christina M. Fitzgerald

Chaucer's Visions of Manhood
   by Holly A. Crocker

The Literary Subversions of Medieval Women
   by Jane Chance

Manmade Marvels in Medieval Culture and Literature
   by Scott Lightsey

American Chaucers
   by Candace Barrington

Representing Others in Medieval Iberian Literature
   Michelle M. Hamilton

REPRESENTING OTHERS IN MEDIEVAL IBERIAN LITERATURE

Michelle M. Hamilton

REPRESENTING OTHERS IN MEDIEVAL IBERIAN LITERATURE
Copyright © Michelle M. Hamilton, 2007.

All rights reserved. No part of this book may be used or reproduced in any manner whatsoever without written permission except in the case of brief quotations embodied in critical articles or reviews.

First published in 2007 by
PALGRAVE MACMILLAN™
175 Fifth Avenue, New York, N.Y. 10010 and
Houndmills, Basingstoke, Hampshire, England RG21 6XS
Companies and representatives throughout the world.

PALGRAVE MACMILLAN is the global academic imprint of the Palgrave Macmillan division of St. Martin's Press, LLC and of Palgrave Macmillan Ltd. Macmillan® is a registered trademark in the United States, United Kingdom and other countries. Palgrave is a registered trademark in the European Union and other countries.

ISBN-13: 978–1–4039–7984–1
ISBN-10: 1–4039–7984–7

Library of Congress Cataloging-in-Publication Data

Hamilton, Michelle M., 1969–
   Representing others in Medieval Iberian literature / Michelle M. Hamilton.
     p. cm.
   Includes bibliographical references and index.
   ISBN 1–4039–7984–7 (alk. paper)
    1. Spanish literature—To 1500—History and criticism.
  2. Go-betweens in literature. 3. Andalusia (Spain)—Intellectual life. I. Title.

PQ6060.H36 2007
860.9′3538—dc22
                                                                      2007001263

A catalogue record for this book is available from the British Library.

Design by Newgen Imaging Systems (P) Ltd., Chennai, India.

First edition: November 2007

10 9 8 7 6 5 4 3 2 1

Printed in the United States of America.

To my mother,
who gave me the strength and curiosity to explore and enjoy life

CONTENTS

Acknowledgments	xi
Introduction: Representing Others in Medieval Iberia	1
1 Palaces of Memory: Mediation, Court Culture, and the Caliphate	15
2 "Many a Zayd and 'Amr": Mediation and Representation in al-Andalus	33
3 Translating Desire: The Violence of Memory in the Judeo-Iberian *maqāmāt*	47
4 Turning Tricks: The Go-Between in Western Europe	89
5 Representing Others in the *Libro de buen amor*	103
Conclusion	147
Notes	149
Bibliography	191
Index	209

ACKNOWLEDGMENTS

Special thanks to family and friends for their patience and time. Also thanks to my colleagues and mentors, Samuel G. Armistead, James T. Monroe, Charles Faulhaber, David Wacks, Sarah Portnoy, Racheli Morris, Elizabeth Allen, Michael Gerli and to the other members of the *Libro de buen amor* working group who read versions or patiently sat through various oral manifestations of this work—often adding invaluable commentary and criticism. Debbie Cordova and others allowed me the time to get this done, although their work, like that of the go-between, remains on the margins and yet holds the whole courtly world together. I would also like to thank the students who participated and contributed to the graduate seminars in which key portions of this study were developed—including on more than one occasion, Tiffany Shinbach. Clinton Armstrong's help with medieval Latin and discussions on Classical culture and literature as well as Church traditions led to unexpected discoveries in the later stages of the study's development. I would also like to acknowledge the support of the Dean of Humanities at the University of California, Irvine, for time off in the form of a sabbatical and a Faculty Career Development Award. I also received funding for this project from the Humanities Center at UCI. I would also like to acknowledge the National Endowment of the Humanities, who sponsored a Summer Seminar on the *Libro de buen amor* in 2003, during which important parts of this work were conceived. Any views, findings, conclusions, or recommendations expressed in this book do not necessarily reflect those of the National Endowment for the Humanities. Thanks also to the University of California Humanities Research Institute for support in the form of a Residential Fellowship. Additional thanks go to the Department of Spanish and Portuguese at the University of California, Berkeley, and to the Graduate Division of the University of California, Berkeley, for dissertation fellowships.

INTRODUCTION: REPRESENTING OTHERS IN MEDIEVAL IBERIA

In a series of narratives produced between the eleventh and fourteenth centuries, the Iberian go-between leaves the Arab court of Cordoba to negotiate the in-between—the hybrid cultural spaces that define medieval Iberia.[1] In *Representing Others*, we witness this go-between as she not only brings lovers together, but also unites the exiled Andalusi authors that created her with the lost courtly world of al-Andalus. The go-between narrative of courtly seduction proved particularly appealing in medieval Iberia, where complex cultural, linguistic, and religious boundaries and constructions were in constant transformation, as historical and social events during the eleventh through the fourteenth centuries brought about a succession of significant changes in political power. The go-between was especially apt at moments of such change as she was the definition of instability itself. Like the exiled courtiers of Iberia, the go-between was always in motion, in a constant process of transformation, and as such she was the perfect vehicle for representing and redefining the changing boundaries of Iberian identity. The go-between's activities in the in-between space of Iberian fiction (between lover and beloved and between Andalusi past and future) become the subject of Iberian narratives of courtly desire.[2]

In *Representing Others* I examine how not only the go-between, but also the narratives within which she moves, represent and are representative of Iberian others. The figure and her narratives underscore the nature of the other as an inhabitant of the in-between, exposing the indeterminacy of the medial, the hybrid, as a source of anxiety. The Iberian go-between and her tales not only embody and portray religious, ethnic, and linguistic others, but, from the vantage point of the contemporary Western literary/cultural critic, they are themselves intermediary others—being products of that "other" time (the Middle Ages, that medial space between the ancient and modern: the temporal other of the modern period into which contemporary thinkers, politicians, and pundits are fond of placing all that is evil, dark, and barbarous), that "other" space (the Iberian Peninsula, geographical bridge between Europe and Africa and not clearly belonging to either) as well as those "other" peoples (medieval Iberians who inhabited the in-between spaces in which different social, linguistic, ethnic, and cultural groups intermingle).[3]

In order to explore the "in-between" spaces of medieval Iberian literature, we must first reorient ourselves. This book requires us to reconsider what/who has become the Other in a post-Said, post-9/11 world—the Arab—as the center, the point of reference according to which the authors of these narratives define themselves and others. In the Iberian go-between tales that I examine in *Representing Others*, the Arab-Andalusi is the center, the ideal but often conflicted home that these displaced Iberian authors recreate in their fiction.

My analysis in *Representing Others* is informed by Homi Bhabha's concepts of hybridity and difference and Edward Said's theories on exile and narrative and explores how the former complement Jaques Lacan, Felix Guattari, and Gilles Deleuze's theories on desire and Mary Russo's reading of the female grotesque. Such a selection of contemporary postcolonial and psychoanalytic theorists is particularly suited to analysis of medieval Iberian culture, which for so long has been left out not only out of discussions of Empire that privilege the modern, but also out of much of North American and European Medieval Studies, whose cultural and discursive models (constructed by eighteenth-, nineteenth-, and twentieth-century medievalists for the study of English and French medieval history and cultural production) are ill-suited to medieval Iberia. Spain is different, and medieval Iberia, too, is different in important ways from much of medieval Western Europe. Far from arguing that medieval Iberia is a postcolonial space *avant la lettre*, the complex social, cultural, and linguistic exchange and conflict that characterizes various groups on the Peninsula between the eleventh and fourteenth centuries can be productively analyzed using contemporary theories on exile, culture, and desire, with the caveat that such theories must be decentered, that is, extricated from the specificity of the modern (post)colonial situation.

It is in eleventh-century Cordoba that the go-between emerges in Andalusi courtly discourse as a uniquely Iberian subject. Ibn Hazm, an exile from the last of the Umayyad caliphal courts that some hundred years earlier had been described as the "ornament of the world," includes the old women he remembers from his youth roaming the streets of Cordoba as the ideal go-betweens of the courtly world.[4] In a succession of Iberian go-between tales these old women will repeatedly be evoked and transformed in the memories of Iberian exiles as the catalyst for and means of accessing the refined world of the lost Andalusi court. This court of memory is also perpetuated in Arabic and Hebrew erotic poetry composed by and lovingly memorized, recited, and elevated to the status of cultural icon by Andalusi exiles forced from the geographical, historical, and cultural spaces where such poetry and the go-betweens who trafficked in it had functioned.

The Iberian authors whose go-between narratives I examine in the following pages, Muhammad al-Saraqustī, Judah al-Harīzī, Judah ibn Shabbetai, and Juan Ruiz, are cosmopolitan intellectuals who share an Andalusi formation/ training, and who find themselves displaced from the courts, the centers of power and culture. These authors use the Andalusi go-between narrative to reinvent themselves in exile. For them the Other is what today we would describe as European; namely the Ashkenazi and Franco-Christian cultures from north of the Pyrenees. These go-between narratives offer us alternative constructions of what it means to be Western at a time when chroniclers across the Pyrenees such as Petrus Tudebodus and Raymond d'Aguilers were beginning to construct the Orient as Other.[5] In his seminal work on the origins of the West's construction of the Orient, *Orientalism*, Said conveniently remains silent on the topic of medieval Iberia—this space that is both "West" and "Orient." He jumps from the eleventh-century French *Chanson de Roland* to fifteenth-century papal activity to argue that the seeds of Orientalism lie in the European Middle Ages, failing to address the complexity of medieval Iberian culture and society, in which hybrid cultural identities dominate and no facile statements about East and West, Arab and Christian can hold.[6]

The centuries during which the go-between tales I examine were produced, the eleventh through the fourteenth, and the very centuries Said elides, are witness to a variety of social and political changes on the Iberian Peninsula (as discussed in detail in the chapters that follow) that result in a shift from an Islamic dominated Arabic-speaking culture to a Christian one whose dominant languages became the Romance dialects of the Peninsula. Despite the dramatic advancements and reversals that unequivocally alter Iberian culture and produce a fourteenth-century Christian Castilian culture that would have been in many ways unrecognizable and incomprehensible to the Peninsula's eleventh-century inhabitants, the go-between narrative continues to be used by learned Iberians to address issues of identity. The continued use and transformation of the go-between narrative in Iberian letters, although not teleological (there is no development from a primitive to a more developed narrative), is testimony to the tale's ability to interrogate the relationship between power and desire. By contextualizing the go-between narrative within specific moments of Iberian history and by showing how different the social, political, and cultural contingencies were in each case, *Representing Others* problematizes modern readings of medieval Iberia and al-Andalus as a flat, unchanging site of harmonious coexistence between the three religious groups of the Peninsula, Muslims,

Christians, and Jews, pointing instead to a more nuanced approach to specific moments and cultures of the eleventh-, twelfth-, thirteenth-, and fourteenth-century Iberian Peninsula.

Al-Andalus and Its Courts

The arrival of the Muslims in the eighth century, most of whom were, at least initially, ethnically Berber, further increased the complexity of the religious, linguistic, and cultural landscape of the Iberian Peninsula, which had, since the time of the Phoenicians, been a geographical site of contact for a variety of cultures, including Greek, Celtic, Basque, Phoenician, Roman, and Germanic.[7] The term al-Andalus was originally used by medieval Arab historians to designate the Iberian Peninsula under the Goths/Vandals and is generally used by contemporary scholars to designate "that part of the Iberian Peninsula in Muslim hands."[8] Al-Andalus looms large in contemporary approaches to Iberian history and culture that tend to focus either on the harmonious coexistence or the conflictive nature of relations between the three major religious groups—Muslim, Christian, and Jew—on the Iberian Peninsula before the Reconquest, the military advance of Hispano-Roman Christians south into Andalusi territories that took place over a period of several hundred years from the tenth to the fifteenth centuries. Such approaches often oversimplify a complex situation marked by periods of both cultural exchange and bitter, sometimes deadly intolerance.[9] The use of the term al-Andalus among contemporary scholars creates an artificial break between Muslim al-Andalus and medieval Iberia, implying not only religious and cultural difference, but also historical and geographical displacement and incongruity. But al-Andalus is Iberia and Andalusis are Iberians. Modern constructions of al-Andalus and medieval Spain stress rupture and marginality, be it religious (al-Andalus is Muslim, Spain is Christian), linguistic (al-Andalus is Arabic-speaking, Spain is Romance-speaking), or cultural (al-Andalus is Other, Spain is European).[10] This study, however, problematizes not only the modern constructions or classifications of medieval Iberians, but also examines how medieval Iberians themselves were wrangling with the complexity of self-definition across, and sometimes against, their own internal linguistic, sociocultural and religious definitions and models of identity.

Although there were, undoubtedly, ideological differences among Muslims, Christians, and Jews in medieval Iberia, there were sometimes equally strong linguistic, philosophic, and cultural differences between factions within these groups as well. Cultural and social division present in the Baghdadi courts of the Umayyad and 'Abbasid Empires (divisions between Syrian, Yemenite, and the Baghdadi Arabs, between Persians, Arabs, and

Jews, and between factions of Muslim religious-philosophical sects) made its way to the Iberian Peninsula, where it complicated existing ethnic and cultural divisions such as those between rival groups of North African Berbers, *muwalladūn* (Muslim Iberians of Hispano-Roman families that converted), more recently arrived Eastern Arabs, Muslims of Slavic origin, Frankish and Basque captives from the northern Peninsula and northern Europe, and Hispano-Roman and Arabized Jews.[11]

In this book I use the term al-Andalus not just as a religio-political term used to distinguish Muslim from Christian Iberia or as a geographical term to identify a specific area of the Iberian Peninsula. I use the term to designate the complex geographical, socioreligious, cultural space in which Iberian intellectuals were formed and in turn within which they helped to create a cosmopolitan identity that cuts across many of the linguistic, religious, and ethnic boundaries that characterized medieval Iberian society. Though parts of the geographical or political al-Andalus fell into Christian hands during some four hundred years of conquest, it continued to live on as an imaginary ideal for several centuries among Andalusi exiles.[12]

Andalusi court culture is defined by a system of values and behaviors ideally enacted between the lover and the beloved. Literature plays a central role in the production of meaning within the Andalusi courts and within Andalusi models of courtly desire, which generated much of that court culture. Poetry is the most important of courtly discourses and the one used to channel desire and codify power in the courtly setting. According to this code, the courtier, like the sovereign, is represented as an ideal lover of refined literary and sentimental tastes.[13] This courtly model of the ideal individual, designated variously as *kātib, zarīf, nadīm*, or *adīb*, is essentially a secular, cosmopolitan one based on the concept of *adab*, the Arab concept of social, cultural, and academic wisdom.[14] The ideal courtier is not just well read in a variety of subjects, including poetry, philosophy, the natural sciences, and theology, he is a poet, a man of impeccable manners, a social wit, and a refined lover. He should also be an expert of rhetoric, possessor of excellent penmanship, knowledgeable in the art of hunting, gambling, and chess, as well as stylish and well groomed.[15] The ambassador of this code of courtly knowledge and behavior, the Persian poet Ziryāb, who came to al-Andalus from the 'Abbasid court of Baghdad in 941 A.D., became the favorite of the Umayyad caliph 'Abd al-Rahman II (822–852) because of the former's mastery of the latest poetic trends in Baghdad. Just as Ziryāb's skill at composing poetry gained him entrée into the Andalusi court, several generations of Andalusi courtiers would also include among their ranks the best of Andalusi poets, including Ibn Zaidūn, Ibn 'Abd Rabbihi, Ibn Darrāj, Ibn Hazm, and Ibn Shuhaid.[16]

An excellent knowledge of Arabic language and poetry was the foundation upon which most of the other aspects of the refined courtly character was built and served as the social glue for the Andalusi court. It was a *lingua franca* for the individual courtiers who came from the many different social, ethnic, religious, and linguistic groups of the Peninsula and became the language of literature among Iberian intellectuals. Non-Arab courtiers such as Moses ibn Ezra, Bahyā ibn Paqūdā, and al-Harīzī composed works in both Arabic and Hebrew, and other Jewish intellectual luminaries such as Maimonides composed many of their works in Arabic.[17] Various *taifa* kings of Berber and Slavic origins maintained courts where the virtues of Arabs were attacked using refined learned Arabic and the conceits of Arabic poetry.[18] Ibn García, a courtier for the Slavic kings of the *taifa* kingdom of Denia, Mujāhid and his son ʿAlī, extols the virtues of the indigenous inhabitants of the Peninsula as being the descendents of civilized Romans and attacks Arabs as base camel herders in an eloquent Arabic that would have allowed him entry into any Arab court from the Maghrib to Baghdad.[19] Members of the different ethnic, linguistic, and religious groups of the Peninsula such as Moses ibn Ezra and Ibn García, had access to Andalusi courts according to their mastery of Arabic, Arabic poetry, and the customs of *adab* (as privileged in that same poetry). These were the basis for a shared courtly identity and for the courtly discourse that these courtiers used to frame their own alternative models of identity. As the works I examine in the subsequent chapters show, the adoption of the Andalusi courtly ideal was not unproblematic, and the tensions between the courtly model and alternative or conflicting models and boundaries defined by the courtier's other communal, ethnic, religious, and/or linguistic identities sometimes results in renunciation of the Andalusi courtly ideal (see especially chapters 3 and 4).[20] Yet, according to different social and political circumstances, the Andalusi courtly model could also offer an attractive alternative to competing, less refined, less cosmopolitan definitions of community for the Andalusi intellectual in exile.

The authors of the works studied in this book recognize the power of both courtier and go-between as negotiators and mediators, and as links to an Andalusi culture that becomes increasingly distant in both space and time. Secular Andalusi courts disappeared after successive attacks by both the religious and socially conservative Berbers of North Africa and by the Latinate Christians of northern Iberia. As the Andalusi courts disappeared, the model of the Andalusi courtier also begins to fade, although managing to survive for some time more in the imaginary of Andalusi exiles. The narratives studied in this book, in fact, trace the disappearance of the imagined court and courtier over the course of some four hundred years. Appropriately enough, the final work examined in *Representing Others*, the *Libro de buen amor (Book of Good Love)* concludes with a eulogy. The passing of the go-between, who is praised by Juan Ruiz as the sacred companion to martyrs, is symbolic of the passing of the Andalusi courtier and the world/culture he both produced and represented.

Going Between

The go-between, like the courtiers and intellectuals who composed the texts studied in this book, gets around. She is portrayed in constant movement. In Ibn Hazm's treatise (chapter 1) she goes from house to house and in al-Saraqustī's *maqāmāt* (chapter 2) she races through an urban landscape—from public baths to private homes; in al-Harīzī and Ibn Shabbetai's Hebrew *maqāmāt* (chapter 3) she travels between hell and earth. Juan Ruiz (chapter 5) not only has her trotting between convent and monastery, frequenting the public areas as well as private homes, but also locates her in paradise with the sainted martyrs. The go-between's constant motion, moving in the liminal, in-between space of the street, the underworld, or heaven, resembles the migrations of the exiled courtiers that incorporate her into their fiction: some of them exiled from the court and their community (Ibn Hazm, Ibn Shabbetai, and possibly Juan Ruiz), others wandering in self-imposed exile (al-Saraqustī, al-Harīzī). The go-between shows how those displaced from, but with access to positions of power can manipulate the margin—the liminal, in-between spaces of exile, to create power.

The go-between's constant movement is destabilizing. And it is this very motion or action that defines her. She is defined not by what she is, a poor, ugly, old woman, but by her actions, her mediation. The Andalusi courtier and the Christian cleric are similarly defined by what they do, by their acts of mediation: the courtier mediates between sovereign and people and between sovereign and text as both translator and author, as the cleric mediates not only between God and sinner, but also between people and knowledge as translator and author.[21] As courtier or cleric, the Iberian is not, or is only secondarily, Berber, Jew, Mozarab (Arabized Christian), or Toledano—he is defined not by his ethnicity, religious, or geographical origin, but instead by what he knows, how he expresses himself, and his role as mediator.[22] This too is the role of the go-between in the courtly erotic that brings lover and beloved together by negotiating in the texts and discourses of courtly desire. Yet she is supposed to remain outside of this desire. She may visit the houses of the nobles and compose courtly poetry, but she is not noble or courtly. She may unite men and women, lover and beloved, but she is neither, being too old, too ugly, and too base to be a desiring subject. Her very inability to be fixed or bounded defines her. Similarly the courtiers and intellectuals composing these works destabilize any attempts at defining a fixed Andalusi or Iberian identity. It is not enough to say that al-Ḥarīzī is a Jew or Juan Ruiz is a Christian cleric; they are these things, but they are also Sephardi and Castilian, Andalusi and Iberian.

The go-between, like the cosmopolitan courtier, smoothes over differences and successfully crosses linguistic, religious, cultural, and even temporal borders. She shows that borders and limits, especially those constructed to curtail her activities such as the convent walls, moral-didactic lessons, and the individual's moral rectitude are artificial, porous, and constantly shifting. It is precisely this ability to "pass" and to transform that arouses not just admiration as is the case within the works of Ibn Ḥazm and Juan Ruiz, but also suspicion and fear as in the works of al-Ḥarīzī, Ibn Shabbetai, and the pseudo-Ovid. As mentioned, the space of the go-between corresponds in many ways to the in-between as defined by Homi Bhabha as that marginal, hybrid space between nations, peoples, and empires. The in-between spaces of the go-between are the exilic and frontier spaces of Iberia. Once exiled from the court, the courtiers and clerics trained in the courtly model reimagine the court from which they have been displaced as an idealized site of intellectual and sensual pleasures as well as of potentially threatening cultural assimilation. These go-between narratives are the products of these liminal spaces. In them their authors define new rules for the courtly subject as well as modify and alter the discursive strategies of the now lost court to better suit their own exilic needs, that is, to better represent their own models of diasporic or exilic identity. Part of this transformation or hybridization is the othering of the court. This is achieved by transforming the beloved, the courtly object of desire, into the monstrous other. Once the beloved is corrupted, courtly desire, the glue that held the Andalusi court together, has been effectively rendered as other as well.

In these works the go-between not only brings diverse subjects together, she also mediates between the lover and his desire. Desire becomes the nexus of this construction of courtly power. In each of the narratives we witness the go-between's manipulation of the courtier/cleric's desire for the courtly ideal, the beloved described by and brokered through the go-between. The beloved, the object of desire in these texts, is not an individual, desiring subject, but a socially constructed fantasy. She is defined by and her body constructed in the poetry of the court. Once displaced from the courts in which beauty and knowledge were both created and trafficked as the discourse of power, the Andalusi courtly discourse unravels. As a result, the beloved's beautiful features become monstrous, refusing "to respect the boundaries that are supposed to limit their form."[23] The discursive construction of the stable, idealized beauty used to seduce the author-cum-narrator belies the monstrously ambiguous, the "unhomely" that lies at the heart of courtly discourse and represents all that is suppressed in the monoculture of the court.[24] The monstrous women that the go-between exchanges for the ordered beauty in thirteenth- and fourteenth-century Iberian works reveal the anxiety of desire that haunt the memories of the Iberian court. Appropriately these monstrous women, like the go-between herself, inhabit the in-between, the liminal spaces of far off lands, the spaces between genders, and the time between youth and old age.

Just as the go-between moves in a shifting, mutable space in which language and discourse loses its stability, so too the constructed beloved. Once displaced from the courtly genres that created her, she becomes a shifting, mutable representative of courtly culture. As I explore in detail in chapters 3 and 4, the juxtaposition of discursive order and disorder, the stable and the grotesque, played out on the female body complement the constructions of the female grotesque that literary critics such as Mikhail Bakhtin, Wolfgang Kayser, and more recently Mary Russo have examined in the context of both Renaissance and classical Greek and Roman literature.[25] The Judeo- and Andalusi-Iberian grotesque beloveds that populate Iberian go-between tales force us to reconsider the theory of the grotesque as the product of Western European culture's response to Greek and Roman aesthetics of order. In these Iberian texts the monstrous is a response to and product of the ordered, codified system of Andalusi court culture, particularly the poetic discourse of desire expressed in Arabo-Andalusi poetry.

The Andalusi go-between will never fully shed her identity as agent of this Andalusi court culture, even as she crosses the borders of al-Andalus itself, north into Western Europe. As the works examined in this book reveal, this Andalusi cultural model and its chief representative, the go-between, will outlive the courts of al-Andalus that created them. Whereas the members of these courts—caliphs, emirs, kings and their courtiers—struggle first against one another and then with the increasingly large and powerful foreign forces from both the south and the north, these old women from Cordoba keep the Andalusi court alive if only as a figurative/imagined space of courtly desire. Each of the subsequent chapters traces the go-between as she is transported one step further away from the geographical, temporal, and cultural space of Ibn Hazm's eleventh-century ideal al-Andalus.

★ ★ ★

Representing Others consists of five chapters, each of which examines how exiled cosmopolitan authors, trained in the Andalusi court model, use the go-between narrative to explore constructions of Andalusi identity. The earliest Iberian versions of the go-between narrative (discussed in chapters 1–3) have received less critical attention, the last version I examine (chapter 5), that of the Spanish *Libro de buen amor*, has been the focus of a tremendous amount of modern Hispanic scholarship.[26] Because the variants of this narrative appear in the different languages of the medieval Mediterranean world, including Arabic, Hebrew, Castilian, and Latin, critics working independently in each of these areas tend to focus on each narrative as unique within the literature of that particular language and/or literary tradition, and not as an Iberian narrative that roams freely across linguistic, religious, and political boundaries. This study breaks down the boundaries created by modern scholarship and asks the reader to focus not on Arabic, Hebrew, or even Spanish Literature (or on Muslims, Jews, or Christians), but on medieval literature produced by a cosmopolitan group of Iberian intellectuals who figuratively inhabited and represented the cultural space of the Andalusi court.

Chapter 1, "Palaces of Memory," deals with the earliest go-between narrative to appear in medieval Iberia, Ibn Hazm's chapter on the go-between (*as-safīr*) included in his treatise on courtly desire, *The Dove's Neck Ring*.[27] Ibn Hazm was an Andalusi courtier who witnessed the fall of the Umayyad Caliphate and the rise of the 'Amirid usurper, the former courtier al-Mansūr.[28] Because of the political and social transformations of his native al-Andalus under the Berbers and *taifa* kings, Ibn Hazm could no longer participate in the caliphal court of his youth except through mediation— through the idealized lens of memory and the imaginary. In the midst of the ethnic and religious factionalism surging across al-Andalus, Ibn Hazm pens an ethical treatise that defines the Andalusi not according to his ethnic origins or religious affiliations, but according to his skills as a courtly lover. In this treatise Ibn Hazm instructs his reader on how to become the ideal lover, and in so doing the ideal Andalusi. Through the lens of courtly love, Ibn Hazm creates an Andalusi literary identity by adapting Eastern literary modes to the cultural context of al-Andalus, evident in the vivid anecdotes of the Andalusi courtiers' love lives with which he peppers the work. The go-between becomes part of Ibn Hazm's discourse of Andalusi identity. He defines the ideal go-betweens as those old, pious women who roamed the streets of Cordoba and gained entry to noble women's homes on the pretext of selling baubles or beauty products. Ibn Hazm's inclusion of the go-between into this national discourse of love reflects Andalusi social mores, according to which many women of the upper classes would not have been allowed in public or to entertain suitors in their homes, as well as the prevalence and importance of mediators/courtiers involved in the most important affairs of state.

Whereas Ibn Hazm, loyal but displaced courtier of the 'Amirid-Umayyad court, had faith that the lover and his desire could be faithfully represented by the go-between, al-Saraqustī, a twelfth-century scholar trained in the *taifa* court of Saragossa, depicts go-betweens as opportunists who skillfully manipulate others' desire and the rhetoric of courtly love for their own benefit. Just as Ibn Hazm had adopted Eastern models to express his notions of Andalusi identity, al-Saraqustī also turns to Eastern literary models, namely the *maqāmāt*, to address political and social tensions in Andalusi society. Chapter 2 traces the process by which courtly desire becomes a pretext for social criticism in al-Saraqustī's *maqāmāt*. His twelfth *maqāma*, "The Persian," critiques the role of singing slave girls, women that form an integral part of Ibn Hazm's courtly world and who were professionally related to the go-between in Andalusi cultural practices. The go-between of al-Saraqustī's ninth *maqāma*, Umm 'Amr, distorts courtly discourse to manipulate and ultimately rob the protagonist. The go-between expands her role from simple mediator or representative to author responsible for the production and representation of desire. Umm 'Amr provides a description of the beloved that conforms to the Andalusi code of ideal beauty, but in the end the reader, like the protagonist, is left to wonder if any such woman existed, or if her description derived only from the idealized discourse of courtly poetry. In al-Saraqustī's *maqāma*, the discourse of courtly love is emptied of meaning, becoming simply a tool used by corrupt intermediaries to satisfy their own desires.

Corruption and the grotesque become central themes in the two Judeo-Andalusi go-between narratives analyzed in chapter 3. In the thirteenth-century go-between tales of al-Harīzī and Ibn Shabbetai, the go-between as transmitter and facilitator of Arabized, secular courtly poetry becomes an agent of assimilation, metaphorically represented as corrupt female flesh. Al-Harīzī and Ibn Shabbetai were both trained in the Andalusi model of the courtier-rabbi; however both lived not among Arabs but among Christians in Castile and Provence.[29] Both embody the transfer of cultural capital from south to north (from Islam to Christianity) that occurred in the wake of the Almoravid invasion. Al-Harīzī worked as a Hebrew translator of Islamic and Jewish texts written in Arabic for the Jewish communities of Provence and France, to whom the intellectual achievements of the Iberian Jews were novel but suspect. The secular prose and poetry of Iberian Jews was suspiciously like that of the Arabs, and even their theology smacked of the rationalism that prevailed among medieval Islamic thinkers. In their go-between tales both al-Harīzī and Ibn Shabbetai address the conflict between the rationalistic, secular courtly discourse of the Judeo-Iberian courtier and the traditional Talmudic (Rabbinic and Tosafist) approach to Judaism that defined the Northern European Jew.

As al-Harīzī and Ibn Shabbetai adapt the go-between tale to changes in Iberian society, they give the go-between a more central position and distort and even reconfigure the message of courtly desire. The object of courtly desire, like the lost Andalusi court, is not as ideal as previously imagined. While al-Saraqustī's *maqāma* leaves us doubting whether the beloved ever existed, in chapter 3, the protagonist encounters the beloved's fractured, grotesque body that belies the go-between's idealized representation of her. Corrupt, dismembered diabolic bodies reflect the fracturing of Arab-Andalusi court culture in diaspora. Al-Harīzī contrasts the decayed Andalusi beloved with a new symbol of unchanging beauty and truth for the diasporic Jew—the gendered embodiment of the Hebrew language and Jewish tradition. And both al-Harīzī and Ibn Shabbetai show Hebrew as a language capable of expressing a unique Sephardi courtly desire.

In chapter 4 the go-between and the grotesque body of the beloved are inscribed into ecclesiastical definitions of gender and enter into what we would today consider, thanks to Foucault, the history of Western sexuality. In this chapter I explore how, as Andalusi culture and knowledge is translated and disseminated (most likely by Iberian Jews in the Diaspora), the go-between reaches into Western Christian Europe. Once she is introduced into thirteenth-century clerical discourses, the go-between, as a vehicle for Andalusi courtly desire, becomes a catalyst for definitions of normative Western sexuality. In Christian Europe the go-between "passes" from the Arabic and Hebrew *maqāmāt* to the Latin elegiac comedy. This process entails significant transformation. As she is incorporated into the Western canon in the late-twelfth to early-thirteenth-century *De Vetula*, the go-between is cleansed of her Arabic and Hebrew lineage. She becomes the product not of Iberian Jews or Arabs, but of the Roman (pagan cum Christian by the High Middle Ages) erotic authority, Ovid. She is now ready for Christian consumption and her subversive and destructive potential is checked.

De Vetula, like the Hebrew *maqāmāt*, is a hybrid text that introduces (translates) Arab philosophical, medical, and erotic knowledge into Latin for a scholastic audience. As in the Judeo-Iberian *maqāmāt*, the go-between functions as the ambiguous locus of this *translatio*. She is a master of courtly rhetoric who not only tricks the protagonist with her description of the ideal beloved but also replaces the beloved in bed. Her body becomes the aged, polluted flesh of the beloved. The anonymous author suggests that this corrupted flesh is not that of a woman, but that of a *spadon* or eunuch, further distancing the Andalusi erotic discourse that the go-between embodies from the normative erotics/sexual desire of Christian Europe. As *De Vetula* shows, both the go-between and the discourse of Andalusi courtly desire translate poorly into the Latin, scholastic culture of Western Europe. The existence of this hybrid Andalusi go-between tale in Latin, though, does attest to the continued existence of the underlying questions of alterity, identity, and assimilation that the go-between is used to address, and that still figure prominently in the intellectual life of the Mediterranean world of the High Middle Ages. These issues, in fact, are at the heart of the Spanish masterpiece, the *Libro de buen amor*, the subject of chapter 5. This fourteenth-century Castilian work, composed by a Mozarab cleric, more likely than not the Juan Ruiz named in the text, brings us back to the Iberian Peninsula to interrogate the cultural border between Andalusi Iberia and Christian Reconquest Spain. In form the work is a *maqāmāt*, but it is composed in the Romance vernacular and, like the *maqāmāt* of Ibn Shabbetai and al-Harīzī whose purpose was, in part, to prove the viability of Hebrew as a literary language on par with Arabic, the *Libro de buen amor* is part of a cultural project that showed that the Castilian language was a worthy contender, not just of Iberian Arabic, but also of the Latin of Christian Europe. The *Libro de buen amor* makes accessible to a Romance-speaking, European audience the translated and transformed literary conventions and *topos* of Andalusi Iberia, similar to the way al-Harīzī introduced Judeo-Iberian material to Northern European Jews. The presence of the go-between, Trotaconventos, in the *Libro* underscores the work's hybridity and intermediacy, having, as it does, one foot in the cultural patrimony of al-Andalus and another in the literary world of the Christian scholastic. Not surprisingly, the go-between is again crucial in negotiating these disparate traditions. Unlike the author of *De Vetula*, Juan Ruiz, the Mozarab cleric who wrote the *Libro*, is not suspicious of hybridity and translation, but instead celebrates them.

Neither Trotaconventos nor the author-protagonist's celebration of her makes sense from the perspective of European Christian Literature, but become recognizable in the context of earlier Iberian go-between narratives. Juan Ruiz's go-between is the faithful and loyal representative Ibn Hazm imagined, as well as the desiring subjects al-Harīzī and Ibn Shabbetai depict with such mistrust. Instead of being threatened by her agency, however, Juan Ruiz eulogizes it. Trotaconventos becomes the lover's best friend and helper. Juan Ruiz, like the protagonists of the *maqāmāt* and Latin comedy, is unsuccessful in his own attempts at seduction through the use of the conventional erotic lyric. Whereas in the previous works, the go-between simply exploited the erotic lyric to her own advantage, in the *Libro de buen amor* Trotaconventos does something new: she creates a narrative of seduction. In her coercions and seductions Trotaconventos successfully translates and transforms the courtly discourse of the erotic lyric into narrative *exempla* and proverbs. As a hybrid text that grows out of the Arabic and Hebrew *maqāmāt* of medieval Iberia and incorporates other Christian European literary material, the *Libro de buen amor*, like the go-between, functions as a cultural intermediary at a moment of intense cultural interaction and exchange.

Representing Others, like the go-betweens and exiled Andalusis it studies, gets around. In it I analyze works composed in four of the languages of medieval Iberia over a course of some four hundred years. The Iberian go-between narrative proved to be a lasting and adaptable allegory for the condition of the Andalusi exile. In each chapter I examine how the go-between figure in a specific work, composed within a particular historical context, functions in the fictional imaginary not only to unite lover and beloved, but also to return the exiled Andalusi author and/or reader, however briefly, to the lost culture of the Andalusi court. This passage—from lover to beloved, from present to past—may be welcome or dangerous, depending on the particular author, but it comes to have transcendent significance for exiles pushed geographically and temporally further from the Andalusi courts of the so-called Golden Age. The go-between used to access this courtly culture is either praised or vituperated; nevertheless, her tales have survived long after the courts and authors that produced them have vanished.

CHAPTER 1

PALACES OF MEMORY: MEDIATION, COURT CULTURE, AND THE CALIPHATE

ويـا جوهرَ الصـين سُـحْقًا فقد غَنيـتُ بيـاقوتة الانـدلسْ

O jewel of China, be far off!
I am content with the red ruby of al-Andalus!

—Ibn Hazm, *The Dove's Neck Ring*

The Andalusi author 'Alī ibn Ahmad ibn Hazm al-Andalusī (994–1064) included the above verses in his treatise on love, *The Dove's Neck Ring* (*Tawq al-hamāma*).[1] Ibn Hazm wrote this work from exile during a bloody and divisive period of Andalusi history known as the *fitna* (1009–1031).[2] This period of civil wars followed the relative stability of the Umayyad caliphate that had established the Iberian Peninsula as a center of Arabo-Islamic culture. The early Umayyad caliphs modeled their courts on 'Abbasid models and their courtiers looked east for the latest literary and social trends. During the last phases of the Umayyad caliphate, however, Andalusi intellectuals and courtiers, such as Ibn Hazm, return their gaze to the Iberian Peninsula and begin to shape in their own work an independent al-Andalus that stands alone as a locus of culture. Whereas ninth- and tenth-century 'Abbasid literature had responded to the literatures and cultures of the East that had come under Islamic domination, the Byzantine in Syria and the Persian in Iraq (and through the Persian those cultures of the even further East, such as India and China), Andalusi poets and theologians begin to adapt Iberian and Western forms to the official discourses of Arabic culture circulating in and defining the Andalusi courts. In *The Dove's Neck Ring*, Ibn Hazm codifies this hybrid Andalusi discourse of love. He states unequivocally that he no desire for the jewels of China, for he has Andalusi rubies. Such a redefinition of the object of desire requires a remapping of the very process of desire itself, and this is just what we find in *The Dove's Neck Ring*. This treatise brings the Eastern rules of desire from Baghdad to the streets, public baths, and women's quarters of al-Andalus. Here these Eastern erotic models must be refitted to suit the diverse Andalusi population of Berbers, *muwalladūn*, Slavs, and slave women from all over the Islamic world. Adapting these Eastern models to Andalusi society requires the skills of a trained mediator. Such a mediator must, like the courtier-author Ibn Hazm, be adept at observing and communicating the desires of others, but also capable of constructing original discourses of mediation that can bridge the religious, linguistic and ethnic differences separating Andalusis.

Ibn Hazm's Andalusi rubies remain hidden in women's chambers and behind the closed doors of the court. The closed quarters and private spaces through which Ibn Hazm will take us in search of these jewels give us glimpses of eleventh-century Andalusi life, and also give us a model for Andalusi society. As Ibn Hazm is composing *The Dove's Neck Ring*, this diverse society is falling apart and breaking into independent factions along cultural, linguistic, and ethnic lines. We see this factionalism behind the Andalusi landscapes described by Ibn Hazm—urban landscapes that affect the lives of the lovers (people separated into quarters, losing themselves in the crowd as they navigate the maze of streets) and landscapes of war that rupture the lovers' happiness (the battlefields and camps where lovers join the enemy ranks and/or are separated by fighting and captivity). The physical and sociocultural landscapes of *The Dove's Neck Ring* consist of boundaries—enemy lines, the closed doors of homes and palaces, and the confusing streets in which the furtive lovers wander. Like the factional and broken political landscape of eleventh-century al-Andalus, Ibn Hazm's erotic landscape is similarly a landscape of division.

The boundaries and divisions between lovers described in *The Dove's Neck Ring* make the use of a mediator necessary. Such a figure is not necessary in the court poetry of the 'Abbasids. It is in the civil war of al-Andalus that such a figure's skills are needed: she is uniquely suited to overcoming the ethnic, linguistic, and social boundaries pulling al-Andalus apart. The Andalusi go-between knows where the rubies Ibn Hazm seeks are located and knows how to get them. Her knowledge of the streets of Cordoba and of Andalusi social realities allows her to mediate between lover and beloved:

> And after this there occurs in love, when confidence had been established and mutual acquaintance had become complete, the entry of the messenger. It is necessary to choose him, and select him, and pick him out carefully, and seek him cautiously, for he is an indication of a man's wit, and in

his hand lies his life and death, his honor and shame—after God, Most High. It behooves that the messenger be ready and keen, for whom a sign is sufficient, who guesses right things hidden, is capable of doing things of his own initiative, and supplies from his own wit what the one who sent him has overlooked, and conveys to the person who sent him everything he witnesses precisely; (capable of) keeping secrets, observing agreements, faithful, contented with little, giving good advice. And if he does not come up to this description, the damage done by him falls back on the one who sent him in proportion to what above qualities he lacks. . . . The kind of people whom lovers use most as messengers to those whom they love are these: either a (low-class) servant. . .or a person of high standing to whom no evil opinion is attached on account of the righteousness he shows or of the high age he has reached. Oh! How many of this type are found amongst women, especially those who have staffs, prayer beads, and wear a double red garment. Indeed I remember that in Cordoba women of good breeding were cautioned against women fitting this description whenever they saw them.[3]

In this earliest recorded description of the go-between from al-Andalus, Ibn Hazm moves from an abstract ideal, the generic "he" of the first section, to the specific, the old women of Cordoba. He tells us that he remembers from his youth many women in Cordoba who conformed to his ideal of the trustworthy go-between. The go-betweens that inhabit Ibn Hazm's memories become part of the Andalusi identity constructed in *The Dove's Neck Ring*. These old women are absent from the Bedouin poetry Ibn Hazm refers to as Eastern and non-Andalusi. Whereas much of the rest of this treatise echoes beliefs and codes of love similar to those set forth by eastern Baghdadi authors, the chapter on the go-between is marked as Andalusi. Ibn Hazm evokes the ideal, trustworthy messenger from his own past.[4] The Cordoba to which Ibn Hazm refers in this passage is that of the Umayyad caliphate—the Cordoba described by the tenth-century German nun Hroswitha as the ornament of the world.[5] By the time Ibn Hazm pens *The Dove's Neck Ring*, this Cordoba, populated by lovers, beloveds, and their go-betweens only exists in memories such as those of Ibn Hazm.

In this chapter I explore how, in response to the ethnic and political divisions that erupted in the *fitna*, Ibn Hazm constructed a portrait of the lost eleventh-century Umayyad-'Amirid Andalusi court, and of the go-between and the courtiers that inhabit it. Ibn Hazm not only codifies what had become a ritualized form of public behavior among the courtiers of the Muslim world, but he makes it a uniquely Andalusi phenomenon—the courtly love of the courtiers of Umayyad and 'Amirid al-Andalus.[6] Ibn Hazm's inclusion of the go-between into this courtly discourse reflects the central role of mediators in the recent Andalusi past.

Courtiers and the Art of Mediation

Mediators were an integral part of medieval Muslim sociopolitical structure in the Iberian Peninsula. Andalusi chronicles are replete with tales of both the betrayals of trusted courtiers and the hubris of courtiers who overstep their position. These tales are recorded by courtiers who self-consciously fashion their narratives according to the politics of their patrons.[7] In the public sphere during the tenth and eleventh centuries, in both literature and collective memory/experience, there were ample examples of the skill, power, and sometimes threat associated with mediators and mediation. The courtiers and intellectuals in the royal courts were the gatekeepers who both produced and controlled Andalusi culture and identity, shaping it from the literature, art, philosophy, theology, and political theory of the Arab-speaking world. However, these same courtiers were often from a different religious or ethnic group from that of the ruler and dominant social group.[8] The culture of the court was open to all, provided they had a mastery of *adab*, the proper behavior and knowledge of Arabic court culture.[9] By the time of the 'Amirids (976–1008), the ambitious courtier, even if he was not of Arab descent, could flourish and advance to the highest levels or power, becoming even sovereign, as long as he mastered the codes of this courtly culture and its literature.

Al-Mansūr, the usurper of the Umayyad caliphate, was proof of this. He gained entrée into the court because of his literary and cultural skills. He began as a scribe (*kātib*), hired to tutor the caliph al-Hakam's son, and quickly progressed up through the court hierarchy.[10] In his capacity as prime minister, Al-Mansūr composed and issued, in the name of the Umayyad caliph al-Hishām II, the very document that granted him effective control of the caliphate. Al-Mansūr's coup was, in fact, a coup of mediation. Al-Mansūr, the patron of Ibn Hazm's father, was a shrewd politician and courtier who used his skills to maintain his power for a period of some twenty years and then to pass control of the caliphate on to his sons. Despite the fact that the Umayyads were betrayed by a courtier trained in their own courts, subsequent Andalusi rulers continued to cultivate courts and maintain courtiers in imitation of the splendor and customs of the Umayyad court.

Ibn Hazm, like al-Mansūr, was proof that the Andalusi court was not populated exclusively by the Arab ruling classes. According to Emilio García Gómez and Miguel Asín Palacios, Ibn Hazm's grandfather was a non-Arab and a non-Muslim, probably a native of Mount Lishām (Huelva).[11] Ibn Hazm's father, Ahmad, however, received an excellent education and became a courtier (*vizier*) in the court of the last Umayyad caliph. As *vizier* to al-Hishām II, Ahmad also served al-Mansūr, who in his capacity as prime minister had by that time effectively usurped royal power. Al-Hishām, living under virtual palace arrest, retained the title of caliph, but al-Mansūr, his prime minister, was the one who exercised control. After al-Mansūr's death, Ibn Hazm's father continued to serve as *vizier* to al-Mansūr's sons, al-Muzaffar and Sanchuelo. Although Ahmad and his son made use of a false genealogy that traced their family history back to Persia in order to legitimate their inclusion in the court, what mattered most in the Andalusi courts, and what allowed access to those courts, was not genealogy but skill and knowledge. Genealogy could be faked, knowledge and skill could not.

In order to break up the Arab hegemony over political and military matters that had characterized the Umayyad dynasty, al-Mansūr had consciously diversified and professionalized his military by employing primarily Berbers and *saqāliba*, slaves of European origin.[12] Hugh Kennedy points out that although there had been a *saqāliba* presence under the Umayyad caliphs, only in the tenth century "did they become a large professional military force as well as forming the most influential group among the palace servants." The most influential group of servants at the 'Amirid court no longer consisted of Arabs, or even Andalusis of Muslim origin, but servants brought as captives mostly from Christian lands, and in the tenth century those lands were increasingly the territory of northern Spain.[13] Some of those palace servants would have come with 'Abda, King Sancho of Navarra's daughter, whom al-Mansūr married, and with whom he had a son ('Abd al-Rahman, known as "Sanchuelo") in 983. Still more may have also come with the daughter of King Vermudo II of León whom al-Mansūr took first as a concubine and later married.[14] Thus we see that, because of al-Mansūr's political alliances and military policies, the 'Amirid court was by no means a bastion of Arab culture, but, quite to the contrary, a hybrid space where Muslims and Christians of various ethnic backgrounds interacted socially and professionally.[15]

Even as al-Mansūr and his sons diversified the Andalusi court and destabilized the Umayyad caliphate, courtiers such as Ibn Hazm and his friends reacted by turning to the Arabic language and "things Arabic" (*'arabiyya*).[16] As the political situation collapsed and al-Andalus was pulled apart by the different ethnic factions of Berber, *saqāliba*, and Arab, Ibn Hazm was among a group of intellectuals that sought to hold the culture together by emphasizing what had held together the ethnically, religiously, and linguistically diverse Umayyad court—*adab* (the Arabic language and traditions from which courtliness was formed). This group included Ibn Hazm's friend, the poet Ibn Shuhaid, and other companions "united by their nobility, their intelligence, their education and—above all—their peerless dominion over that most noble tool of their trade, the Arabic language."[17] This group of young aristocrats and courtiers favored the use of Arabic over local dialects and paid special attention to Baghdadi literary and fashion trends with the goal of ultimately creating an independent Andalusi culture in Arabic based on Eastern models.[18] This group's Arabness is distinctly Andalusi. The language and especially the erotic poetry at the heart of their constructions of Andalusi behavior, though based on the remembered literary world of the Umayyad court, are designed for readers from (and in) the Andalusi courts of the former 'Amirids and the emerging *mulūk at-tawā'if* (taifa kings).[19]

Umayyad caliphate court culture had been highly ceremonial and it was designed to distance members of the court—courtier, public, and visitor alike—from the caliph, which it did by underscoring the latter's elevated status as divinely ordained ruler.[20] With the ascension to power of al-Mansūr, an usurper who could not claim divine right, the ceremonial gave way to a more private and personal court culture focused not on projecting the absolute and divine power of the caliph to his subjects, but on intimate, personal contact between ruler and the most distinguished of courtiers, often in the context of pleasurable activities such as the garden wine party (*majlis al-uns*).[21] These pleasure gatherings replaced the formal ceremonial court gatherings of the Umayyad dynasty, during which courtiers interacted with the caliph in a very limited capacity and only then as part of his official duties. At the *majlis*, in contrast, the 'Amirid rulers participated with the courtiers in the pleasurable activities of wine drinking, composing poetry, and philosophizing on the nature of love.[22] An entire ritual of behavior came to be associated with the *majlis*, and poetry had a central role in it, both reflecting and producing the themes of the garden wine party. The model participant was the *zarīf*, the elegant and refined courtier who was characterized chiefly by his rhetorical abilities and by "his or her adherence to an elaborate and ritualized code of public behaviour which dictated everything from proper greetings for specific occasions to the elegant way to conduct a love affair to the sort of shoelaces one should sport while doing so, complete with the verses inscribed on their tips."[23]

The love affair provided the *zarīf* with a suitable pretext for showing off his elegant manners and literary skills. The object of the courtier's affection could be another courtier, a slave women or even a young *sāqī*, or cupbearer—all apparently part of both the literary and social world of the *majlis* and the court.[24] "Courtly wine drinking and love customs may already have existed in Iraq and Persia before Islam," but it is among eighth- and ninth-century 'Abbasid poets that such customs make their way into the Arabic literature of the court.[25] The Persian poet Ziryāb, who brought the latest trends in Eastern *adab* to ninth-century al-Andalus, also brings the poetry of Abū Nūwās, whose poetry on drunkenness and sex with boys and girls was extremely popular in the 'Abbasid court.[26] Umayyad court poets adapted the forms and motifs of Abū Nūwās's brand of erotic poetry to Iberian strophic forms and to the Andalusi court, developing a hybrid poetry that reveals "an Andalusian nationalism of sentiment yet at the same time a servile imitation of the East."[27]

The Dove's Neck Ring reads as a manifesto for the new poetic conventions popular in al-Andalus. In it Ibn Hazm forges a unique brand of Andalusi court literature out of popular Eastern literary motifs. Though the classical *qasīda* on the topic of love opens with a description of the lover's abandoned campsite (the *nasīb*) typical of the nomadic lifestyle of the Bedouins of the Arabian Peninsula, Ibn Hazm asserts that such conventions no longer apply in al-Andalus; they are from a distinct tradition, "Excuse me from bringing up the tales of the Bedouins and the ancients, for their ways are different from ours. The tales about them are plentiful and it is not my principle to wear out anybody's camel but mine, nor do I adorn myself with borrowed ornaments."[28] Here we see an example of how Ibn Hazm appropriates the subject of classical Arabic poetry and adapts it to his own needs, a changed court life and new role for the courtier. This appropriation is also reflected in the form of the work, for Ibn Hazm composes his treatise on love in the *saj'* (rhymed prose) of the relatively new *risāla* (epistle) form, interspersed with poetry, and not in the traditional verse form and the *nasīb* to which he refers here.[29] Ibn Hazm's systematic reframing of Eastern motifs according to Andalusi models extends beyond the literary forms he uses. Instead of the conventional examples of model lovers (for example, Jamīl wa Buthayna and Majnūn wa Laylā), Ibn Hazm opts to include Andalusi historical figures as examples of the model lover. Al-Andalus does not need Majnūn wa Laylā and the tales of the Bedouin when it has caliphs like 'Abd al-Rahman I, II, and III, and al-Hakam I and II, who, according to Ibn Hazm, were not only great political leaders but also exemplary lovers. This hybrid courtly literature maintained the traditional legitimating function that poetry had had in earlier 'Abbasid, Umayyad, and 'Amirid courts. However, in The Dove's Neck Ring erotic poetry is used to legitimate a court and a way of life that have been replaced by factional fighting and that continues to exist only in memory.

Andalusi Love and Lovers

Ibn Hazm's treatise contextualizes desire in the recent Andalusi past—in the 'Amirid courts and streets of the Umayyad capital, Cordoba. The first chapter of The Dove's Neck Ring includes a list of Andalusi caliphs and their "men of state" that Ibn Hazm claims are model lovers: 'Abd al-Rahman I, II, and III, al-Hakam I and II, 'Abd al-Allāh and al-Muzaffar.[30] All but the last two are Umayyad caliphs. Ibn Hazm legitimizes the son of the 'Amirid usurpur al-Mansūr, al-Muzaffar, by including him in this list. Ibn Hazm is careful to point out here that love is not forbidden by religion. Using the Andalusi caliphs and sovereigns as exemplary lovers reinforces Ibn Hazm's assertion that love is an ennobling and divinely inspired sentiment and legitimates it as the courtly discourse of power.

Ibn Hazm sets forth in *The Dove's Neck Ring* a guide to love designed not only to shape the perfect lover, but also to simultaneously create the ideal member of the Andalusi court. Once he has mastered the rules of love, the courtier is morally prepared to serve beloved and ruler (the caliphs, after all, being model lovers themselves) in the service of the nation. Part of this education includes instruction on how to avoid evil urges like passion and greed. Although Ibn Hazm refrains from naming al-Mansūr or his son al-Muzaffar in the examples of evil behavior he gives, the eleventh-century reader would recognize in Ibn Hazm's examples of failed and evil lovers the same desires and motivations that led the illegitimate 'Amirid and *taifa* sovereigns to exploit their office for personal gain.

The Neoplatonic love described by Ibn Hazm in *The Dove's Neck Ring* is something that can affect all members of the court, caliphs and slaves alike.[31] For Ibn Hazm, love is intimately tied to beauty, and beauty, like love, is divine in nature—an attribute given by God. Appreciation of a beautiful form is the first stage in divinely inspired love.[32] Ibn Hazm is careful to distinguish the Neoplatonic love (*hubb*) that can ennoble even the caliphs, from other similar but much more nefarious urges such as desire (*'ishq*) and passion (*hawā*). Part of Ibn Hazm's instructions to the readers on how to become an ideal lover involve warning them on how to avoid those other urges with which love can be confused. In chapter 29, entitled "Ugliness of Illicit Practices," Ibn Hazm carefully distinguishes love, *hubb*, from passion, *hawā*, using Neoplatonic terminology to explain the spiritual nature of each:

> Many people obey their souls and disobey their reason(s), and follow their passions and abandon their religion; and keep aloof from what God, Most High, encourages (people to do) and what he puts into sound minds in the way of moderation, and forsaking sinful acts, and fighting passion successfully. They oppose God, their Lord, and please Iblis [the Devil] in what he likes in the way of ruinous passions, and practice (illicit sexual) aberrations in their love. We know indeed that God, Most High and Exalted, combined in man two opposite natures: one of them advises nothing but virtue, and incites to nothing but goodness, and nothing is conceived by it except whatever is agreeable: and this is reason and its guide is justice: and the other, its opposite, advises nothing but passions and leads only to perdition: this is the soul and its guide is passion, and God, Most High, says: "Verily, the soul is very urgent to evil."[33]

For Ibn Hazm love and passion are two different types of desire—the first is good and the second is bad. Both involve different processes and different aspects of man's nature. Love is divinely sanctioned and reinforces man's relationship to God, whereas passion leads to evil, sin, and the abandonment of one's religion. As we shall discuss below, for Ibn Hazm the ideal go-between, who is an expert observer, keeper of secrets, and giver of good advice, assists man in attaining good love, whereas the bad go-between, the bad observer, blabber mouth, and source of bad advice, leads to passion and causes shame and damage to the lover's social standing and spiritual health.[34]

Ibn Hazm gives examples of the types of lovers, both the good lover, who loves in moderation and according to reason, and the evil lover, who follows passion, as well as several concrete examples of such men in Andalusi society. In the following passage Ibn Hazm explains what distinguishes the good man from the bad:

> And the righteous man is he who does not mix with depraved people, and does not expose himself to sights which would bring forth passions nor does he lift his eyes to marvelously composed images; and the bad man is he who seeks the company of vicious people, and unfolds his sight to beautifully made faces, and applies himself to seeing evil sights, and loves solitary places which lead to ruin. . . . And as regards a neglected woman and a man who exposes himself, both are lead to ruin and perish. For this reason it was forbidden to a Muslim to take delight in hearing the melodious voice of a strange woman, because the first look would be made at you and the second against you.[35]

The good lover chooses not to put himself into compromising situations, whereas the evil lover deliberately seeks them out. Ibn Hazm identifies the strange/foreign woman as being particularly dangerous and as one of the experiences that the good/proper lover should avoid. The description of the evil lover who chooses depraved companions and superficial beauty in remote locales, particularly the beauty of strange women, could be a description of the lovers examined in *Representing Others* who tell their tales of beautiful women, seduction, and betrayal at the hands of the go-between from exile far from their homes.

The Andalusi Go-Between

Like the 'Amirids who brought about the end of the Umayyad caliphate in al-Andalus from within the court they entered as courtiers and ran as prime ministers, the go-between lies at the heart of Ibn Hazm's treatise on love as a destabilizing force with the potential to subvert the affair and to wreck havoc in the lover's life. In the chapter on the messenger, Ibn Hazm instructs his reader on how to select the best type of go-between in order to seduce the beloved and to minimize damage to the lover: "It behooves that the messenger be ready and keen, for whom a sign is sufficient... And if he does not come up to this description, the damage done by him falls back on the one who sent him."[36] The best go-between is loyal and will faithfully represent the wishes of the lover: one whose wants and desires are as close to those of the lover he/she is serving as possible and someone "faithful, contented with little, giving good advice."

The eleventh-century Andalusi go-between would have had access to women that the male lover could never approach himself. Since in Andalusi society many women were sequestered in their homes, going out only with male family members and then well-covered, the male lover would have had no way of knowing first hand of their beauty.[37] In such a case the go-between was needed to carry messages and to provide the lover with eyewitness accounts of her physical attributes. *The Dove's Neck Ring* is littered with examples that help us specify the exact nature of the go-between's mediation. Part of her job was to provide the lover not only with detailed and accurate descriptions of the beloved but also to deliver poems or statements designed to show the lover's wit. In chapter 4, "Love from Description," Ibn Hazm informs us that love can have its origins in a description of the beloved. The lover's passion may be aroused by such a description without ever having seen the beloved. Once aroused by the description of the beloved, the lover then needs to proceed to the next step of exchanging messages with the beloved.[38] Presumably it would be the go-between who provided the initial description—and thus Ibn Hazm's emphasis on choosing a go-between who can convey all he/she observes precisely. Ibn Hazm further specifies in chapter 8, "About Allusion in Speech," the types of messages and correspondence that love requires between the lovers, including poems, allegories, enigmatic remarks, or "some abstruse verse."[39] The go-between is entrusted with both communicating these poems, allegories, or remarks to the beloved and then giving the lover as accurate an account as possible of the beloved's reaction.

By establishing the go-between figure as essential in the different stages of the love process, Ibn Hazm opens up a space for mediation and for the mediator between lover and beloved. Though love may be a divine force capable of overcoming deep ethnic and political divisions, it is not a spontaneous phenomenon occurring between two persons, but instead a choreographed performance (or production) requiring at least three, but often more people, each with a specific role. In addition to the go-between, whose role, as described above, is delivering messages between lovers as well as providing descriptions of the beautiful form of the lovers, Ibn Hazm also includes the helpful friend, the spy, and the slanderer. The performative and public nature of love as a public spectacle that involves so many set characters is similar to the function of the courtiers in the court—in each the characters have a set role that is based on the code of love as defined in Arab court poetry.

In the chapter on the go-between, Ibn Hazm underscores the necessity of finding a trustworthy messenger ("It is necessary to choose him, and select him, and pick him out carefully"), stressing the harm that results from choosing poorly ("And if he does not come up to this description, the damage done by him falls back on the one who sent him in proportion to what above qualities he lacks"). Ibn Hazm's description of the go-between, which includes loyalty, wit, intelligence, and the ability to keep secrets and to give good advice, could be the description of the ideal courtier, just the sort of person the ruler/lover would want to have on his side and in his court. The go-between's primary function, as described by Ibn Hazm, is as a "sign, proof or guide to man's intellect/reason" (*dalīl 'aql al-mar'*).[40] Yet the go-between is something more, something better, in fact, for he/she fills in the gaps in the lover's intellect/reason (*'aql*) with his/her own.[41] The go-between is adept at readings signs, discerning hidden motives, and recording and transmitting details of observation; in essence, the go-between is a trained exegete of experience. Ibn Hazm, courtier, intellectual, and trained Quranic and legal commentator has created the go-between in his own image.[42] Both move in a world of signs and interpretation, and their performance, like the sword, can cut both ways.[43]

The go-between, like the courtier, is paradoxically both a subordinate representative of the one he/she serves, as well as someone who, in the very act of exercising his/her office, assumes control over the one he/she serves, for he/she has a part in determining their fate: "his life and death, his honor and shame." This go-between, like the passions and justice that guide men's soul and intellect, not only negotiates between the lover and the object of his desire, she also assists in constructing that desire and channeling it toward the appropriate object of desire. If the lover's desire is good (*hubb*) and the go-between faithfully represents his intellect (*'aql*) to the beloved, then the love he receives will give him joy and life. However, should the go-between falter and lead him down the path of passion (*hawā*) by misrepresenting his desire or the nature of the beloved, the go-between will lead him to illicit desire.

Ibn Hazm recognizes the dangers associated with the go-between when, upon remembering the specific sort of women perfect for this in Cordoba, he mentions that noble women were warned against them:

> Oh! How many of this type are found amongst women, especially those who have staffs, prayer beads, and wear a double red garment. Indeed I remember

that in Cordoba women of good breeding were cautioned against women fitting this description whenever they saw them. Women who have professions that cause them to circulate among various people are another type. Among women of this type there is the doctor, the cupper, the thief, the hawker, the hairdresser, the professional mourner, the songstress, the diviner, the instructress, the entertainer, the seamstress and the weaver.[44]

The juxtaposition of social class exposes the tension between those who might be go-betweens (lower-class working women) and potential beloveds (women of good breeding). In addition to hinting in this passage at the potential danger posed by women without breeding, Ibn Hazm ironically also invests the uncourtly workingwomen of the lower classes with a role in the production and creation of courtly meaning.

Nothing can be more marginal to court erotics than the professional women listed here by Ibn Hazm—these women circulating outside of the courtly centers of power. In his treatise, Ibn Hazm brings these workingwomen, doctors, cuppers, thieves, hairdressers, *curanderas* into the company of caliphs. Just as love is a universal force felt by all, Ibn Hazm constructs an Andalusi love such that these displaced, voiceless women outside the purview of the beautiful and powerful desiring subjects of the court have a necessary function in its very production/construction. Like the courtier, these women are professionals who rely on skill and knowledge to fulfill their professional duties. The first of those listed, the doctor, cupper, the thief, the hawker, and the hairdresser, are women whose work brings them into contact with many people. Given the messenger's duty to exchange verse and crafted prose between the lovers, it makes sense that Ibn Hazm also includes the *nāi'ha* [professional mourner], *mughniyya* [songstress], *kāhina* [diviner], *mu'allima* [instructress], and *mustakhiffa* [entertainer]—all women whose professions entail a certain level of linguistic and poetic ability. The songstress and the entertainer recall their courtly counterparts, the so-called slave woman (*jāriya*, plural *jawāri*), or in cases in which the woman was especially trained as a poet and musician, the "singing slave women" (*qayna*, plural *qiyān*). Both songstresses and entertainers seemingly have some of the same professional skills as the *qiyān*, but unlike the slaves, they presumably received a salary for their skills and performance. The knowledge of these workingwomen, like that of the courtiers, can be used as cultural capital to fulfill their own desires.

Unlike the professional women mentioned only once by Ibn Hazm in *The Dove's Neck Ring*, slave women, both *jawāri* and *qiyān*, figure prominently in Ibn Hazm's tales as both lovers and beloveds and are mentioned often.[45] *The Dove's Neck Ring* is teeming with accounts of the relations between aristocrats, courtiers, and slave women.[46] Having relations with these women was part of Andalusi court culture and was not uncommon for men of the upper classes who felt such relations had certain advantages over marriage: "The natural outlet for extramarital relations was concubinage with a slave girl, which, in Islam was perfectly legal. The Christian and Jewish minorities had some difficulty in keeping this disturbance of family life away from their communities. Choosing a female according to one's own taste and to have complete disposition of her could be preferable to a wife selected for the future husband by others and who was constantly watched and protected by her family."[47] And though there may have been no religious prohibition against concubinage with female slaves, relations with them did prove problematic, not only because they were domestic intruders but also because they were often ethnically, linguistically, and religiously different:

> To differences of nature were added differences of culture. All these concubines were of different races, ethnic groups, and "styles": African, Sudanese, European, Iranian, Indian, Asiatic, Slav...Educated in the manners of their own countries, they brought with them an exotic perfume of eroticism and contributed to the acculturation at the base, so to speak. Under the Ommayads and above all under the 'Abbasids, the value of a concubine increased with her beauty, but also with her "skill," her good manners, her poetic gifts, her talent as a dancer or singer.[48]

These slaves may have brought native customs with them, but they also were quick to adopt those of their Arab owners, and their mastery of certain aspects of Arabic culture such as poetry and music determined their value and was part of their appeal.[49]

The education the slave women received, and which was part of their sex appeal, further distinguished them from free Arab women, wives, and sisters, who were usually not only segregated from the company of men, but also left uneducated, or perhaps, at best, given some religious lessons. "[T]he *jawārī* were seen as a means of entertaining men. So those who exploited the *jawārī* took it upon themselves to refine these entertainments in accordance with the demands of consumers. And since the *jāriya* was all the more able to conquer men's hearts in that she was skilled in letter writing (*adība*), music and poetry, no effort was spared to satisfy this demand."[50] Such literary skills as described here—*adība*, music, and poetry—will characterize the slave women represented in the fictional works examined in the following chapters of *Representing Others*, and show these slave women as pertaining to the same literary world as the courtiers. Their training and prevalence in Andalusi courts also reflects the constructed nature of the object of desire.

An even more detailed account of the nature of the skills taught to these Andalusi slave women, as well as insights into their method of training, is found in the Andalusi author Al-Tīfāshī's treatise, *Muta'at al-Asmā' fi 'ilm al-samā' (Pleasure to the Ears, on the Art of Music)*:

> Today, this form of singing is especially prevalent, among Andalusian cities, in Seville, where there are expert old women who teach singing to slave girls they own, as well as to salaried half-Arab female servants of theirs. The [slave girls] are sold from Seville to all the kings of the Maghrib and Ifrīqiya, and each of those slave girls is sold for one thousand Maghribi *dīnārs*; either more or less, according to her singing, not [for the beauty of] her face. She is never sold without an accompanying register containing all [of the songs] she has memorized, most of which consist, essentially, of those poems we have mentioned. Among them are rapid poems suitable for a beginning, and slow poems which experts in the art of music sing only at the end. . . For this reason, those [slave girls] are, among [Andalusians], sold with a warranty, the absence of which necessarily lowers the price of the sale. Among them, a singing girl is required to have an elegant handwriting, and to display what she has memorized to one who can certify to her mastery of the Arabic language. Her buyer reads what is in the register and shows her whatever part of it he wishes, whereupon she will sing it to the instrument specified in her sale. Sometimes she is an expert in all instruments, and in all kinds of dance and shadow play, and comes with her instrument, along with [an entourage of] slave girls to beat the drum and play the reed for her.[51]

The slaves that populate the pages of *The Dove's Neck Ring* are often portrayed as this type of educated woman conversant in Arabic literature and capable of composing courtly poetry.[52] And as in *The Dove's Neck Ring*, in al-Tīfāshī's account (as in the other narratives examined in subsequent chapters), wherever we find the singing slave woman we find the Andalusi go-between. In the above passage we discover that in Andalusi Seville old women owned and trained slave girls. Once the girls had been trained in singing and music, these old women seem to have resold the women for a profit.

These slave women who al-Tīfāshī describes as trained in the culture of the court and who Ibn Hazm includes as participants in courtly love affairs exemplify the intersection of the discourse of courtly love and the discourse of Andalusi power. The slave women and courtiers were moving in the same courtly world and using the same courtly language to forge relationships. The system and language of love described and proscribed by Ibn Hazm, product in part of his own personal history in al-Andalus, was used in the courts for both beloveds and rulers, blurring the distinction between the social and the political relationship. In the Andalusi world of courtly love constructed in Ibn Hazm's treatise, however, *jawāri* and *qiyān* are common, whereas there is only a single mention of these other professional women who mediate for them. The slave women had mastered the codes of love just as the courtiers did, but they could not profit to the degree that the courtiers did—still being subject to the vagaries of their owner's fates and/or desires. The professional singers and entertainers that Ibn Hazm mentions in chapter 11 of his treatise, however, although most likely trained in the same *adab* as the slaves, can make a profit from their knowledge and can be more than simply beloved/desired object—they can act as go-betweens in the courtly production and performance of love.

The go-between could also, as al-Tīfāshī's text quoted above illustrates, actually traffic in more than just cultural capital. The old women of Seville worked as slave traders, trafficking in the very women Ibn Hazm uses to populate his Andalusi court. The professional songstresses and instructresses described by Ibn Hazm may in fact be a description of these slave traders who trained women to sing and memorize poetry in order to get a better price for them. This manipulation of the in-between spaces between public and private, between the court and the commercial life of the Andalusi street, and between the refined love of the court and the ugly reality of the Andalusi sex trade, may explain Ibn Hazm's reluctance to include more about these professional women. The commercial relationship between go-between and beloved does not figure in Ibn Hazm's treatise on love. Where the *jawāri* and go-betweens that enable courtly desire come from is not important for Ibn Hazm, and, in fact, cannot be discussed without causing the whole structure/performance of desire to unravel. Ibn Hazm, while recognizing the existence of these women and their professional activities on the margins, does not elaborate, focusing instead on the female slaves within the court who were appropriate objects of desire because of their well-defined role as slaves and because of their elaborate training in *adab*.

Conclusion

Ibn Hazm's chapter on the messenger gives us a brief glimpse beyond the world of the Andalusi court—a glimpse out onto the streets of Cordoba and a glimpse back, to the Cordoba of Ibn Hazm's youth. In this chapter Ibn Hazm subtly acknowledges the tenuous nature of his constructed site of love. Ibn Hazm simultaneously incorporates the uncourtly old women of the streets of his youth into the courtly *adab* of the Andalusi caliphate, as well as inscribing the go-between into the philosophical discourse of man's ethical decision-making. The old women of Cordoba briefly break into this most refined and elaborate of courtly treatises. In fact, Ibn Hazm acknowledges the centrality of their role, claiming they are essential to the whole performance of love. However, their uncourtly reality—their services rendered in exchange for money—destabilize the courtly love and identity Ibn Hazm is so diligently constructing. These go-betweens are the Achilles heel of courtly desire. By stipulating that lovers must use go-betweens, Ibn Hazm admits an independent desiring subject into the most intimate of relations and assures that the desires and needs of the lover will always be subject to perversions. The go-between will always have the potential to control both lover and beloved.

In the eleventh-century *taifa* courts of al-Andalus, love and the poetry of love continued to be the focus of courtly culture and to serve as the discourse of power. Ibn Hazm's treatise on love is also a treatise on power. The ideal lovers are Ibn Hazm's model Andalusis. Many of the examples offered in the work actually are his Andalusi friends—some living, some dead. *The Dove's Neck Ring* is, in a sense, a work of mediation, an embodiment of the ideal messenger described in his chapter on the go-between. The work is designed to faithfully mediate between the now lost but not forgotten Umayyad dynasty and its 'Amirid continuators—the Cordoba of Ibn Hazm's youth, recreated and reimagined in the personal anecdotes of its now lost inhabitants and out of which the work is woven—and the future al-Andalus, no less imaginary than the Umayyad past. By reimagining the past, Ibn Hazm is providing a model for the future. He dismisses the older 'Abbasid models, the traditional glories of Arabic language and tradition (the Bedouin, their tales and their mounts), for the Andalusis have their own traditions, their own stories. His treatise on love is not merely mimetic—it is not an imitation of Eastern treatises on love. The Umayyad caliphs and 'Amirid usurpers of al-Andalus and their courts, the model lovers he names in the introduction, will be the new locations of culture for al-Andalus, their new center. The Andalusi go-betweens, like the Andalusi courtiers, functioned to make this love—this national identity—work. The lover, like the sovereign, had to make moral decisions, to choose between right and wrong. But he also had to hope that his go-between/courtier was one of the just (an Ibn Hazm, for example) and not one led by Iblis. Once Ibn Hazm has opened up a space for the go-between in his world/text, in the court and in the lover's intellect, she negotiates with and constructs for him the objects of his desire. Her activity, this production of meaning/channeling of desire, engages the very forces of good and evil behind that desire.

Unfortunately neither the past nor the future was as ideal as Ibn Hazm envisioned. As al-Andalus fragmented into a multiplicity of *taifa* courts, several local and often conflicting Andalusi identities arose. Mediation, the courtier, and the love lyric—the core components of *The Dove's Neck Ring*—however, remain central in the fragmentary new Andalusi courts.

The works examined in the subsequent chapters continue to explore what happens when the negotiation of love breaks down and the uncourtly world of the Andalusi street begins to infiltrate the refined atmosphere of the court. In chapter 2 we examine how a twelfth-century Andalusi author, ibn al-Ashtarkūwī al-Saraqustī, takes up the motifs of the slave woman and the go-between and uses them to destabilize further the Andalusi discourse of love/power. The *maqāmāt* that are the subject of chapter 2 address this fragmentary al-Andalus, and unlike Ibn Hazm, whose reimagined Umayyad past gave him a relatively fixed point from which to order his poetry and prose, al-Saraqustī provides us with nothing fixed, nothing sure. His go-between does not mediate, she tricks, and in the end we are not even sure she really existed at all.

CHAPTER 2

"MANY A ZAYD AND 'AMR": MEDIATION AND REPRESENTATION IN AL-ANDALUS

حَرّم على المسلم الالتذاذ بسماع نغمة امرآة آجنبية. وقد جعلت
النظرة الأولى لك والآخرى عليك

It was forbidden to a Muslim to take delight in hearing the melodious voice of a strange woman, because the first look would be made at you and the second against you.

—Ibn Hazm, *The Dove's Neck Ring*

The go-between reemerges in Iberian letters some hundred years after Ibn Hazm created a space for her in the Andalusi courtly discourse of love elaborated in the *Dove's Neck Ring*. The *taifa* courts, the inheritors of Umayyad splendor and culture, were in their infancy as Ibn Hazm was composing *The Dove's Neck Ring*, but by the end of the eleventh century they have fallen to the Berber Almoravids. Unlike Ibn Hazm, whose *Dove's Neck Ring* reflects a hopeful attitude that Andalusi caliphal splendor might be restored, Abū l-Ṭāhir Muhammad al-Saraqustī, al-Andalusī, Ibn al-Ashtarkūwī (d. 1143) (al-Saraqustī) turns a critical eye to Andalusi splendor and its legacy—the literature of Andalusi Arab identity—exposing this cultural model as an illusion no longer viable in a changed Iberian cultural landscape. Mediation and mediators figure prominently in al-Saraqustī's collection of fifty brief narratives, the *Maqāmāt al-luzūmīyah*, both as characters within the narrative and in the very literary form he has chosen for such representation, the *maqāmāt*, which itself is defined by formal and stylistic conjuncture (discussed in detail below). In her new context the go-between is no longer part of a codified courtly discourse. The go-between and the rhymed prose with which she was created have been displaced from the caliphal court and now begin to roam in a new Andalusi landscape, that of al-Saraqustī's *maqāmāt*. In "*Maqāma 9*" we witness as she creates her own erotic discourse, offering the lover fictional accounts of a nonexistent beloved in order to manipulate him to her own ends.

Al-Saraqustī was a learned Andalusi born and educated in the *taifa* kingdom of Saragossa. The patrons of the young al-Saraqustī included the Arab aristocracy of the *taifa* kingdoms, including the Banū Hūd, *taifa* kings of Saragossa, al-Muʿtasim ibn Sumādih, king of Almería, and probably al-Muʿtamid of Seville.[1] Al-Saraqustī's participation in the literary production of these *taifa* courts is significant for it brings him into contact with the Andalusi codes of courtliness as elaborated in Ibn Hazm's *Dove's Neck Ring* (chapter 1). The *taifa* court of al-Saraqustī's native Saragossa was one of the most important twelfth-century Iberian loci of court culture. "The court of the Banū Hūd, represents the site where...'courtliness' as an appropriate and overriding characteristic of the ideal royal *persona*, along with an accompanying 'culture of courtly love,' was elaborated, displayed and, above all, enjoyed for the first time in the history of medieval Western European courts."[2]

Monroe describes al-Saraqustī as "a young Arab poet who associated with and eulogized sovereigns of the politically privileged Arab ethnicity."[3] The subject matter of his early court poetry may have been formulaic and conventional, but that of his *maqāmāt* was not. Unlike Ibn Hazm's *Dove's Neck Ring*, al-Saraqustī's *maqāmāt* do not attempt to unite Andalusis under the pretext of a self-styled, hybrid culture of love, but, on the contrary, illustrate how such a discourse and the courtiers who cultivated it contributed to the divisions and factionalism that would bring about the destruction of Andalusi court culture.[4] In al-Saraqustī's *maqāmāt*, Andalusi desire is not a universal force capable of overcoming linguistic and religious boundaries, but an artifice of the Arabo-Andalusi past. A witness to the fall of the Andalusi *taifa* kingdoms, al-Saraqustī creates a fictional world in which the discourse of courtly erotics—the discourse of Arabo-Andalusi power—proves to be a lie. This discourse, like the voice of the strange woman Ibn Hazm describes in *The Dove's Neck Ring*, tempted the best and brightest of Andalusis away from what al-Saraqustī implies mattered most, their identities as Muslims.[5] The discourse of Arab courtly desire in al-Saraqustī's *maqāmāt* must be read in the context of the arrival of the Almoravids who censured the lax morality of the Andalusis, reframing the debate of national identity in the religious terms of Islam instead of the Andalusi erotic.

Mulūk at-Tawā'if and the Almoravids

Ibn Hazm attempted to self-consciously unite the diverse Andalusis of the caliphate under the construction of an ideal Andalusi court identity, but this construction was shaky at best, and as the caliphate fell apart, the ethnic, religious, and other cultural differences in Andalusi society undermined such a monocultural ideal. The splintering of the caliphate into smaller factional kingdoms under the *mulūk at-tawā'if* (*taifa* kings) helped, if only briefly, to relieve the tensions causing the factional fighting within al-Andalus. In the *taifa* courts Andalusi court culture reasserted itself and briefly found locations amenable to its cultivation. Once *taifa* rulers had established their own courts, they were free to cultivate their own versions of the courtly discourses favored by the Umayyads. This patronage of courtly culture and of the courtiers who were its representatives was not simply motivated by a love of learning and Arab culture, but by very concrete political needs. Several of the *taifa* rulers were ethnic Berbers (for example the Banū Di-l-Nūn of Toledo and the Banū-l-Aftas of Badajoz) or Slavs (Mujāhid of Denia and Labīb of Tortosa) who had been trained as courtiers and soldiers under the Umayyads and 'Amirids.[6] These *taifa* rulers were acutely aware of their own status as illegitimate rulers; that is not members of the Quraysh tribe and not ordained by God as Umayyad caliphs had been, and they realized that the legitimating function of the Andalusi erotic could help solidify their own claims to power. The courtiers at these *taifa* courts were, as the courtiers under the Umayyads and the 'Amirids had been, from various ethnic and religious backgrounds. The *taifa* courts where al-Saraqustī spent his youth remained spaces of cultural exchange where Muslims (Eastern Andalusi and Berber), Jews, and Christians came together, only now the ruler need not be Arab.[7] The Andalusi courtly code of love, which anyone could potentially master, effaced these ethnic, religious, and social differences. The religiously conservative, ethnically Berber Almoravids, who arrived in al-Andalus in the latter half of the eleventh century to help these militarily weak *taifa* kings, viewed Andalusi cosmopolitan court culture with mistrust. The secular discourse of desire that fulfilled the important function of leveling the playing field at the diverse caliphal and *taifa* courts seemed suspiciously profane to the devout Almoravids, and was, in fact, given as a pretext for their invasion of the Iberian Peninsula in 1086 and again in 1090.[8]

Al-Saraqustī's native Saragossa was the last of the *taifa* kingdoms to fall to the Almoravids in 1111. Shortly thereafter in 1118 the Christians gained control of the city. Al-Saraqustī, however, had left some years before to continue his studies with the great teachers of the age in Valencia, Cordoba, Granada, Játiva, Murcia, and Seville. The *taifa* courts of his youth disappeared, on the one hand falling to the encroaching Christians to the north, and, on the other, to the religiously conservative Almoravids who swept up from North Africa, defeating Alfonso VI at the Battle of Zallaqa in 1086 and then taking the *taifa* kingdoms of Granada and Málaga in 1090.[9]

The ethnically Berber Almoravids did establish courts in al-Andalus, but they were not as proficient in Classical Arabic as most *taifa* rulers and courtiers had been, and court culture necessarily changed to reflect the attitudes and abilities of these new Berber rulers. Poets gave up the traditional form of the panegyric, the *qasīda*, in favor of a native Ibero-Romance form, the *zajal*, and Classical Arabic gave way to the vernacular.[10] At the same time that court poetry begins to be composed in the vernacular, prose, which had long taken second fiddle to the privileged discourse of erotic poetry, also becomes more popular. Al-Saraqustī dedicates "*Maqāma 49*" (and possibly the entire *Maqāmāt al-luzūmīyah*) to Tashufin ibn 'Alī, Almoravid governor of al-Andalus from 1138 to 1143. This dedication suggests that al-Saraqustī may have continued to serve at the Almoravid court, or at least curry favor, during his final years.[11] Al-Saraqustī died on December 8, 1143, in Cordoba, the town he had called home since the fall of his native Saragossa.[12]

His shift from erotic poetry during his youth to critical rhymed prose *maqāmāt* later in life would have been a natural transformation reflecting the shift from *taifa* to Almoravid courts. Al-Saraqustī's interests reflect the changing intellectual interests at court as the poetry of the pleasure loving *taifa* kings is replaced by the theological and philosophical treatises of the religious Almoravids. Like Ibn Hazm, al-Saraqustī explored current trends in skeptical philosophy in the relatively conservative Mālikī-dominated al-Andalus.[13] He seems to have been acquainted with several scholars who had been trained in Baghdad and the Middle East, including Abū Bakr ibn al-'Arabī, who himself had personally met al-Ghazālī. Al-Saraqustī's interest in skeptical philosophy and his use of the *maqāmāt* reflect larger literary/cultural trends in twelfth-century Andalusi and Arab society in general. The translation into Arabic of Greco-Roman scientific and philosophic works in Damascus and Baghdad beginning in the ninth century, combined with Persian and Hindu wisdom in vogue in 'Abbasid Baghdad, produced several centuries of profound intellectual ferment and theorizing, as well as the production of secular prose commentaries and treatises. As we saw in chapter 1, this speculative philosophical current reaches the Western outpost of Islam, al-Andalus, in the early eleventh century; Ibn Hazm is one of the first Andalusis to tentatively engage this intellectual trend.[14] The Almoravid interest in speculative philosophy and theology combined with their suspicion of courtly erotics and their lack of abilities in Classical Arabic cause a fundamental change in Andalusi courtly literature. Instead of renouncing Andalusi erotic poetry, however, al-Saraqustī incorporates it into the rhymed prose narrative, the medium of choice for treatises on topics more in line with Almoravid interests, in order to comment on the recent Andalusi past and the political system for which the erotic had served as representative discourse.

The *Maqāmāt al-luzūmīyah*

The *maqāma* form al-Saraqustī chooses for his collection of fictional narratives was a relatively new genre that, shortly after being imported to al-Andalus in the eleventh century, had become extremely popular. As with the *risāla* used by Ibn Hazm, part of the novelty of the *maqāma* was stylistic; it was a hybrid genre that combined rhymed prose (*saj'*), poetry, and pseudo-autobiographic first-person narration. The *maqāma* genre was created by the tenth-century Arabo-Persian author al-Hamadhānī (968–1008), and came into its own at the hands of the twelfth-century writer Abū Muhammad al-Harīrī of Basra (1054–1122), who composed fifty *maqāmāt* in imitation of al-Hamadhānī.[15] Al-Harīrī's *maqāmāt* inspired several Andalusi authors to write *maqāmāt* of their own and were the stimuli for the creation of at least one school (*madrasa*) established in Jerez exclusively for the study and commentary of *maqāmāt*.[16] In fact, Al-Harīrī's *maqāmāt* "became a symbol of Arabic eloquence and stylistic dexterity, and preserved this status until modern times."[17] Al-Saraqustī acknowledges in the prologue to the *Maqāmāt al-luzūmīyah* that these too were inspired by the study of al-Harīrī's *maqāmāt*.[18] Like Ibn Hazm, al-Saraqustī also incorporates Andalusi settings, characters, and poetic forms into what had been an exclusively Eastern genre.[19] His rhymed prose goes beyond al-Harīrī's simple single-consonantal rhyme, using instead a more complicated double rhyme. Al-Saraqustī recognizes in al-Hamadhānī and al-Harīrī's innovative models a form that since its creation had been used to address the complexities of the Islamic Empire under the 'Abbasids with its mix of Persian and Arab, urban and rural, secular and religious. The *maqāmāt* were the ideal vehicle for addressing the complexities of the political, social, and linguistic realities of the Iberian Peninsula at the beginning of the twelfth century.

Part of the complexity of the *Maqāmāt al-luzūmīyah* derives from the use of pseudo-autobiographic narration. The narrator al-Sā'ib is also a character within the embedded tales. Time and time again, in one locale after another, the protean trickster al-Sadūsī offers his services to al-Sā'ib to facilitate some type of interaction, whether social, economic, or criminal, with members of the local population. Each time we discover that al-Sā'ib is a fool who seldom fails to be duped. This unreliable narration—that of the fool—like the other conscious inconsistencies in form and content, impede literalist interpretations of the *maqāmāt*, and conform to the cultural and literary tastes of the late *taifa* and Almoravid periods. In these *maqāmāt*, al-Saraqustī weaves together a series of decontextualized literary motifs and conventions of traditional classical courtly genres including the love lyric, the wine poem, Quranic commentary, Arab horse lore, and legal discourse.[20] In their new literary home, they are not a reflection of the nobility of honorable, learned Arabs (the *adīb*), but merely means to an end utilized by morally bankrupt scoundrels and thieves. The rhetorical virtuosity, traditionally the talent of the *kātib*, courtier, and so esteemed in the Arab courtly milieu, becomes suspect in the *maqāma*, in which the most gifted rhetoricians are the trickster al-Sadūsī and the go-between Umm 'Amr.

"Maqāma 12"

Many of the *Maqāmāt al-luzūmīyah* take place outside of royal or government courts, and reflect instead the prevalence of mediation and mediators as an integral part of daily life in the medieval Muslim world.[21] One of these *maqāma*, the tale of a slave woman, warrants special consideration because it contains elements that subsequent Iberian authors, such as al-Harīzī, ibn Shabbetai (chapter 3), and Juan Ruiz (chapter 5), will fuse with that of the erotic go-between narrative. In "*Maqāma* 12 (The Persian)," al-Sā'ib is duped into buying a woman he thinks is a slave, but who is in fact the daughter of the trickster al-Sadūsī. As we learn at the end of the *maqāma*, the purchase is invalid as a freeborn Muslim woman cannot be sold, and al-Sā'ib inevitably loses his money.[22]

"*Maqāma* 12" begins with al-Sadūsī's caravan arriving in Zafar, Yemen, where al-Sā'ib alights aimlessly. Al-Sadūsī, upon seeing his acquaintance, convinces al-Sā'ib to provide him money to purchase a slave girl whose former owner deeply regrets having sold her. Al-Sadūsī, explains his plan to sell her back to her former owner for a much higher price than the two friends will pay for her. However, al-Sā'ib wants to see this woman before giving any money to al-Sadūsī.[23] Upon meeting the girl, al-Sā'ib is immediately taken by her beauty, describing it in terms typical of Arabic love poetry.[24] Once al-Sadūsī has quieted her down, overcoming her initial reticence and avoidance, al-Sā'ib can explore her body and is even more pleased with what he finds:

> And lo, she had breasts like apples that had been stamped with fragrant ambergris, a waist as narrow as a slender, tightly twisted cord, buttocks as broad as spreading sand-dunes, and flanks that swayed from side to side in the same way that hope and despair alternate with one another. She was gifted with as much pleasant speech as could be wished for, along with coquettishness that was neither unpleasant nor unseemly.[25]

Al-Sā'ib gets to touch each piece of her anatomy, which is then titillatingly described for the readers. Detailed descriptions such as this had become a literary convention, a courtly exercise designed to show off the composer's mastery of the Arabic language and poetry.[26] In subsequent chapters, we will find such formulaic descriptions incorporated into later Iberian go-between tales. Like these later Iberian authors, al-Saraqustī undermines this description's courtly function by incorporating it into this tale of trickery. Al-Sā'ib is not describing his beloved at a garden party, he is feeling up a slave woman he hopes to resell for money in the slave market. While slave women figure prominently in *The Dove's Neck Ring* (as discussed in chapter 1), there they move in an exclusively courtly environment as beloveds of caliphs, emirs, and courtiers (Ibn Hazm's companions). Whereas Ibn Hazm remains silent on the commercial aspects of female slavery, in al-Saraqustī's *maqāma* the seedier side of the slave's life is represented. Slavery as it existed in the Islamic world (including al-Andalus) often blurred the distinction between slavery and prostitution; and, in fact, slave women were not always simply the concubines of their owners, but could also serve as prostitutes for them. The owners of slave women often used them to enrich themselves by prostituting them to others. Al-Jāhiz's treatise on singing slave women, in fact, includes an ironic defense of this practice.[27] Clearly the slave woman was a means to monetary benefit in medieval Islamic civilization, and this is how she is portrayed in this *maqāma*. By giving his inheritance to al-Sadūsī to buy this woman, al-Sā'ib shows he has no moral reservations about participating in the human slave trade. Familiar with the type of schemes al-Jāhiz describes, al-Sā'ib clearly sees al-Sadūsī's plot as a viable way to make money.

He will not get rich this way, however, for al-Sadūsī has tricked him by selling al-Sā'ib his own daughter, a free-born woman and not a slave. Thus the sale is void, and al-Sā'ib loses all hope of seeing his money again. He tries to take his case before a judge, but the latter only chastises him for being so foolish. The trick in "*Maqāma* 12" centers on the sexual slave, which in medieval al-Andalus was associated not only with prostitution and go-betweens, but also with the court and courtiers. Unlike the slave women in *The Dove's Neck Ring* who, as objects of affection and desire, circulate and participate in the courtly desire of Ibn Hazm, here the fictional narrator al-Sā'ib adopts the role of a would be go-between, and fleetingly, that of client (as we see his lustful excitement when inspecting the girl's body) involved in an illicit, but seemingly common act of prostitution—one framed almost exclusively in terms of a financial interaction.

The Go-Between in "*Maqāma* 9": Arabic Tradition and Iberian Fiction

It is the financial—the non-courtly—that also dominates in "*Maqāma* 9." In this *maqāma*, al-Saraqustī introduces us to a female go-between reminiscent of the old women described by al-Tīfāshī as having trained the slave women in Seville (mentioned in chapter 1). Umm 'Amr is not the helpful messenger-confidant that Ibn Hazm tells the lover to find in *The Dove's Neck Ring*, but instead an untrustworthy bawd more interested in fulfilling her desires than those of the lover.

Upon his arrival in Baghdad, a restless al-Sā'ib aimlessly wanders the city in search of diversions:

> When the *jinni* who inspired my youth was a *mārid* [a real devil], and the arrow of my idleness was penetrating, I used to be acquainted with every scoundrel, and sought to drink from every raincloud and downpour of love. I had often heard that the City of Peace [Baghdad] was a seat of knowledge and eminent scholars...so I determined to travel, twisting together the various strands of my resolution. When I arrived there, I did not cease to traverse its quarters and alleys; to explore its commodities and neighborhoods in their various species and kinds; to accost its buxom maidens and lascivious women...While I was wandering about in its lanes and its fair landmarks appeared before me, I suddenly came upon a bevy of women strutting about in mantles and cloaks, swaying like branches, manifesting virtuous beauty, whispering words to one another that were sweeter than honey, and deadlier than misfortune.[28]

Al-Sā'ib is just the sort of evil lover described by Ibn Hazm in *The Dove's Neck Ring*—one who "seeks the company of vicious people, and unfolds his sight to beautifully made faces, and applies himself to seeing evil sights, and loves solitary places which lead to ruin."[29]

Al-Sā'ib spies this group of women leaving the baths and decides to follow them. One woman who seems to be their leader indicates with winks and gestures that she knows what al-Sā'ib wants:

> I suddenly came upon a bevy of women strutting about... swaying like branches, manifesting virtuous beauty...There was one whom I took to be their chaperone, and who had lowered her veil, announcing her stern refusal to be swayed. Yet she did not cease to observe me, and even winked at me.[30]

While presented as the personal experience of the protagonist, it also evokes a literary context—the chance encounter in a public space found in several Andalusi love poems and described by Ibn Hazm in *The Dove's Neck Ring*.[31] Ibn Hazm gives as an example the poet al-Ramādī, who fell in love with a woman he saw at the Gate of the Perfumers in Cordoba. According to Ibn Hazm, al-Ramādī is attracted to the woman because of her actions: "she took possession of all my heart and love for her penetrated into all members of my body."[32] Al-Ramādī follows the woman for quite a while until she finally notices him and asks what he wants.

Similarly in "*Maqāma 9*" al-Sā'ib follows Umm 'Amr: "I pretended not to acknowledge her presence, while actually doing so, and I followed in her footsteps, continually turning away, because I was stumbling from bashfulness, while she proceeded to turn around and indicate to me that all that had transpired was unavoidable."[33] Al-Sā'ib's response confirms that we are in the realm of courtly love, for he claims to be ready to die in order to meet one of the women from her "bevy": "I am complaining to you with a heart that yearns for a long-necked gazelle in the propitious bevy you are leading. Were I to lavish my hidden wealth on my objective, and meet my death over it, it would be of little consequence to me, and I would not consider my sacrifice to be equal to what I can observe in your bevy."[34] Not only do his excessive sentiments reflect similar expressions in the Andalusi erotic lyric, but al-Sā'ib also uses one of the most common motifs of this poetry, the long-necked gazelle, when referring to these women.

In *The Dove's Neck Ring* Ibn Hazm advises finding a messenger who wants little in exchange for serving the lover and helping him achieve his desires; in this *maqāma* al-Saraqustī introduces the needs and desires of the go-between into the affair. Umm 'Amr agrees to arrange a meeting between al-Sā'ib and one of the women, but asks him that he first give her some compensation. Apparently his first gifts are insufficient. Umm 'Amr returns the next day bearing a defiant poem, supposedly from the beloved who is asking for more gifts:

> O you who pine for a coquettish and bashful creature, you have glued your mighty cheek to the dust!
> Beware of the sin of passion (*hawā*), and of its stumbling, for the sin of passion (*hawā*) is unforgivable.
> He who struggles with love (*hubb*) will never gain mastery over it, even though he has many partisans and supporters,
> But as for him who shows up early, with silver as his mediator, how deserving of victory is he![35]

While the affair may have started with al-Sā'ib simply trying to procure a prostitute, with this poem, Umm 'Amr introduces a courtly text full of erotic code words, including *hawā* [passion] and *hubb* [love], and in so doing she takes al-Sā'ib's cue (the mention of his inordinate desire and use of the code word gazelle) and establishes the rules of the game for al-Sā'ib.[36] Now he knows he is functioning in the erotic milieu of the courtly lyric and must follow its norms and conventions, including seeking a companion to assist him in his affair and to whom he can complain of his lovesickness (as dictated in the chapter on the "helpful brother" in *The Dove's Neck Ring*).[37] This poem warns al-Sā'ib not to confuse passion (*hawā*) with love (*hubb*).

By claiming that the victim of love will never gain mastery over it, the poem also foretells al-Sā'ib's eventual fate. In addition to informing the protagonist that he has become a participant in the game of courtly love, Umm 'Amr has also established the horizon of expectation for the learned reader familiar with the courtly lyric genre. Like al-Sā'ib who is duped in the end, the reader too will find his/her expectations thwarted as the courtly lyric is subverted by the parodic prose of the *maqāmāt*.[38]

As she strings al-Sā'ib along, Umm 'Amr may not actually be mediating between him and the woman he desires (who, in fact, may not exist), but she does mediate between the parodic rhymed prose narrative conventions of the *maqāmāt* and those of the courtly love lyric. The introduction of the go-between into the tale creates a rupture in the narrative and allows the author to introduce a different genre, the poetry of courtly love. This is a technique we shall see again and again in the works examined in *Representing Others*. The essence of the *maqāma* is such that it incorporates the erotic lyric, just as, in other instances, it incorporates and transforms so many of the genres of medieval Arab *adab* to meet its own needs and conventions. In "*Maqāma 9*" al-Saraqustī uses the courtly love lyric because it is precisely the genre from which the go-between originates. The erotic poems in this *maqāma*, because of their *topoi* and imagery, as well as the context in which they are exchanged, supposedly between two lovers via a mediator, evoke the Andalusi courtly milieu described by Ibn Hazm.

The beloved's poem makes al-Sā'ib desperate. While he is pondering his situation, he just happens to see al-Sadūsī coming toward him. Al-Sā'ib immediately reveals all, and al-Sadūsī is quick to sympathize, telling al-Sā'ib that he, too, is familiar with love and its snares.[39] Al-Sā'ib asks him to compose a poem in response to the one received from his beloved. Al-Sadūsī's poem combines battle imagery with the typical *topoi* of the Arabic love poem—the gazelle, the distance of the beloved, and the dream-image:

> Whoever desires to catch shying young ladies should not fear arrowheads or sword blades.
> Wonder at the gazelle that stains its claws with blood as it pounces on the lion!
> How excellent would my love-union with one who is inaccessible be, should her dream-image visit me from a distance.
> The more I lavish my love on her, the more she avoids me, like a fugitive in full flight.[40]

Here al-Sadūsī responds to the battle imagery of the beloved's poem, in which the victorious lover is encouraged to show up early with his sword drawn. In this poem al-Sadūsī compares the lover chasing his beloved to a man facing arrowheads and swordsmen. Ironically here it is the prey (the gazelle-beloved) that brutally attacks the hunter (the lion-lover). Such imagery is, in fact, common in the love lyric of al-Andalus, as for example in a poem of the twelfth-century Cordoban poet Ibn Baqī', in which an ardent lover weeps "because he has been given his death-wounds by a wild fawn."[41] Al-Sadūsī's courtly style poem is dispatched in the care of Umm 'Amr to the beloved. Umm 'Amr returns quickly bearing a response from the beloved that warns there will be a battle before any union takes place.

Al-Sā'ib interprets the beloved's response as a trap and again seeks help from al-Sadūsī, who recites the following poem to him. He instructs al-Sā'ib to send it to the beloved as a response:

> O you who yourself sin by accusing me of sinning against passion and our love-union,
> When I am suffering from a wounded heart that is roasting over the live embers of my love for you,
> Will Fate ever grant a love-union to this lover,
> When your memory of him is dimmed by an obstacle that weakens the ties of your affection?
> A mediator, full of glory and virtues, came to you on his behalf.
> Her words were not of the kind that are fashioned and embroidered by al-Hisālī.[42]

Al-Sadūsī again plays upon the traditional themes of Arabic love poetry, mentioning the obstacles to the affair and the lovesick man who pines for the beloved. Central among these conventions is the mediator whom al-Sadūsī praises as being "full of glory and virtues." In fact, al-Sadūsī seizes this opportunity and manipulates the erotic poem and the courtly process of love itself, and instead of creating a love poem dedicated to the beloved creates a panegyric of the go-between and her rhetorical skills. The poem's intended audience is not the beloved, but al-Sā'ib. It is designed to make him appreciate and, we would suppose, give generously to the go-between. Ironically the supposed audience of this poem, the woman al-Sā'ib is trying to seduce and with whom Umm 'Amr has been negotiating, does not exist. The composition of the poem is part of the tricksters' ruse. Al-Sadūsī uses this poem to seduce al-Sā'ib and trick him into believing that the whole affair is real in order to receive further gifts from him.

In the erotic poems of "Maqāma 9," al-Sadūsī and Umm 'Amr are manipulating al-Sā'ib in hopes of monetary gain, and they do so by playing upon al-Sā'ib's sexual desire (hawā) as constructed by and represented in the literature of love, the conventional world of the Arabic love poem. The erotic content of the poems exchanged in this maqāmāt, which al-Saraqustī leads us to believe have all been composed by al-Sadūsī, is undermined by their context in the prose *maqāma*. As readers we know the poems are to be read ironically—that al-Sadūsī and Umm 'Amr are cynically playing with al-Sā'ib's desires. Instead of drawing al-Sā'ib nearer to the object of his desire, the presence of al-Sadūsī and the poetry he composes for al-Sā'ib only serve to prolong al-Sā'ib's fleecing under the guise of following literary and social protocol. The poems have the effect of further removing the protagonist from his desire. He has been exploited by the two supposed mediators, Umm 'Amr and al-Sadūsī, and he never does get to meet the woman he so desired—the woman Umm 'Amr describes as "the pick of an entire kingdom, the unique pearl on a strand; she cannot be matched by any quantity, nor evaluated by any estimate."[43]

Although Umm 'Amr promises al-Sā'ib this incomparably beautiful woman and uses her skills to make his desire grow, she does not come through on her promise. The end of the *maqāma* reveals that al-Sā'ib was merely being strung along. Umm 'Amr uses her persuasive ability to procure money falsely from her victim by telling lies, enticing al-Sā'ib into a business deal with her, in which he relinquishes not only his money but also his will. This surrender of his will to another leads to al-Sā'ib's downfall; it allows him to be tricked, which the final poem, left to him by either Umm 'Amr or al-Sadūsī, points out:

> A superior man is a resolute man, who competes with all mankind in cunning and in hatred. . . .
> I have tested this age and its sons, one and all; both its Zayds, and its 'Amrs.
> Glory is only the *dirham* that your hand clasps, after you have won it in gambling against your rival.
> The real hero is the one who does not cease to milk and to extract the milk of Time, . . .
> Think it proper to defer only to one who can forbid Time's evil or command its good.
> And do not say: "An incompetent has achieved his desires." How different is the lot of the weak and that of the brave.[44]

Whether Umm 'Amr or al-Sadūsī has left this poem is irrelevant, for both have the same function—they are the wily antiheroes who do obtain their desires from Fortune, and who constantly trick al-Sā'ib—keeping happiness and the obtainment of his desires just out of reach.

As this final poem underscores, it is this surrender of his will that makes al-Sā'ib weak and excludes him from the lot of the brave. By deferring to Umm 'Amr, he has allowed her to be the true antihero of the *maqāma*. In the end she is the one "who does not cease to milk the milk of Time." The go-between grows rich by manipulating literary discourses such as courtly love and lovesickness to milk (and bilk) her clients, and thus "obtaining her desires"—money. The ideal old women described by Ibn Hazm prove to be less than model go-betweens in al-Saraqustī's *maqāmāt*. The figures of al-Sadūsī and Umm 'Amr, like the later Iberian go-between figures we will meet in subsequent chapters, are skilled liars. They are motivated by greed, not the best interests of their clients/friends. These go-between figures are a threat not just to their victims, but also to society itself. They arrange love unions, regardless of whether those be adulterous or corrupt the innocent, and in so doing subvert accepted social and literary discourses. In "*Maqāma* 9" the go-between is no longer circulating in a courtly environment as she was in *The Dove's Neck Ring*, she merely uses courtly discourse when necessary to prey upon someone who does accept its authority. The final poem itself is a testimony to the power over such men that both al-Sadūsī and Umm 'Amr have: "I have tested this age and its sons, one and all; both its Zayds, and its 'Amrs." This reference to Zayds and 'Amrs alludes to Umm 'Amr's statement earlier in the *maqāma*: "I am Umm 'Amr, though I have no son called 'Amr, yet many a Zayd and 'Amr have I befriended in this kind of affair."[45] By engaging the services of Umm 'Amr, al-Sā'ib becomes just another 'Amr or Zayd, who has been tested by, and fallen under, the power of the go-between. In this he has made the same fatal mistake that Andalusi rulers—Umayyad and *taifa* alike—had made in their misplaced trust of treacherous courtiers, and the consequences of which both Ibn Hazm and al-Saraqustī had personally witnessed. Al-Sā'ib's fate, namely his fleecing at the hands of Umm 'Amr and al-Sadūsī, reads as a veiled criticism of the Arabo-Andalusi social model in which courtiers and scribes played such an important role—a criticism leveled, ironically, by someone trained as, and who could easily pertain to, that very class of courtiers.

Conclusions

The world al-Saraqustī creates for the reader in the *Maqāmāt al-luzūmīyah* is one in which traditional moral values are inverted. The characters are debauched drunks, greedy mediators, and sexual predators. "*Maqāma* 12" illustrates the custom of sexual slavery, common throughout the medieval Arab world. "*Maqāma* 9" reveals the world of the urban go-between. In both al-Sā'ib is seduced by his greed and by the rhetorical skills of the tricksters, whose primary vehicle is courtly poetry. Al-Sā'ib, the dupe, is an aristocratic Arab who continually makes the wrong decision, often basing those decisions on the bankrupt traditional values of Arabo-Andalusi court society. The protean tricksters, often in league with women and non-Arab others, triumph in this nonheroic genre, by resorting to their own shrewdness and resources.

Linguistic, cultural, and religious differences, so central in medieval Iberian daily life, are key in these *maqāmāt*. As Ibn Hazm showed in *The Dove's Neck Ring*, these differences necessitate mediation, and in al-Saraqustī's *maqāmāt* we find a narrative exploration of what happens when one enlists the help of an untrustworthy and exploitative go-between to overcome these differences; not only is mediation muddled, but also communication is purposefully obscured to the benefit of the go-between. This will be further developed in the works studied in the subsequent chapters. In the case of the Hebrew *maqāmāt*, as discussed in chapter 3, the procuress as surrogate seductress negotiates a love union for the protagonist, although her fidelity lies elsewhere, and the consequences of her betrayal have repercussions that go far beyond the personal, affecting the entire community.

The popularity of the *maqāmāt* in Iberia continued after al-Saraqustī's *Maqāmāt al-luzūmīyah* and "composition of occasional *maqāmāt* became part of Andalusi epistolary practice in the courts of the party kings and their Berber successors."[46] As a genre the *maqāmāt* continued to develop in al-Andalus, taking on new traits and losing others that had characterized the first manifestations of the genre: "Andalusi court *maqāmāt* entirely abandoned specific Eastern characteristics such as the mendicancy theme, two constant protagonists, scheme-based plots, and final exposure."[47] Though certain elements were abandoned as the *maqāmāt* evolved, others were not, and the figure of the go-between not only survived, but flourished in the Hebrew *maqāmāt* of medieval Iberia, as we shall see in chapter 3.

CHAPTER 3

TRANSLATING DESIRE: THE VIOLENCE OF MEMORY IN THE JUDEO-IBERIAN *MAQĀMĀT*

1 שָׂבְתִּי וְתִלְתַּלֵּי זְמָן לֹא־שָׁבוּ / וִימֵי נְדָדִים לַעֲלוּמִים שָׁבוּ
אַחֲרֵי בִלְתָּה הָיְתָה עֶדְנָה לְאֵם / פֵּרוּד וְיַלְדֵי תַאֲוָה יַעֲגֹבוּ . . .
5 אֹמַר לְמוֹכִיחַי לְאַט עֲלֵי עֲדֵי / אֶסְפֹּד וְהַרְפּוּ לַאֲשֶׁר בִּי רָבוּ
הַרְפּוּ עֲדֵי אָסֵב מְכוֹנִים מִן־יְקוֹד / לִבִּי וּמֵי עֵינַי לְבַד חָרְבוּ
דָּמוּ לְעָרִים נֶחֱדוּ לֹא עָבְרָה / רֶגֶל בְּנֵי־אִישׁ בָּם וְלֹא נוֹשָׁבוּ
אַחַר אֲשֶׁר כַּנְפוֹת יְדִידוּת מָשְׁכוּ / בָּהֶם וְשׁוּלֵי אַהֲבָה סָחֲבוּ
צִבְאוֹת צְבָאוֹת מֶעֲטוּ תּוֹכָם וְאַךְ / תַּנּוֹת בְּרִבְעֵיהֶם לְתַנּוֹת רָבוּ . . .
31 צְנוֹף צִנְפָּנִי אֵלִי־אֶרֶץ אֲשֶׁר / נֵרוֹת תְּבוּנָתִי בְּתוֹכָהּ כָּבוּ
גַּם כּוֹכְבֵי שִׂכְלִי בְּמַאְפֵּל עֶלְיוֹנִי / מַדָּע וְעָמְקֵי־פֶה לְבַד הוּעֲבוּ
בָּאתִי גְבוּל רִשְׁעָה וְאֶל־עַם אֵל בְּאַף / זַעַם וְאִתּוֹ הַיְקוֹם קָבוּ
בֵּינוֹת פְּרָאִים אַהֲבוּ מַשְׁחִית אֲבָל / לְדָמַי מָתֵי־צֶדֶק וְתֹם אָרְבוּ . . .
נָא שַׁאֲלוּ מִפִּי מְלִיצִים חָלְפוּ / חַיּוּ תְעוּדוֹתָם וְהֵם רָקֲבוּ
40 גַּם מֵעֲלֵי סִפְרֵי תְבוּנָה תִדְרְשׁוּ / כִּי מִבְּלִי־פֶה הָאֱמֶת דִּבְּבוּ
אִם־יַעֲצוּ אַחִים כְּרָעָה זֹאת וְאִם / שָׁמְעוּ מְזִמּוֹת זוּ לְרַע חָשְׁבוּ . . .
רוּחוֹת בְּשָׂמִים עָבְרוּ נֶשֶׁף בְּבֵית / רִמּוֹן וְעַל־הָרֵי שְׁנִיר נָשָׁבוּ
נָא רַחֲפוּ כִמְעַט עֲלֵי אָחִי וְאַט / הָבוּ לְאַפִּי מֶרְקָחִים הָבוּ
הָבוּ שְׁלוֹם שׁוֹכְנֵי פְאָתַיִם כִּי עֲלֵי / נַפְשִׁי בְּנֵי הַמַּעֲרָב יַעֲרְבוּ
45 אֶשְׁלַח תְּלוּנָתִי אֲלֵיהֶם עַל־יְדֵי / עָב קַל וְעַל־כַּנְפֵי כְרוּב יִרְכָּבוּ

My youthful locks are gone, but I feel again the restlessness of youth.
There is no pleasure for the Mother of Separation, for the children of desire are gone. . .
I say to those who reproach me: "Calm down, for you will soon lament my passing," and to those who recriminate me, "Stop!"
Stop your harsh judgements, for, all alone, my heart has withered and my tears dried up.

These places are like destroyed cities where no human sets foot, devoid of life.

After having had the wings of friendship unfurled in them and the flights of love pass through them.

The armies of gazelles diminished inside, while all around the jackals increased in number to lament. . . .

I have been forced to a land where the lights of my intelligence have been extinguished.

The stars of my mind have been darkened by those whose science is but stammering and gibberish.

I arrived to a land of evil, to a people with whom the Lord is angry and who are cursed above all others.

Among wild asses that love perfidy and who look for opportunities to spill the blood of the just. . . .

Ask the wise ones that have disappeared, those whose testimony lives even though their bodies are rotting;

Inquire also of the books of wisdom, for though they have no mouths, they tell truly

If my bretheren planned such evil, or if they understood the evil of such plans. . . .

O perfumed breezes that pass through Granada in the afternoon, and which blow over Mount Senir,

Hang a little over my brothers, and bring their perfume to my nose, bring it.

Bring greetings from those who live by the sea, for the sons of the West give me pleasure.

I send my complaints to them on a light cloud, on the wings of an angel they go.

—Moses ibn Ezra, "The Poem of Two Exiles"

In this poem the Judeo-Andalusi intellectual, Moses ibn Ezra (ca. 1055–1140), an almost exact contemporary of al-Saraqustī, compares his condition as an exile in northern Christian Iberia to his former life in al-Andalus.[1] Moses ibn Ezra uses the imagery of the Andalusi courtly lyric to express his disillusionment and despair. In Ibn Ezra's poem, al-Andalus has become, much as it was represented in Ibn Hazm's *The Dove's Neck Ring*, an ideal site of memory—an abandoned urban landscape haunted by gazelles, the memories of erotic encounters, and good friends—memories of Ibn Ezra's access to the privileged spaces and discourses of Andalusi power. Moses ibn Ezra's current home, Christian Iberia, is, on the other hand, a hostile space, the cursed territory of brutish men incapable of refined thought or speech, a dark place where the light of Andalusi culture and learning is dimmed. Andalusis have become gazelles of memory wandering in the abandoned palaces of their former splendor, whereas Ibn Ezra's actual neighbors are the stammering Christians and Jews of northern Iberia who bray like wild asses. Inherited wisdom and tradition (Jewish culture), the testimony of the wise, hold no consolation, nor do they offer Ibn Ezra an explanation for his awful fate in exile. The imagery of the Andalusi erotic does, however, offer the poet some relief. The perfumes of Andalusi gardens still come to him as go-betweens traversing both space and time and bearing the greetings of friends and lovers. The perfume of al-Andalus, however, will not be as sweet for subsequent generations of exiled and diasporic Andalusi Jews in northern Iberia. In the narratives analyzed in this chapter we will see how Moses ibn Ezra's idealized al-Andalus is transformed by the following generation of Judeo-Andalusi intellectuals and courtiers in northern Iberia into a nightmarish land whose gazelles have become monsters and whose perfumes have soured.

Like many Andalusi Jews, Moses ibn Ezra fled to Christian Iberia to escape the Almoravids, who not only took over Arabo-Andalusi courts, but also followed a policy of persecuting the previously tolerated *ahl al-dhimma*, Jews and Christians living in Islamic lands.[2] The Almoravids effectively brought an end to the Judeo-Andalusi court life that had flourished in al-Andalus since the time of the Umayyads. Although many Jews no longer had access to Andalusi courts, the memory of a shared court life survived among the culture and literary production of Judeo-Andalusi exiles such as Moses ibn Ezra. Andalusi-style poetry and the rhymed narrative *maqāmāt* continued to dominate Judeo-Iberian literature for some three hundred years after the destruction of the courts where it was first created. Just as Ibn Hazm and al-Saraqustī helped to create a unique Andalusi literature and sense of identity out of the Arabic texts of the Eastern parts of the Muslim Empire, Judeo-Iberian scholars and courtiers living and working in the courts of Muslim Andalusi sovereigns before the Almoravid invasion had similarly mastered the literary and cultural models of the Arab East and adapted them to the Hebrew language and to Judeo-Iberian culture.

The adaptation of Muslim, Arabic cultural models to the Judeo-Iberian context of al-Andalus involved the creation of a series of culturally specific innovations that contributed to a unique hybrid form of courtly discourse that I refer to as Judeo-Andalusi. In this chapter I examine how this Judeo-Andalusi courtly discourse is further transformed in the rhymed prose *maqāmāt* of Jewish courtiers who have left al-Andalus for Christian Iberia. Moses ibn Ezra's poetry shows how one of the first generation of Andalusi exiles begins to create an imaginary space of memory where the cultural and literary values of al-Andalus continue to have value.[3] Subsequent Judeo-Iberian intellectuals and writers, including both al-Harīzī (ca. 1170–1235) and Ibn Shabbetai (b. 1168), use this imaginary al-Andalus and the Judeo-Iberian courtly discourse with which it is associated and within which it is articulated to interrogate their own unique positions as Arabized Jews in Christian Europe. Key in this critical self-examination is the figure of the go-between and the *maqāma* of seduction she orchestrates.

Maqāmāt In-Between

Despite the fact that Judeo-Iberian intellectuals had a well-established tradition of Hebrew poetry modeled on Arabic courtly poetry that went back to the first years of Abd al-Rahman III's reign (912–961), Hebrew adaptations of the rhymed prose *maqāmāt* only began to be cultivated when the Andalusi-Jews came into contact with the cultures of Western Europe. As discussed in chapter 2, the *maqāmāt* had served the twelfth-century Andalusi writer al-Saraqustī as a tool for self-consciously examining the corrupt institutions of power of the *taifa* kingdoms during the very period of their disintegration and destruction by the Almoravids. The Hebrew *maqāmāt* composed in Iberia also explore a recently lost lifestyle and culture, that of the Jewish courtier and intellectual of Muslim al-Andalus. Just as al-Saraqustī's protagonist al-Sā'ib appears in the different locales of the Arab Empire, including Baghdad, China, and North Africa, in al-Harīzī's and Ibn Shabbetai's *maqāmāt* the protagonists are cut loose from the closed erotics of court poetry and travel in both space and time—to allegorical prebiblical lands in Ibn Shabbetai's *maqāma* and across the Jewish Mediterranean world in al-Harīzī's. Al-Harīzī includes in his collection *maqāmāt* set in Damascus, Egypt, and Persia. Crucial for the wanderings of al-Harīzī's protagonist Heman the Ezrahite, as it had been for al-Saraqustī's al-Sā'ib, is his identity as an Iberian and an Arabic speaker. Whereas al-Saraqustī takes great pains to show his dominance and virtuosity in handling and crafting the language of his *maqāmāt*, in al-Harīzī and Ibn Shabbetai's Hebrew *maqāmāt* the Arabic language and the literary traditions of *adab* are portrayed as threatening the Hebrew language and Jewish identity. In these Hebrew works the go-between is identified not only with Andalusi courtly discourse and the secular lifestyle associated with it, but also with the forces of evil that had seduced Judeo-Andalusi intellectuals from their own traditions.

Both al-Harīzī and Ibn Shabbetai are examples of late-twelfth- to early-thirteenth-century Jews born and raised in recently conquered Christian Spain, but whose education and identity are based on the Judeo-Arabic cultural legacy of al-Andalus. The Jewish authorities they cite are those of the Golden Age, including Solomon ibn Gabirol (1021–1070), Bahyā ibn Paqūdā (ca. 1010–1060), and Judah Halevi (1080–1141), whose own scholarship and works, even in Hebrew, are steeped in the political, social, and cultural trends of al-Andalus, with its roots in Eastern (Baghdad and Damascus) fashions and movements. Both Ibn Shabbetai and al-Harīzī use and adapt philosophical works of earlier Judeo-Andalusi scholars such as Ibn Paqūdā and Ibn Gabirol to mold potential Jewish responses to the criticisms of acculturation and assimilation leveled toward Andalusi Jews by the Rabbinic Ashkenazi Jews of Western Europe, and by members of their own community seeking to disassociate themselves from their Andalusi past.[4] Part and parcel of this redefinition of Judeo-Iberian identity is a complicated and often contradictory portrayal of Arabized Andalusi culture and the role of Jewish participation in it. Both Ibn Shabbetai and al-Ḥarīzī reveal a thorough knowledge of and respect for Arab and Arabized Jewish literature and culture as well as a mistrust of this very culture and their own relationship to it. The go-between figure is transformed by both men into a mediator between the Arabized Jew and the fruits and pleasures of the Andalusi courtly lifestyle. In both the works examined in this chapter, the go-between, who had already become associated with the courtly erotic discourse of Andalusi poetry in al-Saraqustī's *Maqāmāt*, is further represented as agent of supernatural forces intent on punishing the Jews for their transgressions. This implicit identification of Andalusi courtly discourse and values with divine punishment reflects a growing Judeo-Iberian reaction to their own cultural heritage and their particular historical situation, precipitated in part by their renewed contact with Western European Rabbinic Jewish communities.

Scheindlin thinks the Judeo-Iberian *maqāmāt* are a unique bridge and intermediary stage between the Andalusi literature of the past and the Christian European literature of the future.[5] This hybrid literary form reflects the changing identity of Judeo-Andalusi intellectuals, such as al-Ḥarīzī and Ibn Shabbetai, who still felt at home in their imaginary al-Andalus, but whose cultural differences from their fellow Jews in Western Europe and the Islamic East, such as Egypt and Iraq, lead them to reevaluate and redefine their Andalusi cultural model. Both *maqāmāt* examined in this chapter reflect the transformation in Iberian Jewish belief and identity that is produced by physical and cultural displacement and relocation. Both al-Ḥarīzī and Ibn Shabbetai inhabit the liminal cultural, temporal, and linguistic spaces of the Andalusi-European frontier. The Hebrew *maqāmāt*—adapted/translated from Arabic to Hebrew by Arabized Jews living in the southern most regions of Western Europe—mediates not only between literatures, but also between languages and cultures. The non-Muslim, non-Arabic cultural atmosphere of northern Reconquest Iberia provided the impetus for the composition of the early Judeo-Iberian *maqāmāt*, such as those of Ibn Shabbetai and al-Ḥarīzī.[6] As Rina Drory points out, Jews living in the cultural milieu of al-Andalus and the East would have had little reason to resort to Hebrew in order to compose a work clearly deriving from the Arabic literary tradition, since their audiences would have been completely familiar with and competent in Arabic, but far less competent in Hebrew.[7] Translators and authors of Hebrew *maqāmāt*, such as Ibn Shabbetai and al-Ḥarīzī, made accessible in a pan-European *lingua franca*, Hebrew—the common language of Ashkenazi and Eastern Jews—the dense and complex tapestry of Andalusi-Arabic learning and customs known as *adab* that provides the backdrop for the formal refinements of meter and rhyme out of which the Arabic *maqāmāt* is woven. As I argue in this and the following chapters, traces of these works can be found in some of the earliest erotic works of Western Europe. However, the traces of these fictional erotic works are much fainter than those left in the Latin didactic literature of Western Europe by Arabic texts of a theological, philosophical, and didactic nature, because the purpose of ecclesiastical translators, for whom these fictional erotic works would have little value, was usually the transmission of "scientific" knowledge. This process of selectively devaluing these texts and their impact and influence on later European vernacular narrative has continued into the present century as literary critics continue to overlook them in studies of the origins of Western European literature. Because these *maqāmāt* are unfamiliar to most contemporary critics working in the literatures of Europe, the Hebrew *maqāmāt* and their important role in the development of medieval and early modern European literature has been neglected.

The Hebrew *maqāmāt* do more than just introduce Arabic *adab* to a Jewish European audience. Because Jewish authors adapted the *maqāmāt* to Hebrew and the literary and religious traditions of Judaism, the focus of the Hebrew *maqāmāt* fundamentally shift from interrogating the discourses of power within a culture to interrogating a competing set of cultural discourses—the discourses of the Arabic tradition in the Jewish context, as well as the often contradictory discourses of Judaism itself—including secular and religious Hebrew poetry, and the differing exegetical models of the Jewish tradition (Midrashic versus Aristotelian). Whereas al-Saraqustī uses poetry to interrogate the courtly culture of Andalusi power (see chapter 2), Ibn Shabbetai and al-Harīzī use poetry within their *maqāmāt* to interrogate Jewish identity, questioning what it means to be a Sephardi Jew. In these *maqāmāt*, profane Hebrew poetry is the embodiment of the secular Andalusi lifestyle and value system in which the Judeo-Iberian intellectual elite were formed. It is at once a badge of their cultural superiority and a symbol of acculturation to a foreign tradition. In both the *maqāmāt* studied in this chapter the authors explore these contradictions at the heart of their own cultural identification as Andalusi Jews.

As mentioned earlier, al-Harīzī and Ibn Shabbetai are both from the first generations of Jewish scholars born and raised in Christian Iberia, but educated and brought up in an Andalusi cultural milieu.[8] The Arabo-Andalusi *maqāmāt* would have been part of that milieu. Al-Harīzī's translation of al-Harīrī's *maqāmāt*, entitled *Mahberoth Itiel*, was completed in Provence and offers proof for the assertion that such Iberian compositions were originally made for non–Arabic-speaking audiences.[9] Andalusi Jews whose linguistic and cultural formation was based in the Arabic tradition of *adab* would have been able to read al-Harīrī in the original. However, Rina Drory speculates that once al-Harīzī left Iberia and Western Europe to travel through the East, his motivation changed and took on nationalist fervor as he encountered Eastern Jewish communities little interested in Hebrew.[10] The encounter with such communities in which Arabic was the dominant language, but among whom Hebrew had not been cultivated as a parallel profane literary tradition, as it had been by Andalusi Jews, inspired him to compose original *maqāmāt* in Hebrew, namely the *Tahkemoni*.[11] Surviving manuscripts, however, also show that the *Tahkemoni* was known among the Jewish communities of Iberia.[12]

Whether al-Harīzī and Ibn Shabbetai chose Hebrew to compose their *maqāmāt* as an assertion of national Jewish-Sephardi identity in opposition to Arabic, or chose it as a means of transmitting the knowledge of the Arabic tradition and Judeo-Andalusi literature to non–Arabic-speaking Jews, or a combination of both, their use of Hebrew entailed a series of modifications and adaptations at both the formal and thematic level. In the twelfth and thirteenth centuries, Hebrew was used only by a small number of learned elites worldwide, mostly for poetry or exegesis, and not as a language of conversation or daily life, for which the vernacular was preferred. Conveying the complex metrics and rhymes of the Arabic *maqāma* into a language of such limited use proved a difficult task.[13] Whereas composers of Arabic *maqāmāt* such as al-Saraqustī or al-Harīrī could draw upon the vibrant Arabic language and the vast field of *adab* literature that had developed in an unbroken progression from the eighth to the thirteenth century, absorbing the various traditions with which it came into contact, such as the Persian, Classical, and even Romance traditions in Iberia, the corpus of Hebrew literature from which *maqāmāt* authors could draw was much smaller, consisting mostly of religious texts and the poetic tradition of the Jews of al-Andalus. Not surprisingly, these two traditions figure prominently in the works of al-Harīzī, Ibn Shabbetai, and the other authors of Hebrew *maqāmāt* in medieval Iberia. Both al-Harīzī and Ibn Shabbetai take up the Andalusi go-between tale and recontextualize it in this new Hebrew landscape tinged with the moral overtones of biblical and Midrashic models. Both authors also explore in the context of the go-between narrative the tension between these two different sources/uses of medieval Hebrew—the secular Arabized poetry of Andalusi courtiers and the ethical, didactic material of the Bible and the Midrash.

These two authors' go-between narratives, *Minhat Yehuda, Sone ha-Nashim* (*The Offering of Yehuda, Enemy of Women*) and the "*Maqāma* of Marriage," Gate Six of the *Tahkemoni*, can profitably be read together given the affinities in theme, content, and imagery between the two works.[14] In both works the use of Arabic and the appreciation of the Arabic literary tradition is addressed in a fictional allegory rife with poetic imagery. Matti Huss dates a preliminary version of Ibn Shabbetai's *Offering* to 1208. A later edition with supplemental material probably appeared in 1228.[15] Al-Harīzī's *Tahkemoni* is often dated to the middle of the second decade of the thirteenth century, sometime after 1216.[16] Judith Dishon includes the *Offering* as one of the sources al-Harīzī used for the "*Maqāma* of Marriage," given the similarities in plot, intertextual allusions, and characters.[17] The striking number of parallels between the *Offering* and the "*Maqāma* of Marriage," explored in detail below, suggest that the former did serve as a model for the latter tale's exploration of Judeo-Andalusi identity.

Judah Ibn Shabbetai on the Frontier

Judah ibn Shabbetai, like his contemporary Judah al-Harīzī, explores issues of Jewish identity and culture, as well as expands the limits of Hebrew fictional narrative in his go-between *maqāma*, the *Offering*.[18] In Ibn Shabbetai's tale, the protagonist is not the comic rogue of al-Saraqustī's *Maqāmāt al-luzūmīyah*, but a pious Jew, son of the only wise man to have survived a mythic battle between Wisdom and Folly. This young man, Zerah, follows his father's advice and shuns the company of women in order to pursue the study of Law. Because Zerah encourages other men to follow his lead and forsake having sex, the women of the community rise up and search for someone to help them make their husbands and lovers have sex with them again. Their pleas are answered by the appearance of an old sorceress who seduces Zerah with a girl that conforms to the secular Andalusi poetic ideal of beauty. In Ibn Shabbetai's work, this ideal woman is more than just a beautiful combination of features, for, like the Andalusi slave girls described by Ibn Hazm and al-Saraqustī, she is also an expert musician and poet, capable of extemporaneously composing Andalusi-style poetry praising Zerah's features. However, the old go-between/sorceress, seemingly with the Lord's blessings, exchanges this beauty with an ugly old crone. Zerah cannot bear his new bride and runs to ask the men of the land what he should do, flee or seek a divorce. He is taken before a judge to have his fate decided. Just as the judge, who is the author, Ibn Shabbetai's patron Abraham ibn al-Fakhkhār, sentences Zerah to death, the author steps into his own story to plead for the protagonist's life.[19]

Ibn Shabbetai's *Offering* inspired other works in addition to al-Harīzī's "*Maqāma* of Marriage." Some contemporary authors responded immediately to the work's misogyny with their own treatises in support of women: *Ezrat ha-nashim* (*In Defense of Women*) and *Ein Mishpat* (*The Fount of Law*), written by an author known only as Isaac in 1210 almost immediately after the *Offering*, and *Ohev ha-nashim* (*The Lover of Women*) (in some translations, *Defender of Women*) written by the Provencal poet Yedaiyah ha-Penini in the last half of the thirteenth century.[20] The number of responses the *Offering* generated attests to its popularity. The work survives in twenty-seven manuscripts and many printed editions. The international literary scandal that it caused among the Jews of Castile, Catalonia, and Provence for almost a century following its composition provides an early analogue for later Western European pro- and antifeminist debates in the fourteenth and the fifteenth centuries.[21]

Ibn Shabbetai also came into conflict with members of the Iberian Jewish communities. In addition to the *Offering*, two of the author's other works survive: one is a satiric debate between wisdom and wealth that lampoons the decadence of the Jewish noble class; the other, a "Writ of Excommunication," *Divre ha-Alah ve-ha-Niddui* (*The Words of the Curse and the Ban*), is Ibn Shabbetai's reaction to having been publicly denounced by five of the most prominent members of the Jewish community of Saragossa (including Joseph ben Isaac Benveniste). These prominent Saragossan Jews led the community to publicly burn one of Ibn Shabbetai's now lost works in the courtyard of the city's synagogue.[22] This work eulogized "the scholars, poets and notables who came to the aid of their people in time of stress, and included an account of the exploits of 'the five kings of Spain.'" Seemingly, Ibn Shabbetai's appreciation of the Christian kings was enough for the religious leaders of the community to excommunicate him. In his retaliatory invective, Ibn Shabbetai characterized his enemies as "Vicious foxes and scorpions. . .stupid and heartless folk."[23] Important for the *Offering* is the fact that in this work Ibn Shabbetai characterizes his attackers as "Men of Folly," and accuses them of the very crime his protagonist Zerah will commit—having relations with non-Jewish slave girls.[24] The Jewish community of thirteenth-century Saragossa was a community within which literature mattered as a tool for political propaganda, for the creation of cultural identity, and, ultimately, as a matter of life and death. Ibn Shabbetai highlights the often contradictory cultural practices and beliefs of the Judeo-Iberian community in the *Offering*. Again it is the figure of the go-between who acts as mediator between the various cultural stances represented in the text. In the subsequent section I explore Ibn Shabbetai's development of this go-between narrative grounded in both the Hebrew secular poetry of the Golden Age and in the Arabic literature of al-Andalus, including the *maqāmāt* of al-Saraqustī, Ibn Paqūdā's ethical treatise *Duties of the Heart*, and Andalusi and Eastern collections of poetry and prose including those of Moses ibn Ezra and Ibn Gabirol.

The Folly of Wisdom in the Offering of Yehuda

The *Offering* begins not with an amorous encounter requiring the services of a go-between, but with a tale of exile. The appearance of the go-between is precipitated in Ibn Shabbetai's narrative by an allegorical battle between Folly and Wisdom. The only survivor from among the ranks of Wisdom's forces is Tahkemoni, who flees from the king of Median (the champion of Folly). Tahkemoni hopes to keep his knowledge alive by passing it on to his son Zerah. Ibn Shabbetai identifies instinct/folly with the Gentiles and names him/it as the king of Median or non-Jews. In Ibn Shabbetai's allegorical battle, the exile of Tahkemoni becomes a parable of the exile and diaspora of Andalusi Jews fleeing the Almoravid invasion of the Iberian Peninsula. Just as learned Andalusi Jews fled from the Almoravids north across the mountains into the medieval kingdoms of Christian Iberia, so too does Tahkemoni flee and escape from the king of Median, lover of Folly, to live among other non-Jewish nations.[25] A seemingly prophetic vision (Ibn Shabbetai is careful to tell us not that the vision/voice are divine, but only that Tahkemoni believes them to be) helps Tahkemoni make sense of the slaughter of his people, Wisdom's defeat and his own exile by blaming these evils on women. In this vision a voice tells Tahkemoni that men have lost their way because their wives have turned their hearts from the "true" path; because of the webs women weave, men have gone astray, doing nothing but quarreling and committing shameful acts.[26] There follows a litany of the evils ascribed to women and a list of evil women culled from the Bible. Implicit in almost all of the examples chosen is the theme of the sexual relation between Jew and Gentile.[27] On the basis of this vision, Tahkemoni convinces his son to swear off women, and the narrative then turns to Zerah and his plight as a righteous young man in a world of angry women. Zerah takes up his father's cause and begins preaching that men should have nothing to do with women and, like his father, blames women for the suffering of Jews in exile. Zerah renounces sex and women and goes with three friends to study the Law.

Before introducing the Andalusi go-between and beloved, both of whom will sway Zerah from his misogynist ways, Ibn Shabbetai offers two models of exile, each of which would have been familiar to Andalusi Jews living in Christian Castile. Tahkemoni's exile, like that of Andalusi Jews who fled the Almoravids, is the result of the political–military advance of an enemy army whose beliefs lead them to persecute Tahkemoni and his companions. His son Zerah's self-imposed exile, though, resembles that of courtiers such as Moses ibn Ezra and second- and third-generation Judeo-Andalusi exiles who maintained their Andalusi culture and often felt alienated from the Spanish Christian society in which they lived (as Moses ibn Ezra so poignantly expresses in the "Poem of Two Exiles"). Ibn Shabbetai shapes these two representations of exile out of Judeo-Andalusi literary models, including a penitential poem by the Judeo-Andalusi poet and philosopher Ibn Gabirol and the ethical treatise, *Duties of the Heart*, by the eleventh-century Judeo-Andalusi pietist Ibn Paqūdā.[28] Ibn Shabbetai's contemporary Judeo-Iberian readers would have been familiar with both these works and recognized his allusions to them. However, by adapting these didactic-moral approaches to Arab acculturation into a narrative that also accommodates the Judeo-Andalusi erotic discourses that are the focus of each text's critique, Ibn Shabbetai creates an original fictional account that reimagines the Judeo-Andalusi exilic condition as a more complex phenomenon than just "us" versus "them," "good" versus "bad," or Jew versus non-Jew.

Both Ibn Paqūdā and Ibn Gabirol, like Ibn Shabbetai, were Saragossan intellectuals trained in the Arabized Andalusi court ideal of *adab* (as was al-Saraqustī, see chapter 2). However, Ibn Paqūdā and Ibn Gabirol both advocate a renunciation of Arabized social and cultural values on the grounds that such values undermine the Judeo-Andalusi's spiritual life.[29] Both these Saragossan intellectuals attack aspects of the Judeo-Andalusi lifestyle, including the use of Arabic, the cultivation of Arabized poetry and song, and the pursuit of advancement and monetary gain in the non-Jewish Andalusi court as a threat to Jewish identity and spirituality.[30] Both Ibn Gabirol's poetry and Ibn Paqūdā's treatise are testimonies of a conflicted exiled subject. Both focus on the internal effects of exile and diasporic assimilation.

From Ibn Gabirol's poem, "On Leaving Saragossa," Ibn Shabbetai adopts the name of Zerah's father, Tahkemoni, the foolish exile who has become so disoriented he believes his foolishness is wisdom.[31] Just as Ibn Shabbetai was excommunicated by the Jewish community of Saragossa because of his beliefs, so too was Ibn Gabirol some one hundred and fifty years before.[32] In this poem Ibn Gabirol reflects on what life had been among people who preferred Arabic to their own traditions. He compares his mental state after the travails he suffered in Saragossa (at that time under the *taifa* kings of the Banū Hūd), to that of the biblical Tahkemoni (2 Samuel 23:8), head of David's warriors and proverbially someone who becomes so confused in battle that in his folly he thinks that he is wise.[33] Ibn Gabirol says that he is similarly confused because he is alone without family and friends among cruel men (ostriches) who tell him to use the common language (Arabic) instead of "Ashkelonite" (Hebrew).[34] In Ibn Gabirol's poem, Folly is associated with the use of the Arabic language and customs and is depicted as cruelly destroying the wisdom of the Jews and the Hebrew language. He implies that Arabized Andalusi Jews, particularly those of the Saragossan community, have betrayed their faith and their people. Ibn Gabirol describes a diasporic subject who, rejected by his own people for not adapting the local Arabic customs, advocates instead a return to Jewish language and traditions. This tension with members of his own community has led to the poet's isolation, and the fight for his culture and language is framed as a spiritual battle. Ibn Shabbetai, writing some hundred and fifty years later in Christian Iberia, and similarly ostracized from the Saragossan Jewish community, takes up Ibn Gabirol's Tahkemoni as symbol of the exiled Jew, but explores what happens when the confused exile becomes a prophet to the next generation—what happens when in his confusion Tahkemoni advises Zerah and his followers to renounce their idolatrous lifestyle and to forgo sex all together.

Just as Ibn Gabirol transposes an Old Testament warrior from the physical battlefield to the mental and spiritual battles of the Judeo-Andalusi community, so too does Ibn Paqūdā offer a metaphoric reading of an Old Testament battle scene to describe the psychological trials of exile. In chapter 5 of *Duties of the Heart*, a work designed in part to lead Judeo-Andalusi courtiers from the Arabized culture of the court, Ibn Paqūdā tells the tale of Ecclesiastes 9:14, the story of a little city besieged by a great king, but saved by a poor wise man. In the *Duties*, Ibn Paqūdā glosses this tale, informing us readers that the city is a man. The people in the story, king and poor man, correspond to various desires or "traits of the soul." "The instinct is called a great king because he has many armies and followers and a great retinue."[35] The bulwarks that the king/instinct builds against man's intellect or will are the evil thoughts inspired by instinct. The poor wise man that saves the city is man's reason or intellect (*al-'aql*). This poor man's little light (*nūr* in Arabic) can expel the great darkness of instinct/folly (*hawā*).[36] The Arabic term used by Ibn Paqūdā to define the evil instinct, *hawā* (*yetser* in Hebrew), that threatens the city and the man in this parable is significant as it also figures in Ibn Hazm's Andalusi courtly construction of the ideal courtier and model lover (see chapter 1).[37] Furthermore, the *nūr al-'aql* used to overcome *hawā* is, for ibn Paqūdā, the light of reason that awakens the soul and guides it to the divine light.[38] Ibn Paqūdā, like Ibn Gabirol, was heavily influenced by contemporary Jewish and Muslim forms of mysticism. In this parable we clearly see how Ibn Paqūdā develops the philosophical-mystical imagery and vocabulary current in contemporary Iberian intellectual circles as part of his own unique system of Jewish personal spirituality. Ibn Paqūdā's spiritual directives and admonitions are, however, contingent upon contemporary sociohistorical events and conditions, and his criticisms of Judeo-Andalusi intellectuals and courtiers is an important context for the elaboration of his philosophical mysticism. Ibn Paqūdā's exegesis transforms the parable into a figurative attack on the precepts of the Andalusi courtly ideal and the Arabo-Andalusi concept of *adab* as adopted by Judeo-Iberian courtiers and uses the same imagery that Ibn Shabbetai will develop some one hundred and fifty years later in his *maqāma* dealing with the same themes. The opening battle of Folly and Wisdom in Ibn Shabbetai's *Offering* provides a Hebrew version of an allegorical battle very similar to the one Ibn Paqūdā describes, suggesting that Tahkemoni's battle and exile are metaphoric descriptions of the mental anguish of the exiled Andalusi Jew.

The intertextual play of the first part of the *Offering*, centered around the name of Tahkemoni and its possible meanings as wise man/wisdom in the sense used by Ibn Paqūdā in the gloss of Ecclesiastics 9:14 and, ironically, as the wise man made foolish in Ibn Gabirol's poem, problematizes the role of Arabized Andalusi-style learning and culture for the Judeo-Iberian exile in Castile. According to Ibn Paqūdā, wisdom is the only hope for a man beset by instinctual desires; however, that same wisdom becomes, like Ibn Gabirol's Tahkemoni, foolish when taken out of context and exiled from its home. What then must we readers think of Ibn Shabbetai's Tahkemoni/Wisdom? Is it the *'aql* if Arabo-Andalusi philosophic rationalism, the inherited wisdom (*hekmat*) of the Jewish tradition, or the ironic "wisdom" of the foolish exile? The multiple interpretative possibilities open to us is part and parcel of the *maqāmāt* and constitutes one of the genre's central aesthetic and hermeneutic qualities.

While Ibn Paqūdā's metaphoric interpretation of the battle between a man's wisdom and the forces of folly suggest that Tahkemoni's opening battle can be read as an allegory for the exilic experience of the Andalusi Jew, another of the central tenets for the Jews in exile that Ibn Paqūdā outlines in chapter 9 of the *Duties* figures prominently in Zerah's personal struggle in the second part of the *Offering*. Ibn Paqūdā's treatise advocates an austere form of asceticism as an anecdote for the sexual licentiousness of the Andalusi lifestyle. Ibn Paqūdā believes Andalusi Jews have special need of asceticism because of their historical submission to instinct and the pleasures of the body:

> As to the obligation of the people of the Law to practice asceticism, it springs from the following reason: the purpose of the Law is to give the mind mastery over the entire soul, with its desires for the pleasures of the body, and to establish the superiority of the mind. It is well known that the dominance of the instinct over the mind is the root of every sin and the cause of all the vices. When that happened, not only did people turn to this world, but they also turned away from their religion. Thus the instinct robbed them of the mainstay of their immunity to sin and deprived them of the way of their forefathers....[39]

Ibn Shabbetai's *maqāma* is a ficitonal adaptation of this advice. Ibn Shabbetai's character, Tahkemoni, witnesses first hand the destruction that ensues when folly and instinct reign, and tries to impart the way of his forefathers to his son Zerah, who follows Tahkemoni and Ibn Paqūdā's directive by choosing to study the Law and renounce women. Zerah does what Ibn Paqūdā encourages Judeo-Andalusi courtiers to do in the *Duties*, namely forsake their worldly positions and to seek "virtues and solitude and the isolation from others" and avoid the evils of being among people.[40] Ibn Paqūdā further warns the courtier driven by instinct to seek the approval of his peers to consult his reason (*al-'aql*). "It will teach you to know that when in matters of the soul you turn away from the study and practice of Law, and approach the other sciences, you will perish, and none of the other sciences you have studied will benefit you before God."[41] Zerah is the fictional embodiment of Ibn Paqūdā's Jewish courtier, for not only does he initially shun his instincts—his sexual desires—in order to study the Law, he later turns away from the Law to follow other sciences, particularly that of Arabized *adab*. Thus Ibn Shabbetai's ficitonal tale offers us two battles between Jewish moral dogma and the secular lifestyle—the first on a national, epic scale, the Battle between Folly and Wisdom writ large, and the second on a personal, individual scale, with the seduction of the pious Zerah by Kozbi and Ayyalah.

Zerah's abstinence clearly conforms to the model of asceticism Ibn Paqūdā proscribes in the *Duties of the Heart*. However, the question of where Ibn Paqūdā got his idea of Jewish abstinence remains, given that, unlike in Christianity, normative Jewish belief and tradition advocates healthy sexual activity.[42] The ideal abstinent student of Torah described by Ibn Paqūdā and whom Zerah resembles recalls the sages of the Northern European and Eastern Jewish communities—not Judeo-Andalusi thinkers. This attitude of sexual asceticism was not common among secular Andalusi Jews.[43] Ibn Paqūdā was heavily influenced by earlier Muslim thinkers such as Muḥāsabī, al-Fārābī, ibn Bājja, the Brethern of Purity (*Ikhwān al-safā'*) and the Muʿtazilites, who also advocated a similar form of physical asceticism as part of the necessary requisites for mystical union with the Divinity or as part of a moral lifestyle.[44] These thinkers, in turn, reveal the influence of Neoplatonism. On the other hand, Ibn Paqūdā's asceticism may also reflect the Babylonian and/or Northern European Rabbinic traditions. The problem posed by a husband's long absence from his wife for the express purpose of Torah study appears frequently in the Babylonian Mishne.[45]

Abstinence is only one part of Ibn Paqūdā's antidote for the Arabized Judeo-Andalusi courtier and his lifestyle—a lifestyle Ibn Paqūdā compares to idolatry. In chapter 9 of the *Duties*, Ibn Paqūdā says Judeo-Andalusi courtiers are wicked sinners like the biblical Zimri, the Old Testament model of the apostate, idolatrous Jew.[46] Ibn Paqūdā underscores the hypocrisy of Judeo-Andalusi courtiers who, like all who seek material profit over spiritual betterment, "ask for the reward of the pious while they do the deeds of sinners; they ask to be ranked with the virtuous while they follow the way of the wicked, as said our ancient sages; 'They commit the transgression of Zimri and expect a reward like that given to Phinehas.'"[47] Again Ibn Paqūdā adapts an Old Testament *exemplum* to the situation of the Jews of al-Andalus. In Numbers 25, Zimri, a Jew who had relations with a pagan, idolatrous Medianite woman, is killed by Phinehas as punishment for corrupting the Jewish people. For Ibn Paqūdā, the idolatry threatening the Jews of Median compares to the *adab* lifestyle and values affecting Jewish identity in medieval Iberia.[48]

Ibn Shabbetai subverts Ibn Paqūdā's model of ideal Jewish piety by having the pious Zerah become traitorous like Zimri. Zerah does not denounce the world and its evils for his religion, he renounces the Law for wordly pleasure. Ibn Paqūdā mentions only Zimri and Phinehas in chapter 9, leaving the Medianite woman with whom Zimri had sex (thus committing idolatry and betraying his people) nameless; Ibn Shabbetai, however, gives this Medianite woman a central role in his narrative. Like Ibn Paqūdā, Ibn Shabbetai adapts this Old Testament account to medieval Iberia, making Kozbi, the Medianite woman, an Andalusi go-between and the textual representative of the Andalusi court culture and lifestyle. In the second part of Ibn Shabbetai's tale, the initial struggle between Folly and Wisdom is recast as a struggle between men and women. The gendering of the initial tension provides a textual opening for the go-between, whose function in Andalusi courtly discourse (as we have seen in chapters 1 and 2) is not only to bring men and women together, but, perhaps more importantly, to help construct desire by manipulating courtly discourses such as poetry and formulaic description (*wasf*). In the *Offering*, however, the go-between is much more than a member of a courtly love triangle. She is at the center of the larger cultural struggle between Folly and Wisdom, Jews and non-Jews, men and women, and the extremes of the exilic Jew's identity. Ibn Shabbetai focuses on this woman and her role as an essential agent in the construction of Jewish identity. Ibn Shabbetai's selection of Kozbi as go-between works across the several levels of signification in his work and unites the complex intertextual web he is weaving throughout this *maqāma*. In the biblical episode of Baal-Peor, evoked by Ibn Paqūdā, Kozbi is a princess, daughter of the king of Median. Relocated into Ibn Shabbetai's narrative her name alone relates her not only to the biblical whore, but also possibly to the king of Folly, the king of Median who defeated Wisdom and exiled Tahkemoni in the first part of the tale. Since in Ibn Shabbetai's text the king of Folly/Median is also, according to the conventions of the Judeo-Andalusi lyric, a metaphor for the non-Jewish rulers of Iberia, Kozbi is also therefore associated with the Muslim and Christian cultures of medieval Iberia and with the forces that led the Andalusi Jews into exile. The tale Ibn Shabbetai develops in the rest of the *maqāma* shows the process by which Kozbi, agent of folly and pleasure, seduces and brings low Zerah, the model Jew. Because Zerah has convinced the other men of the land to forgo sex, the women band together and seek out Kozbi to help them. Kozbi makes a dramatic entrance, arising from among the gathered women in flames of sorcery: "There arose from amongst them a wise woman, a mistress of necromancy and deceit. The rivers could not wash away the sparks of the immensity of her sorceries and whoring. And her name was Kozbi bat Yeresha, 'Lying, daughter of Inheritance' because she held deceit as an inheritance."[49] Kozbi's origins among sparks of sorceries and her portrayal as a master of necromancy further mark her as a Gentile, a non-Jew.[50] In his treatise, Ibn Paqūdā attacks those Andalusi Jews who chose to study Astronomy/Astrology, claiming they are following the ways of the Gentiles, preferring sorcery to the Law/Torah. Ibn Shabbetai's learned audience, upon hearing Kozbi's description would recognize that Kozbi embodies these Gentile ways designed to seduce Zerah away from the Law and Jewish traditions.

As he gives voice to the Medianite woman, Ibn Shabbetai also gives voice to the women of the land, who come to have a central role in this *maqāma*. The women who summon Kozbi to assist them are "filled with gall and venom" because their husbands and fiancés have abandoned them.[51] As Zerah puts into action the Jewish lifestyle that Ibn Paqūdā and, to a lesser degree, Ibn Gabirol advocate, we witness a community torn apart. Ibn Paqūdā's advice is for educated males. Ibn Shabbetai, however, shows us that there are many other members of the community, and their voices and behavior also affect communal well-being. Ibn Paqūdā does not explore the consequences of the abstinence he preaches, but this, in fact, becomes the subject of the second part of Ibn Shabbetai's *maqāma*. The women proclaim, "Lo, Zerah has transformed us into sources of terror and fear. Seven women seize one man. Think of us and see that our misfortune is enormous. Every virgin is a house all shut up, and there is no coming and going from her prison. . . . Death to this man, may he be stoned, with no deliverance, for he has slandered the virgin of Israel."[52] The women describe themselves as legitimate virgins of Israel and as an integral part of the Jewish community. Zerah's abstinence and homosocial behavior, modeled on Ibn Paqūdā's ideal as elaborated in the *Duties*, is here portrayed as harming the nation of Israel. In fact, Ibn Shabbetai shows us how Zerah and his followers' extreme behavior leads from licit sex with the virgins of Israel to desire for illicit relations with an Andalusi bride.

Ibn Shabbetai offers us in the character of Kozbi an alternative to the inherited discourse of Jewish identity represented by Tahkemoni. Like

Tahkemoni the Wise, Kozbi is also a powerful and learned figure who, despite her identification with non-Jewish figures and traditions, is ironically dedicated to ensuring the survival of Judaism. Tahkemoni, believing he has had a prophetic vision, seeks to steer his son Zerah away from the enemies of Judaism; namely women. Kozbi, on the other hand, follows a completely different path. In response to the legitimate appeals of the women of Israel, Kozbi sets about discrediting Zerah and the abstinence he is preaching in order to reestablish sexual relations between men and women so as to ensure that the Jewish race will continue to multiply. Whereas Tahkemoni believes he has had a prophetic vision informing him of the evils of women, Ibn Shabbetai informs us that Kozbi speaks, prophet-like, directly to the Lord:

"Lo! Instead of peace, bitterness, I have, bitterness bitterness.[53] O thou who built the upper chambers within the waters;[54] who gave us private parts: the upper and the lower; who chose men and rejected women; who caused to sprout in man the beard and penis for his fame and glory, and who gave the daughters of Eve passion and the lust of death (the uterus). Fatten the heart of this man and blind his eyes in order to destroy his transgression." She ended her prayer and went out to Zerah's tent. And Zerah, as his pleasantness turned to pain, did not know the Lord had abandoned him. And Kozbi the cruel stood before him. And Lo! Plague stood before him.[55]

In Ibn Shabbetai's *maqāma*, the Lord listens to Kozbi's prayer and does her bidding. Kozbi prays to God for assistance with her plan. She curses the fact that she is a woman, and gender differences in general, lamenting the sorrows of women and the power of men. She reminds the Lord that He established the hierarchy according to which women rank lower than men, and therefore He must assist the women to defeat Zerah and the other men who have renounced women, for women cannot defeat the men alone. Behind the supposed teleological superiority of men that Kozbi emphasizes in her prayer is the obligation that men have toward their inferiors/the women, as well as their obligation to procreate as mandated by the Fall. Women as part of their natural condition (their identity defined by the pangs of childbirth) must procreate, and in order to do that the men must have sex with them. Kozbi points out to God (and the reader) that Zerah's abstinence goes against God's own plan. Zerah's transgression is further underscored in the final scene when the judge before whom the people bring Zerah claims, "He deserves to die for scorning the beauty of women and for destroying the mighty, the holy nation."[56] In Ibn Shabbetai's tale, sexual abstinence as advocated by Tahkemoni and Zerah—the textual representatives of the anti-Andalusi Rabbinic tradition—is incompatible with Judaism. Kozbi, the Andalusi-style go-between, becomes the tool/intercessor by which the Lord saves the Jews, which she does by manipulating the discourses of Andalusi erotic desire.

Ayyala, Hind of the Dawn

Kozbi, the helpmate of God, tells the women what they need to do in order to stop Zerah. She describes the ideal woman they will need to seduce him. Ibn Shabbetai has brought Kozbi, the textual representative of Arabized Andalusi discourse, into the moral universe of pietists such as Ibn Paqūdā, and she immediately gets to work. Kozbi describes the ideal woman with imagery typical of Judeo-Andalusi poetry. She is a "maiden complete in her beauty, entirely perfect and without blemish. . . Shining like the sun, fashioned from myrrh and cassia. Formed (as a mosaic) from grace and beauty." Additionally Kozbi specifies her social skills and musical talents: "She receives all who gaze upon her with delight. She should be endowed with morals and sound advice and understand proverbs and enigmatic/satirical poetry. She should speak with a mastery of rhetoric and bewitch with her song, and her speech should be pleasant like a sprinkling of dew and like a mirror of strong metal . . . and she should know how to play the lute and the lyre."[57] This most desirable woman conforms to the ideal Arabized poet according to Moses ibn Ezra.[58] She is the embodiment of just the type of Andalusi-style learning that Ibn Paqūdā warns his readers about in the *Duties*. Ibn Shabbetai's incorporation of this description of *adab* into the description of the perfect woman makes it clear that Kozbi is here introducing the discourse of the secular Andalusi courtier.

Kozbi takes her idols and works her sorceries/spells, and "conjures the maiden endowed with secret knowledge and the life of the souls. She is the gazelle taken from Eden, the garden of God. And her name is Ayyala Shluha, Hind of the Dawn."[59] Ibn Shabbetai's use of *'ofra* (fawn) and *ayyala* (hind) establish this ideal as part of both the erotic Jewish past—the beloved of the Song of Songs—and the secular Arabized Andalusi erotic poetry. The image of the gazelle/deer was central in the Arabized Hebrew poetry of Iberia and is ubiquitous in Andalusi poetry composed in both Arabic and Hebrew.[60] The image of Ayyala being conjured into being by Kozbi, further plays with the semantics of both women's names as well as Andalusi beliefs concerning poetry. In his poetic treatise *Kitāb al-Muḥādara wal-Mudākara*, Moses ibn Ezra cites a pseudo-Aristotelian aphorism that was widely cited in Arabic scholarship claiming that the best aspect of poetry is the most false.[61] Maimonides also attacked poetic imagery (syllogism and analogy) as a means of deception and lying.[62] Ayyala—the poetic hind of Judeo-Andalusi verse—is created by Kozbi, whose name literally means "Lying, daughter of Deception." Kozbi's conjuring of Ayyala is a metaphor for the poetic process itself as defined in Judeo-Andalusi letters and recalls Umm 'Amr's seductive lies. With the introduction of Kozbi and Ayyala, Ibn Shabbetai inscribes the discourse of Arabized erotic poetry into the heart of Tahkemoni and Zerah's spiritual parable of instinct and folly. Kozbi mediates/joins these two discourses—pietist and erotic—functioning in both as interpreter and creator of desire.

Ayyala's actions immediately show us that she fulfills Kozbi's ideal description. Ayyala makes a dramatic entrance with her retinue of servants and her lyre: "And she came and stood like the breaking dawn and the setting sun. She walked to and fro. She advanced with her maid servants, and, she made the heart that desired her beat. She condemned righteous men to wrong doing, yet she was innocent/righteous. Her eyes widened and she kept silent, drawing near and then backing away. She took the lyre and tightened its strings and she brought forth the elegance of its tones. She stood before Zerah and graced him with her voice." Ayyala's first words to Zerah are in verse typical of Judeo-Andalusi secular poetry: "The hair of my beloved and the light of his face is like the sun covered by a cloud. /. . .Come, my beloved, and join/keep company with faithful ones. Go down in the gardens and pick roses/lilies and plant pleasantries![63] For the buds are already showing themselves. Open the blossom of the vine! The two pomegranates, breasts that have never been caressed, are budding."[64]

By referring to Ayyala's ability to play the lute and lyre, as well as to sing and compose Andalusi-style poetry, Ibn Shabbetai is also locating her in the tradition of the Arabo-Andalusi singing slave woman as discussed in chapters 1 and 2.[65] Here Ayyala is the fictional incarnation of the slave girls of Seville who were trained by old women in the art of singing and music as described by Al-Tīfāshī (see chapter 1). Ayyala fits al-Tīfāshī's description well: she has an old woman as a teacher (Kozbi), is skilled in rhetoric and singing, and has an entourage of hand maidens and her own lute, which she plays quite well. Unlike the slave woman in al-Saraqustī's "*Maqāma* 12," who represented the pleasures of illicit sex and the ugly realities existing outside the discourses of courtly desire, Ibn Shabbetai paradoxically frames the illicit desire Ayyala represents as a tool in the larger narrative of Jewish redemption. One of the issues dividing the northern Iberian Jewish communities was the practice of owning non-Jewish slave women.[66] Opponents to this custom saw these women as a threat to the community, and it was the wealthiest and most distinguished members of the community who most often had relations, and children, with such Gentile women.

Confronted with the beauty and charming words of Ayyala, Zerah forgets all his father's advice and engages her in an Andalusi-style poetic exchange in which both lover and beloved reveal a thorough familiarity with Judeo-Andalusi courtly poetics. Zerah takes up the imagery used by

Ayyala in her first poem to describe her beautiful hair and face: "Your hair is like the dark of night, / Your face as morning fair; / Let not your brilliance startle you or your raven-colored hair."[67] He has responded to Ayyala's description of his countenance with one of hers: both descriptions, which contrast the dark hair against the shining face, are reminiscent of the Arabic and Judeo-Andalusi poetic traditions.[68]

The next several poems/verses that the lovers exchange follow the habit of Judeo-Andalusi poets of mixing allusions to the Torah, Numbers, and the Song of Songs, with imagery typical of Arabic erotic poetry.[69] The threatening eyes of the fawn mentioned by Ayyala ("Fear no fawn's eyes although they threaten death to every man alive; / Their eyes may sting, but when victims see them they at once revive") correspond to imagery discussed in Book 4 of Moses ibn Ezra's treatise.[70] Ayyala further claims that Zerah derives his name from the brightness of his face that shines both day and night, simultaneously revealing her familiarity with the conventions of Judeo-Andalusi poetry and an advanced knowledge of the Hebrew language.[71] Zerah, in turn, calls Ayyala a gazelle of grace, and claims that he is a faithful lover who wants nothing more than "to pasture/graze amongst the roses of your cheeks as the seraphim observe from above."[72] Ayyala complements Zerah's long, noble neck, and he returns in kind with a similar verse: "The neck of the graceful gazelle is like an ivory column on a stone floor of porphyry and red marble."[73] Zerah completes this literary portrait with verses dedicated to the beauty of Ayyala's breasts.[74]

The poems exchanged by Ayyala and Zerah are descriptive love poems that focus on the lovers' bodies. The images are commonplaces of Judeo-Andalusi Golden Age poetry and follow the standard order, descending from the hair to the breasts, conforming to the canonical description as summarized by Raymond Scheindlin.[75] However much his father may wish it were not so and try to dissuade him, Zerah is an Andalusi Jew, and as such, his desire is shaped by those cultural forces that determine Andalusi identity. Ayyala constructs Zerah as an ideal Judeo-Andalusi courtier, both desiring subject and ideal beloved, and uses the Andalusi discourse of courtly love to channel his desire. We see in the lovers' exchange of poems the process Lacan describes as the creation of desire in the Symbolic, the "social world of language and culture."[76]

Zerah's desire for Ayyala springs from his condition as an Andalusi Jew, with the specific contingent cultural conditions and histories that entails. His father, the voice of a particular strain of Jewish tradition and wisdom, may tell him such desire is wrong, but Zerah seemingly has no other vocabulary to describe his desire. Zerah resembles the Lacanian subject who does not/cannot control or define the object of desire, but, on the contrary, is defined by it. Zerah is overcome by desire, and he bows his knee to acknowledge Ayyala's superior poetic talent. Zerah calls the go-between to arrange a dowry, for he must wed Ayyala. He tells Kozbi he is willing to pay any price. Zerah succumbs to Kozbi's plan and to the beauty and skill of Ayyala, despite his father's warnings:

> Upon seeing the glow of her face and hearing her songs and reasonings, the maiden raised in his estimation, and she was good before him. Zerah replied, saying: "The heart of a maiden is bound to folly, but from God comes a woman who acts wisely. She has taken Prudence and Beauty as an inheritance. This is the one He calls 'woman.'"[77] He forgot all of his father's words and commandments, and he perverted/twisted all his ways.[78]

It is Kozbi, the go-between, who has created this object of desire and set it before Zerah, but in this passage Ibn Shabbetai reveals that she has done so according to God's plan. Zerah quotes Genesis in his praise of Ayyala, comparing her to the beautiful wise woman created according to the Lord's ideal of womanhood.[79] Zerah reframes Ayyala and her talents, which in the previous episode were characterized as typical of the *adab* education of both the *qiyān* and the Judeo-Andalusi courtier, as conforming to the Jewish ideal of feminine grace and strength. Ayyala is Zerah's ideal mate, but he will not be allowed to enjoy a life with her, for he must pay for his transgression, namely following the advice of his father, Tahkemoni. In this passage Ibn Shabbetai takes us back to Genesis, to the book that not only establishes gender differences, but instinct—the drive to copulate—as part of the human condition. It is precisely Zerah's former denial of desire that is his sin and for which he is now punished.

Final Judgment

Kozbi does not allow Zerah to enjoy the fruits of his Andalusi bride who, paradoxically, embodies the ideal of the Jewish woman and the Andalusi ideal of beauty, and, at the last moment, exchanges Ayyala with the ugly hag Ritzpah.[80] Zerah thus finds himself married to a woman who is the antithesis of the beautiful Ayyala. "And Kozbi took the girl [Ayyala] and gave in exchange for her a woman distressful like a black crow. Her lips are swollen like a water skin. The hair on her flesh rough and scratchy, nettles covered her mouth. She shunned infants and babes. She was contemptible in the eyes of all. Her name is Ritzpah bat Ayah (Coal, daughter of the vulture)."[81] Ritzpah's black countenance, swollen lips, and frightful appearance contrast the beautiful features of Ayyala enumerated in the poetry discussed above. While Ayyala is the incarnation of the most appealing elements of Arabized poetry and the Andalusi lifestyle as well as the perfect Jewish woman, Ritzpah is its antithesis. She is the grotesque female body, "loaded with all the connotations of fear and loathing around the biological" processes of sex and aging.[82] Like Rabelais's carnivalesque female bodies described by Bakhtin, Ritzpah's body "is blended with the world, with animals, with objects."[83] As Mary Russo points out, images of grotesque bodies like that of Ritzpah "are precisely those which are abjected from the bodily canons of classical aesthetics."[84] The Andalusi courtly ideal as embodied by Ayyala allows no room for features like those of Ritzpah.

Zerah was enticed by the promises of Kozbi and the canonical Andalusi beauty of Ayyala, but finds himself trapped, and legally bound, in an insufferable state of servitude to an almost subhuman wife. Zerah cannot believe his ill fate and begins to curse in both prose and poetry. In response to his outburst Ritzpah tells him neither his moralizing prose nor his poetry has any effect on her. Just as the description of Ritzpah's body lets the reader know she cannot be identified or contained by the "high" or official culture of the Andalusi court, she informs Zerah that she wants nothing to do with the literary world of either Ayyala or Tahkemoni: "Stop taking up your rhyme! Do not even raise your voice. I have no interest in wisdom or culture...Your poems and your lyrics mean nothing to me."[85] In addition, Ritzpah threatens Zerah, saying that if he fails to supply her with all she demands something so horrible will happen to him that it will drive him mad. She also intimates that this list of demands is only the beginning. Ritzpah and Ayyala's speech further reflects the dialectic between "high" and "low" culture mapped out in their features. Unlike Ayyala, whose speech is always couched in poetry, the language of the court, this woman only speaks in prose. Ritzpah immediately assaults Zerah with a very prosaic list of demands: "Do not give your eyes a rest! Don't disobey what I say! Go get for me [the following]: objects of silver and gold, dresses and pearls, bracelets and veils, a house and an apartment, a chair and a lamp,...anklets and bangles, and most of all, special clothes for feasts, Shabbat, holidays, etc. Such will your hands deliver up. And if you should weary from having to do all that, you'll go crazy from what your eyes see."[86]

The grotesque, disorderly figure of Ritzpah resembles the exilic conditions of Andalusi Jews (lovers of Ayyala's type of discourse) in Christian Iberia who find themselves in an alienated abject state, misunderstood by a society with different cultural values. Ritzpah, the demanding and coarse old woman, lambastes Zerah and his courtly lifestyle, and the narrator tells us that his soul is destroyed in this life. He instantly ages, becoming an old man overnight; his hair becomes white and he groans in pain, "He wept for the days of his youth, now in decline, and for his hair, gone white with him in his prime."[87] Ibn Shabbetai here plays with the image of the compunctious poet who repents for the mistakes of his youthful excess and erotic adventures, an image common in Judeo-Andalusi Hebrew poetry.[88] Ibn Shabbetai is playing, then, with the conventions of Arabized erotic poetry, from the descriptions of the beloved, the erotic imagery of wine poetry, and the renunciation and grey hairs typical of the poems of repentance written by middle-aged poets who had led a licentious youth and composed profane poetry.

Zerah cannot believe what is happening to him and frames his response in the biblical language used by the Jews of the Diaspora to describe the Babylonian Captivity.[89] "And as Zerah was listening to these words he let out a terrible cry, saying: 'Is Israel the slave? Does it [Israel] have no messiah/redeemer? Have the concubines raised up over the viceroys and prefects? Do pierced ears have dominion over turbans?' Heaven and Earth, and its hills, cried, and let tears fall because of this. The freeman and the son of plenty is a slave to the one with pierced ears."[90] Zerah's fate is equated with that of the Jews of the Diaspora and both are framed in the same sexualized terms. Just as Zerah must serve his bride Ritzpah, viceroys and prefects (the chosen ones) are forced to serve slaves/concubines (Arabs and Christians). Zerah's frustration at the situation in which he now finds himself, being a "favored son" subject to "one with pierced ears," also echoes the situation of the Jews in medieval Iberia or Western European communities, who found themselves, the "chosen ones," the intellectual elite of al-Andalus subjected to Christian monarchs who did not possess their own cultured background and could not fully appreciate their illustrious cultural patrimony, and who suspected them of being too Arabized. Just as Moses ibn Ezra asks in his exilic lament, "On Leaving Saragossa," if his bretheren planned such evil, Zerah wants to know how this has happened. This world upside down parallels the triumph of Folly over Wisdom in the opening episode of this *maqāma*.

The tale, however, is further complicated by a final and unexpected turn. Zerah runs from his new bride. The people of the land are torn between allowing him to divorce her and stoning him to death. They seek judgment from a wise judge, Ibn al-Fakhkhār, Ibn Shabbetai's own patron. Ibn Shabbetai ends his tale with a final rift in the narrative frame. The author, Ibn Shabbetai, enters the diegetic narrative to plead Zerah's case before Ibn al-Fakhkhār, who likewise has been transformed into one of the tale's characters. The judge finds the tale so amusing he breaks into laughter and dismisses the case.[91] Ibn Shabbetai utilizes this final judgment scene within the narrative as a palinode to the work's overt misogyny. It is a final act of subversion in a work defined by both thematic and formal subversions. In his defense of Zerah, the author as character claims that Zerah and all the characters of the work are fictional, "[N]ot one of these characters ever existed. I made them up out of my own inspiration; on a foundation of falsehood is their existence built. More than anyone who has ever lived, I love my wife and children."[92] Ibn Shabbetai's final plea for Zerah and assertion of his own marital situation suggests that Zerah's lapse in judgment had to do not with his choice of a sensual Arabized lifestyle, but with his initial decision to shun women and sex. In this tale Ibn Shabbetai has shown the two extreme positions on sexuality and Jewishness taken within the Jewish communities now coming into contact in Western Europe, Ashkenazim and Sephardim. Neither of these extreme positions conformed to traditional Judaism. By composing his work in Hebrew and including sexual behaviors present and increasingly under attack in both the Andalusi and the Rabbinite communities, Ibn Shabbetai has constructed a narrative whose readers, regardless of their stance on the philosophical-theological spectrum, will be brought by the very act of reading into dialogue with the views and opinions of the other community, and forced, at the same time, to acknowledge and recognize the extremes of their own.

Ibn Shabbetai carefully weaves together these contemporary and traditional moralistic sources and manipulates the narrative frame of the *maqāma* to create a subversive text in which the go-between becomes the agent of destabilization. Ibn Shabbetai systematically deforms inherited moralistic discourse, such as that of the previous generations of Judeo-Andalusi moral reformers, including Ibn Paqūdā and Ibn Gabirol, as well as the foundational text of Jewish belief, the Torah. Ibn Shabbetai manipulates these sapiential authorities to create a "subversive intertext to structure his work," just as some hundred years later the Iberian author Juan Ruiz will (see chapter 5).[93] In the *Offering*, Ibn Shabbetai relexicalizes the moral didactic discourse of the Jewish tradition in order to problematize traditional Jewish/Judeo-Andalusi views of exile and community. This systematic subversion and ironic reframing of traditional beliefs, particularly those expressed in Ibn Paqūdā's treatise on Jewish ethics, reveals the fissures and slippages in Judeo-Andalusi exilic identity.

Ibn Shabbetai takes Ibn Paqūdā's moral gloss of Ecclesiastics 9:14 and Ibn Gabirol's poem on exile, both seemingly straightforward didactic pieces aimed at admonishing Andalusi Jews from the secular lifestyle of the Andalusi courtier, and inscribes into them the Andalusi discourse of courtly erotics. Ibn Shabbetai opens up Tahkemoni's narrative, which begins with the allegory of Folly and Wisdom based upon Judeo-Andalusi and biblical material of a moral-didactic character, and introduces into it the very Other it sought to keep out—Andalusi-style poetry and courtly erotic discourse. Ibn Shabbetai exposes how elements of Ibn Paqūdā's model of ideal

Jewishness are merely definitions of Otherness. Key parts of Ibn Paqūdā's treatise focus not on what actually constitutes the ideals of Jewish belief/identity, but on what threatens them, namely Andalusi culture and lifestyle. Whereas the opening battle of Wisdom and Folly locates Ibn Shabbetai's tale within the imagery of two of the most important Saragossan Judeo-Andalusi ethical and moral authorities of the twelfth century, the second half of the work dramatically transforms that imagery by accommodating it to the Andalusi go-between tale used by another Saragossan writer, al-Saraqustī (as discussed in chapter 2). This relocation of traditional Judeo-Andalusi didactic moralizing material into the world of the Arab *maqāmāt* is destabilizing, and the go-between, who acts as agent of this destabilization, uses the Andalusi courtly discourse of erotic poetry to seduce Zerah and save the nation of Israel.

Kozbi becomes the vehicle by which Ibn Shabbetai weaves together the various discourses—the moral didactic (Ibn Paqūdā/Ibn Gabirol) and the Andalusi erotic—into a hybrid exilic narrative. She does undermine Zerah, but she does so with the help of the Lord. Andalusi Jews may have erred by being too sensual, but the asceticism of mystic Islamic, Neoplatonic and/or Rabbinic Jews is equally as appalling and far from the Jewish path (as defined by Ibn Shabbetai). Ibn Shabbetai salvages the go-between from Andalusi literature—she "passes" from al-Andalus and Arabic literature into the Hebrew *maqāmāt* and becomes the mediator between the secular lifestyle and the will of God. In al-Saraqustī's "*Maqāma 9*" we saw how Ibn Hazm's faithful messenger became an independent composer of texts. Whereas Umm 'Amr was the creator of the courtly description of the nonexistent beloved, in the *Offering* the go-between gives the lover not just a description, she constructs the ideal woman herself—Ayyala. Ibn Shabbetai further develops the go-between's role as author and desiring subject by locating her in the discourse of Jewish identity. This agent of Arabized secular culture does not simply expose the social and political shortcomings of the victim she is seducing as was the case in "*Maqāma 9*," she redefines the Judeo-Andalusi conceptions of folly and wisdom—key to the Jewish intellectual's spiritual health and religious, ethnic, and cultural identity.

Al-Harīrī/Al Harīzī: Arab to Jew

Whereas Ibn Shabbetai, adapting Ibn Paqūdā's didactic parable, uses his go-between narrative to focus on instinct, wisdom, and folly as the forces at work behind the Judeo-Andalusi's exile, in the *Tahkemoni* Judah al-Harīzī focuses on the Jews' relationship to their language as emblematic of their exilic condition. Although al-Harīzī does not allude to Ibn Shabbetai or his work by name, several elements of the *Tahkemoni* reveal its indebtedness to the *Offering*. Al-Harīzī's "*Maqāma* of Marriage," the sixth episode or "gate" of the collection of fifty *maqāmāt* entitled *Tahkemoni*, reflects a deliberate reworking of many of the themes and motifs of the *Offering*. The title of al-Harīzī's collection, *Tahkemoni*, is in all probability an allusion to Zerah's father, which in turn is an allusion to the poetic altar ego of the exiled Ibn Gabirol (as discussed above).[94] Similarly the name of the narrator of the *Tahkemoni*, Heman the Ezrahite, refers to the son of the biblical Zerah mentioned in 1 Chronicle 2:6, and thus establishes yet another link to the characters of Ibn Shabbetai's work. The biblical Heman the Ezrahite is an official musician and seer under King David and the composer of Psalm 88, which is the plaint of a distressed man in captivity abandoned in a deep pit by his kin, community and God.[95] Al-Harīzī establishes a patrimony between the characters of Ibn Shabbetai's tale, Tahkemoni and Zerah, and both the title of his collection of *maqāmāt* and its narrator, Heman the Ezrahite. The "*Maqāma* of Marriage" also follows the same narrative structure as the second half of the *Offering*, consisting of the tale of the duped protagonist and the exchanged bride. Al-Harīzī, like Ibn Shabbetai, was learned and well read in Judeo-Andalusi literature and we find in his text the same intellectual indebtedness to the major Judeo-Andalusi poets and their imagery as in the *Offering*. In both works the images and tropes of Judeo-Andalusi erotic poetry become short hand for important concepts of acculturation. And, as in Ibn Shabbetai's work, in the "*Maqāma* of Marriage," it is the go-between who mediates not only between the Jewish man and the object of his desire, but also between the competing discourses of Jewish identity.

Whereas Ibn Shabbetai takes the abstinence Ibn Paqūdā proposed as a personal reponse to the battle of Folly, Wisdom, and Instinct, as the point of departure for his ironic treatment of the Iberian Jew, in the introduction to his collection of *maqāmāt* Al-Harīzī adopts the Neoplatonic imagery of Ibn Gabirol, and describes the mystical union of soul and intellect in the terms found both in Ibn Gabirol's philosophic works and in erotic Judeo-Andalusi poetry. As discussed in detail below, the protagonist of the introduction is al-Harīzī's own divinely inspired intellect who seeks out and weds the soul, whom he characterizes as the embodiment of the Hebrew language. Al-Harīzī uses the Neoplatonic theory of divine emanation, according to which the intellect mediates between God and man's rational and animal souls as an allegory for the Jew's relationship to the Hebrew language.[96] In the work, both the relationship between intellect and soul and Jew and language are eroticized. As was the case with Ibn Shabbetai's narrative, al-Harīzī's *Tahkemoni* uses sexual desire as a metaphor for the Judeo-Andalusi courtier's intellectual desire for Arabized learning and poetic composition. Whereas Ibn Shabbetai developed this message by identifying

Andalusi traditions and learning with the go-between and the beautiful woman, Al-Harīzī makes the beautiful woman into the very language in which the work is composed. This identification of sex and language reflects al-Harīzī's own cultural activities as one of the principle translators of both Arabic and Judeo-Andalusi religious-philosophical texts into Hebrew for consumption by the Jews of Western Europe.[97]

Ibn Shabbetai's *Offering*, Judeo-Andalusi poetry, and Ibn Gabirol's works, however, are not the only texts that have left traces in al-Harīzī's *maqāmāt*. Al-Harīzī tells us he wrote *Tahkemoni* as a reaction to the Arab writer al-Harīrī's *maqāmāt*, a work considered the epitome of Arabic stylistic excellence. Al-Harīzī had previously translated al-Harīrī's *maqāmāt* into Hebrew.[98] For his own Hebrew collection al-Harīzī adapts the same form used by al-Harīrī—a collection of fifty *maqāmāt*—the only such Iberian example in Hebrew of the classical *maqāmāt*. Al-Harīzī's goal, in part, was a nationalist one, to prove that Hebrew could rival if not exceed Arabic as a vehicle for literary production.[99] Rina Drory maintains that al-Harīzī's original Hebrew *maqāmāt* cannot be considered independently of his work as a translator and that, like his translation, his original work is designed to allow Jews living north of the Pyrenees access to Andalusi literature and to prove to Jews in Babylonia and Palestine that Hebrew could be used for a variety of purposes, not just ceremonial or religious works.[100]

In the introductory preface to the *Tahkemoni*, Al-Harīzī reveals to the reader his misgivings about having translated al-Harīrī's Arabic *maqāmāt*. He felt compelled to compose an original work in Hebrew that could rival the former work.[101] The contradictory manner in which he speaks of al-Harīrī's *Maqāmāt* and its translation reveals his evident pride at having accomplished the translation of such a difficult and brilliant work, but also guilt at not having composed an original work in Hebrew instead. His depiction of Jews sleeping in a land of folly recalls both Ibn Shabbetai and Ibn Paqūdā's use of similar imagery:

> Now many of those that slept in the soil of folly awoke and they made the chariots of their tongues race through the road of song. They planned to translate the book of this Arab Harīrī, from the Arabic tongue into the Sacred Tongue, Hebrew, and they came in prosaic garments to serve in the sanctuary of the muse.... For by the power of the metaphors of the book they were dismayed and terrified, and at the sound of its thunders and hailstones they perished and were exterminated, and the hail came down upon them and they died....Until I arose and wrought its armor. I translated the whole book with fitting prose and poems like pearls, pure and salty... And I spoke to the rock of song and it gave forth its waters. For the nobles of Spain, when they heard the words of the Arab's book (Harīrī's *Maqāmāt*) marveled at them. And they sought of me while I was still among them to

translate this book for them and I was not able to turn them away. Now when I had fulfilled their desire and had translated the books, I forsook my home and I wandered on roads, I sailed on ships. . . . And I saw that I had done foolishly and my iniquity was greater than I could bear having neglected to compose a book of our own poetry, and had undertaken to translate a book of foreign poetry, as though the Word of the living God were not amongst us. I had hastened to keep the vineyard of strangers, but mine own vineyard I had not kept. Therefore, I composed this book with new poems, hallowed by the Holy Tongue, with new themes which will revive souls and refresh dry bones.[102]

Again the battle between folly and wisdom, here the metaphors al-Harīzī creates to rival those of al-Harīrī, is an allegorical one depicting the translation of a difficult text.

The warrior-translator al-Harīzī describes here the very collection of *maqāmāt* being read. Although designed to show the beauties of Hebrew, al-Harīzī still couches his new poems in a form and style determined by the Arabic language and literary tradition, that of the *maqāmāt*. The Lord, acting through the author's own intellect, puts the words of the *maqāmāt* in al-Harīzī's mouth, telling him: "Behold, I have put my words in your mouth and for the vision of poetry I have set you as a prophet unto nations. See I have appointed you to pull down the houses of folly and to build and to plant the palaces of poetry."[103] These *maqāmāt* are palaces of poetry built on the destroyed ruins of folly. Poetry here is identified with both the rhymed prose *saj'* of the *maqāmāt* and the intercalated lyric poetry composed in Hebrew. In the context of the denigration of Hagar and the tongue of Kedar/Arabic (discussed below), al-Harīzī is fashioning Hebrew rhymed prose and poetry as superior to the folly of Arabized Andalusi poetry and *maqāmāt* written in Arabic.

In the first *maqāma* of the *Tahkemoni*, the narrator, Heman the Ezrahite, offers yet another alternative metaphoric explanation for how the author, al-Harīzī, came up with the idea of composing the work. Now recounted from the perspective of one of the characters embedded in the narration, we are told how one day Heman was spending time with the best and brightest of Jewish youth, and one among his group was extolling the praises of the Arab poet and father of riddles and metaphors, al-Harīrī. His praise of al-Harīrī is outdone only by his praise for the Arabic language itself, which "in the sweetness of its words and in the pleasantness of its metaphors has no tongue that can compare to it."[104]

The author-narrator, al-Harīzī, interprets these words as a challenge, becoming physically upset: "My heart was upset within me, neither was there breath left in me."[105] He manages to control himself and respond civilly, acknowledging Arabic as a superior language excelling above all others except for the Holy Tongue. Al-Harīzī continues to praise the Hebrew language as superior to Arabic or Romance vernacular dialects: "[O]ur language is a wonderful language and its words are words of prophecy. For although it is in straits, it enlarges itself for us, and though it is insufficient, it suffices for all of us."[106] This argument is inevitably couched in a discourse of Hebrew cultural nationalism—not only making the assertion that Hebrew is more than sufficient to create compositions comparable to the best of the Arabs, but also providing a brief synopsis of the linguistic effects of the Diaspora: "But from the time that we were exiled from our land, we learned the languages of the nations and forsook our own language, and this was the cause of the shortcoming of our tongue and its deficiency following its perfection and its superiority."[107]

This description of the Diaspora could apply equally to Sephardic and Western European Jews who had similarly adopted vernacular dialects as well as maintaining Midrashic Hebrew (considered inferior to biblical); al-Harīzī, however, then makes it clear that he is most concerned with Andalusi and Eastern Jews like himself who have adopted Arabic as their daily language: "Only from the time that our people mingled among the nations and dwelt among them and learned to speak in their tongues, they forsook the Hebrew language and they tottered in judgment. And their souls despised the son of Sarah, the Hebrew woman, and desired the son of Hagar, the Egyptian."[108] Al-Harīzī is talking about Judeo-Iberian intellectuals' use and preference for Arabic—the language used by the descendants of Hagar, mother of Ishmael. This imagery complements that used in the introduction, in which al-Harīzī eroticizes Jews' relationship to Arabic, describing the enslaved Hebrew as a scorned lover:

> And the tongue of Kedar blackened her, and like a lion, tore her. An evil beast devoured her. All of them spurned the Hebrew tongue and made love to the tongue of Hagar. They embraced the bosom of an alien. They desired the wife of a stranger. They kissed her bosom, for stolen waters were sweet to them. Their hearts were seduced when they saw how excellent was the poetry that Hagar, Sarai's Egyptian handmaiden had bourne. And Sarai was barren! The spirit of jealousy passed over my soul for wisdom had far from us fled.[109]

Al-Harīzī's sexualization of the relationship between the speaker and his language is key in understanding the "*Maqāma* of Marriage." The depiction of the Jew who prefers Arabic as a man who sexually desires Hagar over

Sarah further makes the question of language usage part of what it means to be a Jew. Had Abraham not chosen Sarah and had sex with her there would be no Jews. Far more is involved in the adoption of a language other than Hebrew than a simple linguistic shift. In the introduction al-Ḥarīzī frames his initial preference for Arab works, namely by having translated al-Ḥarīrī's *maqāmāt* before having composed original ones in Hebrew, as tending a stranger's vineyard, whereas here the choice of Arabic is an erotic one. Al-Ḥarīzī frames the use of Arabic not only as a renunciation of the Hebrew language, but as a sexual desire for Hagar—mother of the Arabs. The Andalusi Jews who chose Arabic "totter" (*paku pliliya*) in their judgment and that costs them a meaningful relationship (a licit sexual relationship?) with their rightful bride/mother.

This first *maqāma*, in fact, functions like a gloss, or counterpoint to the allegory of the preceding introductory *maqāma*, in which the author, al-Ḥarīzī, describes his choice to take up Hebrew instead of Arabic in mystical allegorical terms familiar from both Ibn Paqūdā and Ibn Gabirol. As discussed above, Al-Ḥarīzī tells us of how Intellect aroused him from folly, entrusting him with a divine mission to "build and to plant the palaces of poetry." Intellect's role in fighting against folly recalls the *nur al-'aql* of Ibn Paqūdā's *Duties*, but here al-Ḥarīzī introduces poetry as the alternative to wordly foolishness. Al-Ḥarīzī tells us that the Hebrew language, once shaped by his genius and set forth in the *Taḥkemoni* will be as beautiful as a bride bedecked with her finest bridal jewelry.[110]

Al-Ḥarīzī further elaborates the connection between language, literature, and sexual and religious desire, by describing Hebrew's clothing and the power of her gaze: "Poetry is her garment and the spice of myrrh is on her skirts. When she takes off her veil, every eye hangs upon her and every heart is bound by her cords. Giants are held captive by her fetters and the heroes of war are her slain."[111] Despite the power of her beauty, Hebrew has been neglected by contemporary Jews. "But today filthy, violent persons among our people have stabbed her with swords and with spears from the flint of their tongue. Righteousness lodged in her, but now murderers. All her sons have forsaken their tongue and become stammerers. Their silver is become dross. Every day she weeps bitterly."[112] These are the stammerers Ibn Ezra describes in his "Poem of Two Exiles," who violently "spill the blood of the just." Like Ibn Ezra, al-Ḥarīzī equates poor linguistic skills with deadly violence. Al-Ḥarīzī compares the Jews' neglect of the Hebrew language to the abandonment of a helpless young bride to murderers and rapists. Al-Ḥarīzī represents the Hebrew language as a spurned beloved, describing in detail her horrible treatment at the hands of feckless lovers, comparing the Arabized Jews of the Diaspora to a pit full of ravenous, lustful beasts who torture their own bride, Hebrew.[113]

The abandoned bride entreats her audience: "What wrong have you found in my deeds that you have gone far from me?" Despite her importance and holiness she finds herself betrayed: "And yet your children have spurned me and embraced the tongue of strangers, in that they have burned incense unto other gods." The narrator tells us, "They have enslaved the tongue of the Israelites to the tongue of Kedar and they said: 'Come and let us sell her to the Ishmaelites.'"[114] According to the beautiful Hebrew, Jews have enslaved her to the tongue of Kedar, the language of the Ishmaelites/ Arabs. Hebrew eroticizes her relationship to the Jews, putting them into the position of deceitful lovers who embrace foreign women. The Jews have not just abandoned Hebrew, they have enslaved her to Arabic, the language of non-Jews. The image of an enslaved Jew recalls Zerah's cries at the end of the *Offering*, when he bemoans the fate of the nation of Israel forced to serve slaves. Here, though, it is a female representation of Jewish identity, Hebrew (al-Harīzī's soul), that is enslaved.

Al-Harīzī, like Ibn Shabbetai, takes the trope of the slave girl, which was part of the formulaic *adab* material of the classical *maqāmāt* (discussed in chapter 2), and inscribes it into his discourse of Jewish nationalism. In Ibn Shabbetai's *Offering* and al-Saraqustī's "Maqāma 12," as in the treatises of Ibn Hazm and Ibn Shuhaid, the poetic description of the slave woman is used because it is emblematic of the Arab court. In al-Harīzī's first *maqāma*, however, the slave girl, object of erotic desire in Andalusi court poetry, is redefined as a Jewish queen ("the crown of royalty")—as the object of Jewish literary and religious expression, and as the embodiment of Jewish identity itself.[115] Whereas in the *Offering*, it is the women of Israel who vow to change the situation and take revenge on Zerah, in the introduction to *Tahkemoni* it is the author, al-Harīzī, who proposes vindicating the Hebrew language, textual representative of the Jewish tradition. In both works it is the behavior of the Jewish men toward their own tradition that causes problems and threatens Judaism itself. Unlike Zerah who shuns the virgins of Israel and preaches against them, al-Harīzī will use his literary skills to extol Hebrew's virtues and betroth her.

The Poetic Bride

After these detailed descriptions of the Hebrew language's degradation at the hands of Jews, al-Harīzī has a prophetic vision in which he has an erotic encounter with the beautiful bride, Hebrew. Out of this union is born the work itself. This encounter is an answer to a prayer in which he had asked to meet a maiden of understanding and mysteries, such that she would be the vehicle of his mission to redeem Hebrew literature and to make it rival the wonders of Arabic literature.[116] Hebrew language incarnate appears instantly, offering herself to al-Harīzī: "Drink, my lord, from the running waters of my thought, for honey and milk are under my tongue. . . . I was the crown of royalty but behold, today I am trodden under by every foot. I am the Holy Tongue, your mistress. And if I be pleasing in your eyes, I will be your companion. But only that you will be zealous for the name of God. . . ." Al-Harīzī is ecstatic: "Then I bowed my head and prostrated myself before God for I had found grace in her eyes. And I placed earrings of my praises in her ears and a necklace of my poetry about her neck. And I betrothed her unto me in righteousness and in reverence without contract or intercourse. I went unto the prophetess, and she conceived and bore a son in the likeness and image of God. And the government was upon his shoulder. And the spirit of the Lord began to move him. He gathered unto him all his people."[117]

Al-Harīzī weds his beautiful bride and gives her offerings, his literary compositions—praise and poetry. As in his earlier description of Hebrew, in which he describes her as a bride wearing her finest jewels and clothing, here al-Harīzī compares poetry to jewelry and lays special emphasis on the act of adorning the bride with a necklace and earrings, his verses. Al-Harīzī appropriates the topos of the poem as jewel and garment, used in Arabic and Judeo-Andalusi poetry as object of exchange between poet and patron, and redefines it as a function of Hebrew nationalism.[118] Jewish poets should write in Hebrew with the goal of creating a Jewish literature capable of rivaling the Arabic poetic and literary tradition, and not merely adapt Arabic literary conventions to participate in an Arab-style courtly milieu.

The representation of the Hebrew language as source of erotic desire developed in the introduction and first *maqāma* of al-Harīzī's *Tahkemoni* is essential in understanding the function of the go-between as mediator and manipulator of courtly discourse in Gate Six, the "*Maqāma* of Marriage." The image of the ideal erotic encounter and spiritual union depicted in this introductory material is a divinely ordained intellectual one between a Jew and his holy language. This representation of the ideal union becomes the standard against which other erotic relationships in the *Tahkemoni* must be measured. Naturally the relationship between man and woman, the theme of "*Maqāma* 41," pales in comparison to the ideal intellectual union of poet and muse described in the introduction and first *maqāma*. However, it is the marriage arranged between the protagonist and a foreign woman in the "*Maqāma* of Marriage" that proves to be the antithesis of, or counter model to the ideal encounter described in the introduction.

The Go-Between in Al-Harīzī's "*Maqāma* of Marriage"

The "*Maqāma* of Marriage" reflects not only the plot and imagery of Ibn Shabbetai's *Offering*, but also the erotic metaphors of al-Harīzī's introduction and first *maqāma*. Many of the tropes and images developed in the introduction and first *maqāma* to describe the author's marriage to the Hebrew language are later subverted in the "*Maqāma* of Marriage." While in the introduction God serves as the go-between or broker who brings together author and personified language, in the "*Maqāma* of Marriage" it is the go-between, Sitnah (a female Satan) who mediates between the protagonist and the beloved. In the introduction God provides the author, al-Harīzī, with a prophetic vision in which he encounters the beautiful Hebrew, to whom he gives poetry as a bride price, but in "*Maqāma* of Marriage," Sitnah exchanges the promised virgin for an ugly old hag whose horrible countenance inspires a lengthy invective. Just as God is juxtaposed with Satan, the antithesis of the ideal bride (Hebrew) resembles the ugly hag Hagar of the introduction. The introductory material and "*Maqāma* of Marriage" serve as model and counter model for Jewish intellectuals, illustrating how to engage properly in cultural activities. Al-Harīzī looked to Ibn Gabirol's works for a model of Jewish spirituality, and he looks to Ibn Shabbetai's *maqāma* for his counter model.

The "*Maqāma* of Marriage" begins as a flashback: Heber runs into his old friend, the narrator, who welcomes him and offers to look for a woman to comfort him. Heber reacts violently to this offer, and in response narrates to his friend the story of his ill-fated marriage. The tale of his seduction opens in a manner similar to that of al-Saraqustī's "*Maqāma* 9." Like al-Sā'ib, Heber arrives in a strange city, lovesick and suffering. He wanders around the city until coming upon the go-between: "Lo! I encountered an old hag with evil visage and ugly form. She looked as if Fate had stolen her from the demons to be part of him. And he called her name 'Sitnah' [the female form of Satan's name in Hebrew]."[119] Al-Harīzī, like Ibn Shabbetai, gives his go-between a name that belies her association with the forces of evil.[120] Sitnah's name contrasts her with God and his role in the author's first erotic encounter with Hebrew as described in the introduction of the *Tahkemoni*.

Sitnah's association with evil is further underscored by the description Heber gives us of her speech. The cords of beguilement that characterize Sitnah's speech offer a stark contrast to Hebrew's beauty and her glances that entrap and subdue giants and great warriors: "She spoke fair and fell upon her knees, and her mouth was smoother than oil. Honey was upon her tongue but deadly poison was in her throat. . . Now when I heard her speech, my heart was drawn by the smoothness of her words, and I was bound by the cords of her beguilement."[121] Like Kozbi the liar and Ayyala the poetess, Sitnah is a master of (false) rhetoric. Here al-Harīzī, whose emphasis in this *maqāma* is on speech and language, uses the same image of deceptive, sweet speech used by al-Saraqustī to describe the go-between's speech in "*Maqāma* 9" (see chapter 2), and which had become common stock among Judeo-Andalusi poets in describing Tevel, "the allegorical personification of the world's evil."[122]

Al-Harīzī exploits the new cultural and literary contexts this image from al-Saraqustī's go-between tale has in the Judeo-Iberian context. Al-Saraqustī's description of the honeyed speech of the Umm 'Amr alerts us to her rhetorical ability and propensity for lying. Al-Harīzī exploits the same image's currency in Judeo-Iberian literature and culture to relate Sitnah to the dangers of Arabized erotic poetry and to the most destructive of forces, Mother Earth, the corrupt material world.[123] Al-Harīzī adapts the go-between as the agent of this seduction from Ibn Shabbetai's narrative; in both al-Harīzī and ibn Shabbetai's *maqāmāt* she is the textual representative of the acculturated, Arabized Judeo-Andalusi poet/intellectual. Her identification with Tevel and Satan reflect the same anti-assimilatory attitude al-Harīzī expresses in the introduction. The description of Sitnah's speech also acts as a counterpoint to Hebrew's speech as described in the introduction. Hebrew offers up the honey and milk under her tongue to the author-narrator in a kiss, which he uses as raw material to compose ornate poems of exquisite workmanship.[124] In the introduction, Hebrew's honey and milk produce beautiful verses, and the marriage of author and language produces a handsome son/text. In the "*Maqāma* of Marriage," however, Sitnah's false promises, the deadly poison hidden in her throat, lead Heber to marry a hideous creature and to commit a horrible crime.

Sitnah immediately sets about her ruse. First she gives Heber the honey, namely the description of the beautiful woman she offers to procure for him:

> I will give you from among the daughters of the noblemen, a lovely hind (*ayyala*) whose cheeks arouse the dawns and whose hair brings the evening twilight! . . . Her cheeks will glow as a candelabra and her mouth as a jarful of manna. You will walk in darkness by the brilliance of her countenance, and her lamp will not go out by night. Her merchandise is better than the merchandise of silver, and her worth is far above rubies. She has eyes as the eyes of gazelles; they are drunk with the wine of desire. Her body is luscious and supple as a sceptre studded with pearls, mingled with purity and holiness. It will smite the heart of he who beholds her and will send fire within him. Her cheeks are luminaries, her eyes young lions. Sapphires are the rows of her teeth, and her breasts are as two fawns.[125]

Just as Kozbi did in the *Offering*, Sitnah constructs her description of female beauty from the imagery of Judeo-Andalusi poetry, which in turn adapts many images from the Arab rhetorical tradition. As discussed above, love poems often concentrated on descriptions of the ordered beloved's body, enumerating each feature from the head down. Sitnah's description follows these convention and conforms to the Judeo-Iberian poet and scholar,

Moses ibn Ezra's manual, *Kitāb Zahr al-Riyāḍ*, which outlines the content and method for such descriptions.[126] The subsequent imagery, including the glowing face of the beloved, her "eyes of gazelles" that attack the lover (that also compare to Ayyala's powerful fawn eyes), the comparison of her body to a jewel-studded scepter, and her fawn breasts, is not only common in Andalusi poetry, but also corresponds to imagery discussed in Book 4 of Moses ibn Ezra's treatise, *al-Muhāḍara*.[127] Sitnah's description of the beloved, in contrast to the biblical description of Hebrew elaborated in the introduction, derives from the secular Andalusi poetic ideal of beauty.[128]

In this *maqāma*, Al-Harīzī introduces the secular erotic imagery of the Arabic tradition, as adopted by Jewish poets of the Golden Age, as part and parcel of the go-between's deceptive speech. These images are those used by Sitnah to seduce and undermine Heber. Al-Saraqustī similarly inscribed Arabic erotic poetry into "*Maqāma 9*" to criticize the class of courtiers that cultivated such poetry in the *taifa* courts of al-Andalus, as well as the value system to which they ascribed, and Ibn Shabbetai, following in this tradition, included Arabized Hebrew poetry in his *maqāma* in order to create a critique of Judeo-Andalusi courtiers. Similarly, al-Harīzī here subverts the Judeo-Andalusi courtier-poets among whom Hebrew poetry modeled on the Arabic-Andalusi model had become a form of social currency and whose lifestyle reflected the secular values extolled in the poetry. This is the poetry of Hagar described in the introduction as leading Jewish men away from the Hebrew language. As Ibn Shabbetai did in the *Offering*, in the "*Maqāma* of Marriage" al-Harīzī is giving us an *exemplum*—a case study of how Jews are seduced by Hagar and the terrible consequences. Sitnah's seduction of Heber is an example of how Jews forsook Hebrew to make love to Hagar, "seduced when they saw how excellent was the poetry that Hagar" produced.[129]

Sitnah's constant claims of veracity play upon contemporary Andalusi attitudes toward poetry. Careful readers who recognized Sitnah's description as the secular Andalusi poetic discourse would have also recognized that her claims to veracity could not be true, for, as discussed above with regard to Kozbi, poetry in and of itself is false and poets are liars.[130] To religious scholars and philosophers, Sitnah's use of rhetoric and typically poetic imagery (like that used by Ayyala in the *Offering*), including the mimetic description of the beautiful woman, would have marked her not only as a liar, but also, like the Judeo-Andalusi poet, "a dangerous, even depraved, word merchant whose lies extended a false promise of fleshly gains to the higher bidder."[131]

Heber, like al-Sā'ib in al-Saraqustī's "*Maqāma 9*," does not see past the lies and proves to be one of those interested in bidding on love—a dupe who misses all of these sociocultural and literary clues and allows himself to be seduced by Sitnah's poetic and false description of the beautiful woman. He tells Sitnah that if the woman is as she describes he will give any amount for the dowry and throw in a special gift for Sitnah. In response, Sitnah assures him that she has not exaggerated: "When you see the beauty that tears like a lioness, you will know that there is no deceit in my tongue."[132] In "*Maqāma* 9" beauty was embodied by bloodthirsty gazelles, and here it is compared to the lioness. Al-Harīzī's ideal reader would remember from the work's introduction that it is Arabic (the tongue of Kedar) that tears like a lion, and realize that Heber has become enmeshed in the trap of Arabized poetry and desire. This last veiled allusion to the threat of Arabic poetry and culture, understood only in the context of the introduction, is another of the various textual clues included in the narrative that alert us to Sitnah's evil nature and Heber's impending fate.

The Daughters of Ham

Heber soon realizes his mistake in trusting Sitnah, discovering that the beautiful woman Sitnah described is in fact an ugly, old hag. Unlike al-Sā'ib in al-Saraqustī's "*Maqāma* 9," Heber arranges to marry the woman before having seen her. Heber's exchanged bride recalls Ritzpah from Ibn Shabbetai's *Offering* and further reveals al-Harīzī's indebtedness to the Judeo-Iberian *maqāmāt*. Like Zerah, Heber deals not only with the procuress and bride, but also with the bride's family. The bride's father and the elders of the community come to Heber's house, where he sets his daughter's dowry at two thousand pieces of silver. Heber accepts and signs the kettubah, the marriage contract, in front of all present.[133] Heber's marriage arrangements contrast with those of the author-narrator, al-Harīzī, as elaborated in the introduction. In the introduction al-Harīzī depicts his relationship with Hebrew as that of a man with a loving, obedient bride. In the "*Maqāma* of Marriage" the relationship is exactly the opposite. Heber, unlike al-Harīzī who met his bride before marrying her and spoke with her directly, accepts the services of a go-between and, like Zerah, finds himself entrapped—married to a woman who is the opposite of the lovely Holy Tongue as described in the introduction.

Once he has married the woman described by Sitnah as the epitome of poetic beauty, he discovers that she is the antithesis of this. The honey words of Sitnah's description did, in fact, hide poison. The woman described as a lovely fawn is in truth a hideous old hag like Ritzpah:

> Then I turned to her and I stripped off her mantle and I took off the veil that was on her face and I brought the lamp close to her face. And lo! her face was of fright and her voice was as the sound of thunder. Her figure was like

Jeroboam's calf, and her mouth was like Balaam's ass, and the breath from her nose was putrid. The natural bloom had fled from her cheeks as though the devil had daubed them with blackness, and worked them with coals, so that I thought her of the daughters of Ham. But if her visage was blacker than coal, her hair was white, and her days had waxed old—and her lips protruded lightly from above—and her teeth were as the teeth of wolves or bears. And her eyes were the eyes of scorpions.[134]

This apparition appears more monster than woman, and her features reveal she is the antithesis in every way of the beautiful virgin described by Sitnah. Physically this woman recalls the grotesque Ritzpah from the *Offering*; however, al-Harīzī's description is much more elaborate than Ibn Shabbetai's. He includes a long list of horrible animals and terrifying creatures with which this woman's fractured body compares. This woman is an old hag with a weathered hide that has become blacker than coal. Her eyes, instead of being those of gazelles or young lions, are those of scorpions; instead of having a mouth like a jarful of manna, her breath is putrid like Balaam's ass. Her teeth are those of wolves or bears, not rows of sapphires. Instead of being the "lovely hind" described by Sitnah, this woman is a terrifying demonic beast-like daughter of Ham.

This image of the female grotesque must also be read in contrast to the description in the introduction of the ideal bride Hebrew. As Tova Rosen asserts, this monstrous woman embodies the inherent misogyny of the medieval Hebrew literary and cultural tradition.[135] But she also embodies the perceived cultural threat of Arabic learning and poetry. Heber claims that her hideous appearance leads him to believe she is one of the daughters of Ham, a common Judeo-Andalusi expression used to denote Muslim women. Al-Harīzī calls this woman a descendant of Ham to emphasize that her skin color is black. Al-Harīzī reconfigures the Andalusi ideal of the white beloved by using a common Andalusi racial stereotype that relied upon a fictitious biblical genealogical mapping of Arabs as the descendants of Ham, thus also equating them with Africans.[136]

This grotesque image of the Muslim woman clearly figures into the same system of images developed in the introduction. When al-Harīzī encounters Hebrew, his bride in the introduction, he finds a beautiful maiden whose mouth of milk and honey inspire him to write exquisite poetry. This second bride inspires only invective. This is the Hagar (Arabic language) of the introduction unveiled. Like the Jewish men described by al-Harīzī in the introduction, Heber has been seduced by the poetry and poetic discourse of Arabic. Heber's poor judgment, in combination with the maliciousness of the go-between, leads the protagonist into a terrible situation, comparable to that of the Andalusi Jews of Christian Spain, whom al-Harīzī depicts as having neglected their own language and culture. Following in Ibn Shabbetai's footsteps, in this *maqāma* al-Harīzī exposes the destiny that awaits such men.

The beautiful Hebrew of the first *maqāma* inspired al-Harīzī to compose not only the refined ornate poems with which he adorned and clothed her, but also the work we are reading. Their union also produces powerful and beautiful male offspring. Heber's bride, however, only inspires a lengthy invective, a verbal attack that does not help to dispel his anger. He first responds by composing a poem on this woman's ugliness in which he gives us a deconstructed version of Sitnah's earlier itemized description of her features:

> She resembles in her teeth the teeth of bears
> That devour and cut off whatever they find.
> Her head is full of boils and her eyes
> Rob and destroy the mirth of the heart.
> Her stature is like a wall and her legs
> Are like two tree stumps of the forest—cut off.
> And her cheeks are black as coal but her lips
> Are the crooked lips of a large-boned ass.
> Her figure is the shape of the angel of death
> All they that touch her will fall down dead.[137]

Heber then asks the woman what riches she has in her dowry, but once he finds out that she is poor, he can no longer contain his anger and once again launches into an even more scathing verbal attack. Heber relates the ugly hag to Lillith and the Angel of Death, and asks if is she is in league with demons.[138] Then he again begins enumerating her monstrous features:

> Your lips are as the lips of bullocks
> And your mouth is a grave but your belly is a cave.
> And your teeth are like the teeth of a filthy bear,
> And in them filth and slime are as a heaped-up dish.
> . . .
> You have a belly like a belly of a bottle
> And your shape, like your star, is black.
> Your hands are the hands of a hairy ape
> And fingers like fire brands in the cooking stove,
> And the sound of your speech is like an earthquake at midnight,
> The breath of your mouth is a whirlwind.
> And your mouth is a tomb for your eating and drinking—
> They turn in your belly to the bitterness of gall.

Heber is brutal in his attack. In his anger he redoubles his efforts to describe the spiritual and physical ugliness of this woman. He expands upon some features already mentioned in the first poem, including her teeth (here they are not just those of a bear as in the first poem, but those of a "filthy bear") and her figure (in the first she is "like a wall" and in this like a bottle). In addition, new and detailed elements are added in this poem, further enhancing the image of this woman's ugliness: she is black like a star, has hairy ape-hands, firebrand fingers, terrible breath, and speech like an earthquake. She is the boundless grotesque female body that oozes and transforms. She cannot be contained. The similarity between her evil countenance and that of Sitnah is here underscored, not only by relating this figure to the Devil, but also by comparing it to a mediating gift between Fate and Lillith.

After composing this scathing poem/song, Heber comments that it did not heal him, or take away his trouble. Not comforted by his words, Heber resorts to physical violence, beating his new wife until "her heart's blood came out of her mouth," and she died:

> I saw that my pangs would not be healed by my poem, nor my anguish be removed by my meditation, and that my song had not taken away my trouble. Then my fury arose up in my nostrils, and I took three rods in my hand and I rose at midnight, and I gagged her mouth with a rag, and I broke all the sticks on her back until her heart's blood came out of her mouth. And I tore all her flesh from off her and I caused the blood of her virginity to come forth on her body.[139]

Heber's invectives cannot heal his wound or bring him relief so he resorts to physical violence. The fact that his poems do not protect him from this monstrous woman's image, again illustrates that he has chosen unwisely and lacks a proper muse and/or the skill for poetic composition. According to Moses ibn Ezra, the wise man can use his pen like a sword fighting for wisdom. He can put the poison of his thoughts into his poetry to slay his adversary, as if it were the tongue of a viper.[140] Heber as poet cannot compare to al-Harīzī who in the introduction chooses wisely in selecting Hebrew for his bride. The union of al-Harīzī and Hebrew produces a warrior who excels all others in fighting for Wisdom, whereas Heber's union with this embodiment of Arabic (like that of Zerah and Ritzpah in the *Offering*) only produces invective and despair.

After killing his wife, Heber praises the Lord for having rescued him from Hell at the last minute, and vows to praise Him with his every breath. The narrator, Heman, laughs off Heber's tale as "misrepresentations" and "lies." Rosen reads the final humor of the episode as a patriarchal reduction and limiting of the female grotesque as a means of controlling it.[141] The emphasis Heman places on Heber's tale as being falsification and lies, however, again locates it within the Andalusi literary valorization of poetry and poetic imagery as lies. Al-Harīzī plays with the diegeitc narrative in order to double the trickster figure. Just as Sitnah is the vehicle for the Andalusi poetic discourse (i.e. fabrications and lies) within the tale, so Heber as narrator of the tale becomes, especially after his final poetic compositions, the creator of recognizably false discourse. In the Andalusi tradition, lying and fabrication may be the domain of poetry, but in this nascent Hebrew *maqāmāt* tradition, which is still intimately tied to the poetic tradition, lying and fabrication become an aspect of the literary fiction of the rhymed prose itself. We saw the beginnings of this transformation in al-Saraqustī's "*Maqāma 9*," in which Umm 'Amr becomes fictional creator of poetic texts, but both Ibn Shabbetai and al-Harīzī further expands this movement outward to the fiction of the frame. Al-Harīzī has the narrator of the frame comment on the embedded tale and narrator's fiction, whereas Ibn Shabbetai breaks the frame himself in order to declare it and its inhabitants nothing more than the products of his imagination.

Seduction, Betrayal, and Western Europe

What we find in the Judeo-Iberian works written in Christian Iberia analyzed in this chapter—Ibn Shabbetai and al-Harīzī's go-between tales, as well as Ibn Paqūdā's treatise, *Duties of the Heart*, Moses ibn Ezra's and Ibn Gabirol's poetry—is a recognition that the Andalusi discourse of power, love poetry expressed in Arabic, is no longer viable for Jewish intellectuals in Western Europe. In Ibn Ezra's "Poem of Two Exiles," al-Andalus is an ideal site of memory, a place haunted by gazelles and the memories of erotic encounters—memories of his access to the discourse of power, erotic poetry. The Andalusi palaces and *majlis* exist only in these authors' memory, though. These Judeo-Andalusi authors retain the imagery of Andalusi courtly erotic discourse, but, just as Ibn Hazm and al-Saraqustī had done centuries before, they adapt this imagery/discourse to suit their own needs and to serve in the construction of a new identity suitable to their new environment in the Diaspora.

Just as the palaces and *majlis* have become the stuff of memory, so too have the beautiful hinds and gazelles that wandered in them. These beautiful memories, though, become dangerous apparitions that threaten to undermine Jewish intellectual and spiritual development. Whereas Ibn Hazm (chapter 1) remembers real Andalusi courtly women, and al-Sā'ib's quest for the beautiful wild cow (chapter 2) is initiated by witnessing a group of real women leaving the baths, in the *Offering* and the "*Maqāma* of Marriage," the Andalusi erotic object of desire is nothing but a description/ a spell, conjured from the tropes of Judeo-Andalusi poetry that were still memorized, recited, and culled over by Judeo-Iberian authors as part of their cultural heritage and as symbols of their former prestige. In Ibn Shabbetai's go-between tale the Andalusi lifestyle is no longer viable for Iberian Jews, because it no longer functions in the Christian environment of Iberia, an environment in which the beautiful Ayyalas have been replaced with monsters. Al-Andalus and the Judeo-Andalusi poetry that describes and creates it are only a memory, not a viable guide for interacting with Christian society, and more importantly the Jewish communities of the Diaspora.

Ayyala is conjured by Kozbi, the mediator between the Andalusi past and Christian Iberia, but she is out of place in the new moral didactic landscape of Ibn Shabbetai's tale, formed as it is from moral literature that is itself a hybrid concoction of Muslim and Jewish philosophic and religious texts and possibly even Ashkenazi pious discourse. Ayyala, a fabricated illusion brought to life by the sorceress Kozbi/Lying, is little more than the discursive construction of beauty Sitnah gives Heber. Both are but the memory of al-Andalus, its lifestyle, and the cultural superiority and power of the Andalusi Jewish courtier. Like the gazelles running through the empty house of memory described in Moses ibn Ezra's opening poem, these beauties—al-Andalus—no longer exists, and its memory has now become a source of perversion among the Jews of Christian Iberia. The memory of al-Andalus leads to punishment, self-pity, or worse, destruction and violence. It is a constant reminder to the Andalusi Jews that the Romance-speaking "European" inhabitants of Christian Iberia are but violent, unrefined "stammerers" whose cultural achievements and discourses pale in comparison to the al-Andalus they have left behind. All that remains of al-Andalus is the memory of gazelles like Ayyala. Ritzpah and the she-ghoul of al-Harīzī's "*Maqāma of Marriage*" are the ugly reality of Judeo-Andalusi exile. Jews may work in Christian courts because of their Andalusi knowledge, but the Christian courts of Iberia are not the *majlis* of al-Andalus. They are the ugly, mundane sites of basic desires and degradation where Judeo-Andalusi poetry no longer functions as a discourse of power, but simply marks their creators as Other. In chapter 4 we will examine how this threatening go-between tale developed by Judeo-Andalusi authors leaves Iberia and is adapted by the Latin culture of Western Europe to address definitions of gender and competing models of identity among Christian clerics.

CHAPTER 4

TURNING TRICKS: THE GO-BETWEEN IN WESTERN EUROPE

> *barbarus hic ego sum, qui non intellegor ulli*
> *et rident stolidi uerba Latina Getae;*
> *meque palam de me tuto male saepe loquuntur,*
> *forsitan obiciunt exiliumque mihi*
>
> Here I am the barbarian, understood by no one,
> and the stupid Getae mock my Latin words;
> often they malign me openly in safety,
> perhaps they reproach me with my exile.
>
> —Ovid, *Tristia* 5.10.37–40

These verses describe the loneliness of the exiled Roman poet Ovid, who was banished by the Emperor Augustus to the cold northern city of Tomis on the west coast of the Baltic Sea.[1] Ovid characterizes Tomis as a strange land whose language he does not understand and whose people mock him. These sentiments are similar to those expressed by Judeo-Andalusi exiles in Christian Iberia such as Ibn Gabirol and Moses ibn Ezra. It was in such an exilic environment that we witnessed the Andalusi go-between pass from the Arabic to the Hebrew tradition in chapter 3; in this chapter we will examine how in thirteenth-century Western Europe a clerical author recreates in medieval Latin the exilic landscape of Ovid's *Tristia* in order to provide a new space for the Andalusi go-between—an ancient but recognizably familiar space in Western culture and literature, which the Andalusi go-between can inhabit and in which she can put on the garb of Roman culture and adopt the Latin that medieval clerics attributed to Ovid. The Roman poet may not have been able to communicate with the Getae in the *Tristia*, but in *De vetula*, a thirteenth-century Latin elegiac comedy composed of some two thousand four hundred lines of rhymed prose dactylic hexameter, he has no problem understanding the Andalusi go-between. The anonymous author of *De Vetula* resuscitates the exilic Ovid of the *Tristia* as author-narrator of this unusual treatise that combines observations on the newest trends in science and philosophy with fictionalized accounts of key episodes of the Roman poet's life, chief among them his encounter with a deceptive, old go-between.

By the twelfth century Ovid was considered the Western authority on love and in Europe was one of the most widely read and cited of classical authors. *De Vetula* was composed during the three-hundred-year period known as the Age of Ovid because of the popularity of Ovidian and pseudo-Ovidian works and because of the inclusion of these works into the school canon.[2] The first recorded allusions to *De Vetula* suggest that it is from the thirteenth century, probably composed some years after al-Ḥarīzī's and Ibn Shabbetai's go-between tales were known in Provence.[3] Yet the anonymous author of *De Vetula* distances the work from this contemporary Semitic tradition by attributing it to the most popular classical Western authority of the period, Ovid. The anonymous author ensures that his fellow clerics will have no pretext for dismissing his lessons on love/sex, for not only does *De Vetula* record the pagan author's final years in exile, but also his supposed prophetic visions of Christ's birth.[4] The description of how the great Roman poet of love adopted Christian beliefs late in life does away with the pesky label of pagan leveled against other classical (Greco-Roman) authorities such as Aristotle and Virgil.[5] Furthermore, attributing the work to one of the most popular and important classical authors of the Middle Ages, now safely Christianized, helps to hide its Andalusi roots. Yet Andalusi courtly culture, despite remaining unnamed, lurks behind the diverse parts of *De Vetula*. The Andalusi go-between appears in this unusual treatise that includes under the rubric of this Christianized pseudo-Ovid's autobiographic narration a selection and critique of the intellectual trends in thirteenth-century scholastic culture, many of which had developed as a response to, or adaptation of, material recently acquired via Arabic–Latin translations from Iberia.[6] The translations of numerous Arabic texts throughout the thirteenth century made many classical works (or Arabic editions and commentaries of them), including treatises on philosophy, theology, and the natural sciences, increasingly accessible to Western Europe. It is in this context of learned exchange between power elites that, not surprisingly, the Andalusi go-between appears. She passes into Latin Europe with her other Andalusi companions, namely the discourses of philosophical rationalism and scientific empiricism. Just as these discourses had proven unsettling in the increasingly religious milieu of al-Andalus and among the Arabized Jewish communities of Christian Iberia, so too in Latin Europe. The representation of the go-between as a suspicious, but extremely powerful force bent on the ultimate violation of the protagonist reflects the thirteenth-century Latin author's attitude toward this growing body of Arab secular knowledge and its use among Western European laymen.

This Latin version of the go-between tale, by adapting the go-between and her courtly environment from Andalusi Arabic and Hebrew into the ecclesiastical rhetoric of medieval Latin and by redefining the author-narrator as a repentant pagan who foretells the coming of Christ and who prays to the Virgin, effectively makes both the pagan narrator Ovid and the go-between he includes in this treatise ready for Christian consumption. Just as the Hebrew *maqāmāt* reframed the basics of Andalusi education and cultural formation (*adab*) for a new context (Christian Iberia) and a new audience (Jews), the anonymous author of *De Vetula* introduces/translates Arab philosophical, scientific, and erotic knowledge into Latin and frames it for a scholastic Western European audience using existing ecclesiastical models. In this chapter I examine how the go-between tale enters the Latin literature of the scholastics under the guise of Ovid in a pseudo-autobiographic treatise on rational philosophy, the natural sciences, and the scholastic lifestyle. As in the earlier Andalusi go-between tales examined in the preceding chapters, in the Latin go-between narrative the relationship between procuress, language, and identity is framed in the context of exile.

Latin Crosses: Ovid, Exile, and the Andalusi

In the medieval Latin *De Vetula* the line between beloved and bawd is blurred. The unnamed go-between replaces beloved as desiring subject by taking her place in bed with the lover. In *De Vetula*, the old bawd is deceitful and untrustworthy, and in Book 2 we witness her string along, dupe, and ultimately rape the lover. As in both al-Harīzī's "*Maqāma* of Marriage" and Ibn Shabbetai's *Offering*, in *De Vetula* the beloved is exchanged for an old hag. After arranging for a meeting with his virgin beloved, the pseudo-Ovid arrives in her bedroom only to discover that it is not the beautiful woman he expected waiting in bed for him, but the old go-between. This go-between commits the ultimate transgression only hinted at in works such as Ibn Shabbetai's *Offering* or al-Harīzī's "*Maqāma* or Marriage": the violation of the courtly lover and thus of courtly discourse itself. This violation transforms the tale into a Christian Latinate *exemplum*. The Hebrew *maqāmāt* are ambiguous narratives that negotiate between courtly lyric and didactic prose and between Arabized secular Andalusi culture and the Rabbinic traditions of Iberia and Europe, creating a liminal literary realm of hybrid discourse. *De Vetula* shifts the go-between into another hybrid space; again, one between East and West. The distant East remains the Arabized culture and learning of al-Andalus, but this time the West is not the Jewish traditions of medieval Iberia, but the scholastic learning of Latin Christendom.

De Vetula is thought to have been composed in France, where the works of both al-Harīzī and Ibn Shabbetai were known during their lifetime. Al-Harīzī made translations for the Jewish community of Provence, and Ibn Shabbetai's *Offering* stimulated responses by French and Provencal authors such as Isaac and ha-Penini.[7] It is a French intellectual, Richard de Fournival (1246–1260), who is often credited with composing *De Vetula*.[8] The major works known to have been written by Richard de Fournival include the *Bestiary of Love* and the *Biblionomia*, an annotated bibliography of the ideal thirteenth-century library.[9] *De Vetula* is not included in the *Biblionomia*, leading Robatham to exclude Richard de Fournival as potential author.[10] However, the material covered in *De Vetula* shows that the author is someone with de Fournival's breadth of knowledge and similarly someone with access to the type of library that de Fournival catalogues in the *Biblionomia*. The works included in this catalogue show us that the ideal thirteenth-century French library included works on philosophy and theology and reflects interests comparable to those current among Judeo-Andalusi intellectuals.[11] Though this cleric includes few works of fiction in the official list of library items, we know that such works were transferred in translation from al-Andalus to Europe.

In *De Vetula* the pseudo-Ovid tells of his erotic adventures, and of the composition of his final work, *De Vetula* itself, which the narrator stipulates should be left in his tomb. As mentioned this narrator is the aged Ovid exiled to the frontier town of Tomis. Ralph Hexter points out that this banishment was a trip from the center of the Roman Empire to a "barbaric outpost on the periphery."[12] As Ovid makes clear in the *Tristia*, this exile was like a trip in time and space, to a land where Latin, the source of Ovid's fame and identity as a poet, was not spoken. Just as the Judeo-Andalusi intellectuals Moses ibn Ezra and Ibn Gabirol had been active as courtiers in the Arabized courts of al-Andalus before being exiled to the Christian north, before his exile Ovid had participated in Roman cultural life as a courtier.[13] On the frontier, though, Ovid's refined skills as courtier and rhetor are useless, and he has become the barbarian whose fellow men cannot understand him. In a letter to the Emperor Augustus, Ovid begs forgiveness for the two causes of his exile—a poem and a mistake (*carmen et error*).[14] The poem is the *Ars amatoria*, but Ovid failed to disclose during his lifetime what the mistake was. In *De Vetula*, however, a repentant Christianized pseudo-Ovid suggests his mistake may have been the pursuit of material desires. He informs us that after a life of enjoyable sex with women, his encounter with an old go-between (*vetula*) caused him to renounce sex and to henceforth live a life of celibacy devoted to the study of philosophy.[15] In exile, the pseudo-Ovid (supposedly the great Praeceptor Amoris) renounces both women and sex, and turns instead to the meditative life of the philosopher-theologian.

This pseudo-Ovid's narration alternates between erotic adventures or opinions on love and sections on contemporary knowledge and science, such as gaming, statistics, mathematics, philosophy, alchemy, and law. The final section of Book 1 (lines 722–840) particularly resonates with the Hebrew *maqāmāt* in that it includes a critique of intellectuals who use their knowledge for worldly gain. Such men, like the Judeo-Andalusi courtiers attacked by Ibn Paqūdā, are represented as using philosophy and rhetoric for evil purposes. The narrator of *De Vetula* laments this sorry state of affairs and describes how lawyers have subverted their learning in the quest for material wealth. These greedy lawyers are False Praisers/Hypocrites that have come to rule in place of Justice and have enslaved the young virgins Philosophy and Rhetoric:

> But Philosophy has been exiled from her homeland, and Philopecunia (the Love of Money) rules in her place. And Philosophy's daughter, Rhetoric, is not free, for she has been sold into slavery. While Justice lived, the chaste study of Rhetoric was the rule. But now Rhetoric has been taken by country bumpkins to the city to there be used by the greedy before a judge.[16]

Philosophy's exile recalls Tahkemoni's fate after the allegorical battle of Folly and Wisdom that opened Ibn Shabbetai's *maqāma*. This passage also recalls al-Harīzī's introductory metaphor in which he describes the enslavement of Hebrew and the exultation of Arabic/Hagar. In both Judeo-Iberian texts the metaphor of enslavement and the allegorical battle represents Jews' relationship to Arabized Andalusi culture, but in *De Vetula* the narrator uses these metaphors to attack his lay counterparts, lawyers.[17] The narrator goes on to describe the evils of lawyers who subvert language and rhetoric for their own benefit and who do not care if their clients lose their cases. These evildoers intentionally abuse rhetoric, and the act is characterized as the prostitution of a virgin: "Then they prostituted you, oh very just virgin. You should not have been exposed to these captors, for they had no right to enslave you—you who did not deserve to be enslaved. Oh with what fervor those hateful ones follow Alchemy, whose fruit they so desire."[18] Reminiscent of the manner in which al-Harīzī portrayed Jewish intellectuals who chose the discourse of the Andalusi court, Arabic language and poetry, as enslaving the Hebrew language and as whoring with Arabic, here the pseudo-Ovid sexualizes both lawyer and layperson's relationship to knowledge. Lawyers act as pimps by forcing Rhetoric against her will to service others. Their maltreatment of Rhetoric is designed to bring them material gain. In *De Vetula*, lawyers and laypersons shun or enslave rhetoric and philosophy, the "true" sciences, for a false science, alchemy, that will make them money. Alchemy and alchemical treatises had long been associated with Arabic language and sciences in medieval Europe.[19] The pseudo-Ovid is setting up an opposition between the culturally and spiritually true path of philosophy (the ultimate goal of scholastic study—the *trivium* and the *quadrivium*) and the false path of alchemy and philopecunia (the foreign, non-Christian sciences).

Spadons, Go-betweens, and the Monstrous

Book 2 of *De Vetula* turns from the hypocrite lawyers and lay persons who pervert knowledge to serve their earthly desires to what the narrator characterizes as sexual deviants that similarly pervert the laws of nature. The anonymous author continues for some hundred and sixty lines on the topic of *semiviros* (half-men), which he identifies with *spadons* (eunuchs). Continuing the pseudo-scientific discourse of Book 1, the narrator gives a graphic description of the ways in which one can be made into a eunuch.[20] The narrator then classifies the different ways in which eunuchs can be defined as monstrous. Because eunuchs are gender neutral they are grammatical monsters. They are neither a "he" nor a "she," a "him" or a "her," and thus befuddle anyone trying to describe or call to them.[21] In addition to being offended by their grammatical indeterminacy, the narrator also declares that eunuchs are moral and natural monsters because their indeterminate sex defies Nature's biological order. The anonymous author thus appeals to Aristotle's hierarchical model of the natural world, according to which the biological imperative of all living things is to procreate.[22] In *De Vetula* the anonymous author weaves both contemporary theological and medical knowledge, much of it recently translated from Arabic into Latin, into his discourse on sex and procreation.[23] The grammatical categories of language and Nature's hierarchy of being prevalent in the natural sciences informed contemporary scholastic readings of key biblical passages on the sexes and in *De Vetula* become central in how this supposed Roman poet defines the parameters of sexual identity.

Some of the examples given by the pseudo-Ovid as proof for the classification of the eunuch as a monster of divine and natural laws can be found in the Judeo-Andalusi *maqāmāt*. The pseudo-Ovid underscores both the genitalia and the beard as markers of male identity. Nature has privileged man with the testes and the beard: "est honor ergo / Barba viro, testis virtutis testiculorum" (The beard is honor and proof of the virtue of the testes).[24] *Spadons* cannot grow a beard or will soon lose theirs, and therefore are not men. In the *Offering*, Kozbi similarly stresses the beard and genitalia as the markers of gender and power, telling the Lord he "caused to sprout in man the beard and penis for his fame and glory." In addition to pointing to the beard and penis as exclusively male attributes, Kozbi's prayer further calls attention to the Lord's role in creating gender differences. Men were given a penis just as women were given a uterus and the pangs of childbirth in order to procreate.[25] According to the pseudo-Ovid, *spadons* are not women because they lack a vulva and they are not men because they cannot grow a beard, produce semen, or procreate. In the *Offering*, Zerah is attacked because although able, he refuses to procreate. Kozbi's prayer anticipates the arguments articulated in *De Vetula* and later thirteenth-century Western European ecclesiastical texts, arguments taken from the natural sciences and used in the theological discourse of medieval Christianity to support misogynist church doctrine. Ibn Shabbetai uses these same misogynist discourses (Aristotle's privileging of the male and the Lord's infliction of childbearing on women as punishment for the Fall) to undermine Zerah and Tahkemoni's supposedly divinely sanctioned celibacy. The pseudo-Ovid, however, uses these discourses not to attack celibacy, which was at least theoretically obligatory for the clergy, but to undermine and defame a possible rival—the eunuch—in order to show the superiority of the cleric's celibate lifestyle, which is the result of mental and spiritual control and not of having the testes physically removed or impaired.[26]

In the subsequent verses on the *spadons*, the anonymous author sets up a dialectic between "whole" priests, those who are virile and have a fully functioning penis and testes, and eunuchs who have been rendered impotent. According to the pseudo-Ovid these *semiviros* are not men, but more like old women whose brow is deeply furrowed and whose voice is high and feminine.[27] The pseudo-Ovid describes the monstrous eunuch as resembling old women very much like both the go-betweens and the exchanged brides of the Judeo-Andalusi *maqāmāt*. Identifying the go-between with the male eunuch makes sense in the homosocial world of Christian clerics. Like the female slaves of al-Andalus, the eunuch was also associated with the enslaved others of the Muslim East and with the lifestyle of the Andalusi and Eastern courts.[28]

Whereas Ibn Shabbetai and al-Harīzī create fictional worlds in which the go-between and exchanged hags practice sorcery and have dealings with the devil, in *De Vetula* this distancing of the go-between and hag to the supernatural is built upon the "scientific" discourse of the philosophical, grammatical, and theological arguments presented in the text. The narrator, supposedly a product of the classical world in which the sexual activity of such *spadons* occurred, distances himself and his culture from the *spadons* by claiming that such people have no right to serve as priests or priestesses in the temple.[29] He further elaborates on the moral nature of the *spadons*, claiming they are monsters that investigate the nature of God and that their rite or Law consists of old stories.[30] This striking critique reads as a veiled attack on Jews and their beliefs, including either the rationalist philosophers such as Maimonides, the centrality of Midrash and Talmud in Rabbinic Judaism, and/or the Kabbalah and its corpus of Neoplatonic texts concerning the nature of God.[31] That the pseudo-Ovid is attacking specifically Judeo-Andalusi rationalism is supported by lines 156–186 in which the pseudo-Ovid attacks a race of people who follow the law of the first-born and the patriarchs. He then compares the deceptive Jacob, who tricked his brother Esau, to the monstrous eunuch. The biblical passages describing the rivalry between Jacob and his older brother Esau and its consequences for the Jewish people, that is, the king of Edom's refusal to allow Moses and the Jews into his kingdom (Genesis 25–35, Numbers 20), were read allegorically by medieval exegetes as analogous to the conflict between Judaism/the Jewish people and Christianity/Rome.[32] The eleventh-century exegete Rashi (1040–1105), like his contemporary Iberian coreligionists, identified Esau/Edom with Christianity and Jacob with the Jews in exile.[33] The pseudo-Ovid is subverting the Jewish exegetical model by identifying Jacob, the exilic Jew, with the *spadon* and making Esau, who in the Jewish exegetical tradition is identified with idolatry and with Christians, not the aggressor and persecutor of Jacob/the Jews, but the victim of the latter's deception. This inversion of the meaning of Jacob and Esau's relationship and Jewish interpretation of it, combined with the attack of those who respect the law of the first-born and investigate the nature of God, suggests that in *De Vetula* the *spadons* are stand-ins for Jews.

In the section on the *spadons* the pseudo-Ovid identifies the monstrous *spadons* with both old women and religious Others (Jews), as well as excludes them from the classical discourses of power—they are outside of the Latin language, the laws of nature, and the realm of religion. The *spadon* is outside of this medieval Latin pseudo-Ovid's classificatory systems, and because of its indeterminacy becomes monstrous. This monstrosity is conflated with that of the go-between who enters into *De Vetula* precisely in those verses following the description of the *spadons*. Whereas Ibn Shabbetai and al-Harīzī create female grotesque Others in their works, in *De Vetula* the author further displaces the grotesque Other from the ordered, controllable Western European Latinate world of language and civilization by locating it outside of language (it is neither he nor she) and outside of categories (it is not man, woman, or animal). Ironically the *spadon* is both outside and in-between—being neither man nor woman, neither *hic* nor *haec*, but something in-between and unnamable. It is the simultaneous displacement and mediacy that makes the *spadon* the perfect representative of the Andalusi go-between. Whereas Ibn Shabbetai hints at Kozbi's non-Jewishness by having her practice the Gentile art of sorcery as defined by Ibn Paqūdā, the pseudo-Ovid makes the *spadon* a stand in for non-Christian Others. Despite the differences in discourses, both the Latin and the Hebrew texts arrive at a monstrous representation of the old woman and of sexual desire.

As proof of his own functioning masculinity, the pseudo-Ovid tells us that in his youth he enjoyed coitus very much, and that he had sex and pursued women until he had a sudden change in lifestyle.[34] He begins the go-between tale as a way of explaining what caused his change in attitude. This tale opens with a description of the beautiful woman with whom he has fallen in love and because of whom he has sought out the help of an old woman or *vetula*. The pseudo-Ovid's description of his beloved offers a stark contrast to the monstrous *spadons* described in the preceding lines. Again, as in chapter 3, we see how the poetic description functions to create desire in the Symbolic—both employing and reiterating a network of cultural and linguistic signifiers recognizable to the thirteenth-century Western European reader. The pseudo-Ovid's ordered and formulaic enumeration of conventional, accepted features is the antithesis of the *spadon*'s grammatical, linguistic, and rhetorical indeterminacy. The act of describing both creates and satisfies desire, and the pseudo-Ovid tells us that even if he were to describe each of her features, his words could never fully communicate their beauty.[35] Though his descriptions pale in comparison with the physical reality of her attributes, just enumerating them will bring him joy.[36] His beloved has thick golden hair, a broad forehead as white as lilies, and dark, arched eyebrows. The space between her brows is particularly appealing: "At the same time each brow stands out notably in its own right and separates the placement of the eyes from the forehead. Between them, however, where the nose continues on from the forehead, set deeper than the nose as well as the forehead and the brows, a certain small space is evident; it is free of hair and is similar to the privet for whiteness." Her tear-rimmed eyes are bright; her nose is not too long or too short; her cheeks are like red apples, and her complexion is a combination of red and white.[37] She has full cherry-red lips that "[s]ince they are shaped a bit outwardly they seem to want to be ready to offer themselves for the taking of kisses." Her teeth are perfectly ordered and brighter than silver and her neck is smooth: "there is no rigid sinew, no puffy vein. Her complexion is free of any roughness; no blemish disfigures it."[38]

In *De Vetula* this listing of the woman's features establishes the narrator as a desiring subject and defines the object of his desire as the most traditional of heterosexual beloveds.[39] This list of features also recalls the description of the beautiful beloveds in the Iberian *maqāmāt*.[40] In the latter, however, these descriptions were based on Arabo-Andalusi poetic conceits (often not gender specific), while this Latin description corresponds to twelfth-century Latin and French vernacular treatises that codify the rhetorical description of specifically female beauty and that require detailed descriptions of the woman's head and occasionally the breasts, but seldom go below the waist.[41]

The pseudo-Ovid, however, continues his description of the beloved's body to include both her breasts and her behind. He admits that he has not, of course, seen the beloved's body. However, based on what he has seen and knowing that what is unseen must be better, he can imagine what it must be like:

> I suppose that on the flat of her chest, rising like twin swellings, are her smallish breasts. They are firm, curvaceous, and seem to admit that they want to be squeezed in an embrace and want, of their own accord, to proceed to the man giving the embrace. Her long slim arms are fine, soft and full; the upper part descends in a straight line from the beginning to end. Her torso is slender; her loins appear to be full and graceful in her girdle; her buttocks are modest but ample in extent. And then there is the movement of her legs, the bend in her knees, her small feet, well shaped and moving forward with an even gait. All these demonstrate the quality of that part which I desire so much.[42]

Based on his own construction of the beloved's beauty, the pseudo-Ovid can further imagine the perfection of her private parts. This image of the beloved's breasts, posterior, and body is strikingly similar to the description of the slave woman revealed by al-Sā'ib's probing hand in "*Maqāma* 12."[43] Just as the slave woman who excited the lover was part of the trickster al-Sadūsi's plan to deceive and rob the desirous al-Sā'ib, this description of the beloved (based on contemporary literary models of beauty) so excites the lover that he immediately enlists the aid of a go-between. Like Zerah, the lover defined by his own desire, this pseudo-Ovid will find that his expectations of pleasure are not fulfilled.

The go-between, as we might expect, deceives the desirous pseudo-Ovid. Claiming to have arranged a midnight rendezvous with the beautiful beloved, the old go-between waits in the beloved's chamber for the lover. The lover sneaks into the beloved's dark room to consummate the affair. Only afterward does he find that the woman with whom he has had sex is not his beloved, but the old go-between in his beloved's bed:

> It was terrible: how unlike the limbs of a young woman were these limbs: the jerky movement of her frame, her sinewy neck, her scrawny shoulders

were suggestive of an elderly woman. Her tough breast of stretched leather was not really a breast but a shepherd's bag, empty and slack. Her stomach had been furrowed by a plow, her buttocks were dry and lean, her legs were coarse, her swollen knees were as hard as diamond. The weak confused motion of the ensemble was like that of an old woman. Pulling myself together I got up and resolved to go at her with my sword. But the good name of my young lady came to mind: so as not to expose her to a scandal I restrained myself. All hope of possessing her had come, however, to an end. I took no action, and my love, though suppressed, was able to compensate for my intense suffering.[44]

Not only does this description of the old go-between resemble descriptions of the old women in the *maqāmāt*, but also the preceding descriptions of the monstrous *spadons*, whom the anonymous author made a point of telling us were like old women with wrinkled faces. In fact, this description emphasizes the wrinkled, tough skin of the old woman the protagonist finds in bed, suggesting this may be an admission of intercourse with a *spadon*. Ovid's supposed exilic memory is tarnished by the old woman who tricks him into having sex with her (him?)—seemingly spoiling forever his erotic fantasies. Ovid, the poet of Love, is exiled from the erotic universe of pleasure by the tricks of the go-between, just as the Christian cleric was banished from the pleasures of the flesh by twelfth- and thirteenth-century canon law and ecclesiastical culture. The inclusion of this go-between tale in the corpus of Ovidian works that circulated in the Latin culture of Western European scholastics also brings it into dialogue with contemporary debates about sex and love taking place among the European clergy. Celibacy was often not practiced by twelfth- and thirteenth-century clerics, who preferred to have an active sex life. This activity was frequently carried out with wives and concubines; the latter often held a special legal status and frequently bore the clerics' children. The Fourth Lateran Council of 1215 put an end to some of these practices, at least in theory.[45] Perhaps the pseudo-Ovid offers this monstrous go-between as the ultimate antidote to the continued urges plaguing the virile cleric, such as, we must imagine, the anonymous author.

This lover is duped into an embarrassing sexual encounter. After having sex with the old go-between he feels violated, but, unlike Heber in al-Harīzī's Gate Six, he decides against killing the old woman because it would tarnish his beloved's honor. However, the description of the old woman's body, post-coitus, recalls the descriptions of both Ritzpah and the she-ghoul in the Judeo-Iberian *maqāmāt* and, given the number of other formal and thematic parallels between *De Vetula* and the Judeo-Iberian works, suggests that the author of *De Vetula* was aware of these Hebrew works.[46] The go-between tale is used by the anonymous author of *De Vetula*, as it was by Ibn Shabbetai and al-Harīzī, to self-consciously address the ethical choices regarding the use of language, rhetoric, knowledge, and desire made by members of his elite group of intellectual peers. The pseudo-Ovid frames these linguistic and sexual choices as cultural options within the scholastic discourse of medieval Latin. Yet the go-between once again opens up a space for alternative discourses. Clerical identity, based in part on abstinence, is problematic for a church that holds procreation as a tenet. Despite this pseudo-Ovid's claims at virility within celibacy, the existence of *spadons*—those half men that prove indistinguishable from old women—lurk behind the narrator's remembered erotic adventures and break into this final erotic escapade of the Praeceptor Amoris just at the moment that should most be enjoyed.

The go-between, the other face of the *spadons*, transforms coitus that would be considered natural according to both Aristotelian science and Christian theology (i.e., between a young man and young woman) into the unnatural and transgressive union of young man and sexually ambiguous older woman. After the encounter the pseudo-Ovid goes home and, believing death insufficient for her crime, fantasizes about the misfortunes and infirmities he hopes will befall the old *vetula*:

> Let her be wretched, and not find a pitying hand to help her; if something is given to her, let it be paltry and bad; let her eat no bread unless it was produced with rotten grain; let her eat no meat except that which is aged or putrid; let her eat no fish which is not contaminated by a stench in all parts; let her partake of no wine unless it is pasty or sour; may she cough for all eternity; may gout wear down her joints; may she have a fever, and while she burns, suffer from an unquenchable thirst; may she have persistent chills and also strong heat spells; if possible, may she have both at the same time, or at least one right after the other; may she weep continually, and have perpetual tears in her eyes; may she have sudden fits of sobbing and sighs and have these often and repeatedly; may she gasp for breath while racked with stiffness; may she belch out a foul smell; may she be unable to clear her nose, and may sordid matter flow down into her; may she not spit it out; but swallow it and then regurgitate; may her bladder and rectum not contain her urine or waste: rather, let there be a constant flow back and forth.[47]

Here the protagonist wishes upon the old go-between a host of physical illnesses centering on the biological functions of the woman's body: weeping, bad breath, flatulence, and a series of gastrointestinal ailments—recalling Heber's final poems in the "*Maqāma* of Marriage."

The old go-between, like the *spadons*, slips into in-between spaces. She sneaks into the beloved's bedroom and has sex with the lover, revealing that the order and control that the protagonist believed he exercised was an illusion. Like Zerah and Heber, the pseudo-Ovid, the great master of love, does not control his desire. His invective, like that of Zerah, reveals an alternative monstrous physicality displaced from the constructions of beauty and desire—the monstrous go-between whose body oozes and flows across the boundaries designed to keep it out.

Conclusion

De Vetula offers a tantalizing example of the go-between tale as rendered into the Latin of European scholastics. The anonymous author reveals a breadth of knowledge typical of a thirteenth-century cleric trained in the Liberal Arts (the *trivium* and the *quadrivium*) and the newest cutting-edge Arab sciences (algebra, astrology, philosophy) recently made available in translations from Iberia (often made by Andalusi Jews as discussed in chapter 3). He also, though, shows an awareness of the fictional tradition of the Judeo-Andalusi tradition. This author may have been a Judeo-Andalusi convert to Christianity, similar to any number of well-known cases such as Moses Sephardi (Petrus Alfonsi) and Abner of Burgos (Alfonso de Vallodolid).[48]

Whereas Judeo-Andalusi authors used the go-between tale as a parable reflecting Judeo-Iberian adoption and assimilation of Arabic language and philosophical ideas at the expense of Jewish customs and traditions, *De Vetula* positions the go-between tale in a text that holds both Christian Latin sources as well as Arabic sciences as esteemed traditions and sources of knowledge. The pseudo-Ovid frames the go-between tale as part of the same debate about the use and purpose of knowledge within the larger culture. Al-Harīzī and Ibn Shabbetai used the go-between tale to engage and explore different possible models of identity available to the Judeo-Andalusi courtier in exile (celibate Torah scholar, secular Arabized Andalusi courtier). The author of *De Vetula* similarly develops the go-between tale as an examination of different modes of thirteenth-century clerical identity. Like Ibn Paqūdā, this pseudo-Ovid focuses on the ethical decisions of the learned subject. Just as the cleric is superior to the secular lawyer because he has chosen to pursue knowledge for a greater/divine purpose, he is also superior to the eunuch for he is a fully functioning man who has chosen celibacy instead of having it thrust upon him.[49] According to the pseudo-Ovid, *spadons* have no place in the church, in his community. The author of *De Vetula* redefines the urges of the learned cleric—the urge to use his acquired knowledge in the pursuit of money or to approach his fellow clerics to vent his sexual desire—as invalid options. The ideal for the learned cleric, or so says the repentant exiled Ovid, is a life of celibacy studying the true doctrine, the truest light of philosophy.[50]

This Latin work reflects the tension created when the Andalusi model of courtly desire is displaced from the Arabized courts of Iberia and inscribed into a system in which the poetic discourse of desire is no longer the discourse of power. Unlike the laws of geometry and statistics that the anonymous author of *De Vetula* translates from the Arabic to Latin, Ibn Hazm's Andalusi desire does not translate into the often overtly misogynist discourse of Western Latinate culture. It fits so uncomfortably in fact that the author, after attempting to explain how such desire (embodied in the *spadons*) defies the ecclesiastical classificatory systems designed to order the world, interrupts his "scientific" treatise with a go-between tale that exemplifies the threatening nature of Andalusi desire.

The privileging of Andalusi culture and texts, including philosophical treatises and poetry, that is at the heart of the Hebrew *maqāmāt* has been displaced in the Latin text. Unlike Ibn Shabbetai and al-Harīzī, the anonymous author of *De Vetula* does not engage with the Andalusi, but, on the contrary, erases the overt signs of al-Andalus and the Arabs. By making the exilic Roman author Ovid a mouthpiece for the natural sciences, mathematics, philosophy, and medical knowledge made available throughout thirteenth-century Europe in Andalusi translations, the anonymous author elides the role of Andalusis in the shaping and transmission of this material. However, as we would expect, the go-between as product and disseminator of the Andalusi courtly erotic brings with her traces of al-Andalus, despite the anonymous author's attempts to purge them. From divine or demonic helpmate and gateway of idolatry she is transformed into the sexual deviant. Her ability to transform and seduce allows her to become the embodiment of medieval Christian sexual anxiety—the eunuch or *spadon*. This suspicious being that defies clear categorization continues to exercise the go-between's subversive and transgressive actions from outside the epistemological boundaries of the learned thirteenth-century Christian cleric. Despite the church's increasingly rigid policies on gender, clerical sex, and the natural order, the go-between, like the *spadon*, thrives simultaneously outside of and in-between the scholastic's defined boundaries. The medieval cleric's obsession not with acculturation and idolatry but with sexual deviance reveals the slippages in the church's official discourse. However, this monstrous sexual ambiguity does correspond to medieval Christian depictions of Arabic sexuality and culture and suggests that, despite the anonymous author's best attempts, the specter of the Arab lurks just below the surface in *De Vetula*.[51] In chapter 5 we will explore how the tension between Western European scholastic identity and Andalusi erotics makes its way back to Iberia. In the fourteenth century the peninsula where the Andalusi go-between was born witnesses her demise. Before her sudden death and comic funeral, Juan Ruiz frees her from the confines of her tale, allowing her to roam free throughout his collection of Romance *maqāmāt*, where she will come into contact and transform a serious of disparate Western European discourses and genres.

CHAPTER 5

REPRESENTING OTHERS IN THE *LIBRO DE BUEN AMOR*

> *Assí fue, ¡mal pecado!, que mi vieja es muerta:*
> *Murió a mí serviendo, lo que me desconuerta;*
> *Non sé cómo lo diga, que mucha buena puerta*
> *Me fue después çerrada que antes me era abierta.*
>
> It's come to pass—sad fate!—that my old crone is now no more.
> She died while in my service, which afflicts me with great pain.
> I don't know how to say it, but many a good door
> Has now been closed to me, which used to be wide open before.
>
> —*Libro de buen amor*

The go-between in his/her different iterations as courtier, procuress, and even text formed an integral part of official Iberian culture during the Middle Ages. The authors of the works studied in the preceding chapters were themselves courtiers who manipulated the official discourses of Andalusi culture to explore the mediator's (and thus their own) essential role as sociopolitical and cultural intermediary. The fourteenth-century Castilian work, the *Libro de buen amor* (*LBA*), underscores the importance of the traditionally Andalusi role of mediation and the mediator in the construction of Iberian identity. The work reveals that despite official attempts to distance the increasingly Christian-dominated fourteenth-century court and church literatures of Castile from the Arabic and Hebrew traditions of Iberia, the Andalusi go-between and the cosmopolitan worldview of which she is both product and representative survived in Castilian vernacular literature.[1] In a Castilian culture increasingly influenced by Western European religious trends from beyond the Pyrenees, the author of the *LBA* uses this go-between to open up a space for a secular Andalusi-style erotic at odds with the moralizing and often misogynist discourse of Western European scholasticism, for which the reconciliation of sexuality, desire, and religious sentiments proved a perennial difficulty (as it also proved for Iberian Jews as discussed in chapter 3). Juan Ruiz's go-between, as representative of the secular Andalusi cultural heritage of medieval Iberia, offers a counter model to those nationalist ideologies being constructed in both the Castilian court and Church that had begun to systematically exclude and push to the margins (or across them) the Andalusi (Arabic and Hebrew) heritage and traditions of medieval Castile. Early Castilian works such as the *Cantar de Mío Cid*, the *Caballero Zifar*, and the *Castigos del Rey Sancho* set about shaping a new, non-Arabized Christian ideal—a soldier of God in the Western European mold; the *LBA*, on the other hand, offers a model for a distinctly secular Iberian lover whose potential beloveds represent the plurality of Iberian society. In the late Middle Ages and Renaissance this pluralistic society, celebrated and acknowledged by the official discourses of the first generation of post-Reconquest Castilian kings, gives way to a courtly and church ideal that increasingly privileges a homogenous Christian construction of Castilian identity. The mid-fourteenth-century author of the *LBA* witnesses the cultural doors of Castile closing on the differing cultural, ethnic, and religious traditions excluded from this new Castilian cultural model. The *LBA* provides an alternative, fictional model where those doors remain open, however briefly, for the protagonist and his representative, Trotaconventos—the last mediator capable of bridging the ever-widening cultural divides separating Jews, Muslims, Berbers, Mozarabs, and northern Christians in medieval Castile who converse, seduce, and experience one another in the pluralistic and varied society of medieval Iberia. By the work's end, however, the death of the go-between, described in the stanza opening this chapter as the closing of many good doors, signals the final closing of official Castilian culture to the many other cultures of medieval Iberia. With the death of the mediator the possibility for dialogue and mutual experience in the Spanish court disappears.

In this chapter I explore how the cultural, linguistic, and religious Others of fourteenth-century Castile—the various potential beloveds of Juan Ruiz, which include a Moorish woman, a shepherdesses on the northern Frankish border, possibly a Jewish woman, and a Mozarab nun, as well as the go-between herself, an older woman with supernatural powers—are represented in the *LBA*. The old *alcahueta* Trotaconventos is like the messenger described some three hundred years earlier by Ibn Hazm. Her skills and manipulations are part of the Andalusi past and as such are part of the author's cultural heritage. This now disintegrating model of a plural Iberian society is a model in which mediation is possible. The *LBA* appears in the fourteenth-century as Castile establishes its dominance on a growing expanse of Iberian and Andalusi territories acquired by Christians from the north—both Iberian and Frankish—during the preceding two centuries of Reconquest. There is still a large presence of Muslims and Jews in Castile, but more liberal policies of coexistence established in the first decades of the Reconquest and continued under Alfonso X during the second half of the thirteenth century have given way to an ideology of military domination and the supremacy of Christianity. In the *LBA*, however, *moras*, Jews, and Christians sing, love, and live together—not always effortlessly or painlessly—but successfully, provided they have mediators. Trotaconventos can reach and communicate with women guarded as jealously as the Torah, Moorish women in the market, and nuns in the convent. She truly overcomes all barriers, and in the *LBA* this successful negotiation of linguistic, cultural, and religious boundaries is celebrated.

The *LBA*, whose title, "buen amor" (Good Love), is also the name of the go-between, "For love of the old woman and to speak the truth, I named this book 'Good Love' and her too from this time on" (933), is itself a mediator.[2] It mediates between the Semitic past and culture of Iberia and the European Latinate Christian ideals taking hold among the courtly circles of fourteenth-century Castile and among the Iberian clergy. The author of the *LBA* inserts the increasingly monologic Christian discourses of Castilian Church and courtly literature into the open *maqāmāt* frame of the *LBA*, exploiting the latter's tendency to multivalency in order to rewrite those moralizing discourses within the context of Iberian Andalusi secular erotics. The scholar's work of interpretative glossing and exegesis becomes the purview of the would-be lover. Like the go-between, the *maqāmāt*-form used in the *LBA* opens doors by opening dialogue between literary models and tropes that normally remain confined to their own particular narrative/poetic, cultural, and linguistic traditions. Just as in the day to day life of medieval Iberia—life in the market, street, and bedroom—people of different ethnic, social, and religious traditions met, fought, fell in love, shared stories, hardships, holidays, and celebrations, so too in the *LBA* Western European erotic genres come into contact with and are transformed by Andalusi erotic material. The go-between is not merely an element of this Andalusi erotic, she transcends it and manages to mediate between the seemingly incongruous moralistic scholastic tradition of Western Europe, Judeo-Iberian pietism, and the Andalusi-style erotic literary forms and philosophical approaches of medieval Iberia. The go-between, like the book in which she is represented, transforms these traditions and forces them to accommodate the seemingly incompatible Other.

The go-between in the *LBA* becomes emblematic of the reading process that the *LBA* both teaches and requires from its would-be audience, the act of good loving by which the reader is forced time and time again to choose between two or more possible readings/interpretations for the same passage, moral or motif. Whereas fourteenth-century Castilian clerics and kings may have adopted the techniques and attitudes of Western European moralizing scholasticism at the expense of the Semitic traditions of Iberia in order to legitimate their own tenuous claims as "Europeans" or "Christians," the author of the *LBA* forces the reader to engage the variety of often contradictory literary and cultural traditions of medieval Iberia. The *maqāmāt* proves amazingly useful as an open-ended frame capable of accommodating representative European narrative and poetic elements that range from the orthodox Christian sermon to the secular erotic lyric or fabliaux. Native poetic forms like the *zajal* and *mester de clerecía* also firmly establish the work as an Iberian text. But it is the go-between herself who makes the work not only function, but transcend the sociocultural and political contexts of medieval Iberia. This old bawd, whose presence pulls together the disparate and seemingly unrelated discrete narratives from which the *LBA* is formed, also, as she inscribes herself into the center of the narrative displaces both the authoritative discourse of the narrator and the book itself, transcending the historical moment and anticipating the crisis of the subject and the polemics of identity that characterize contemporary postcolonial and postmodern theory.

Trotaconventos is not the treacherous mediator of al-Harīzī's and Ibn Shabbetai's *maqāmāt*. Her translation and transformation of desire is not a threat to the author-narrator's identity, but on the contrary, she is a part of his identity—part of his Andalusi/Iberian heritage. Al-Harīzī and al-Saraqustī inscribed the go-between and her erotic negotiations into only one episode of their *maqāma* collections, but Juan Ruiz transforms his collection into a vehicle for the go-between. Mediators are present in all but four of his erotic encounters, and those in which she is absent end disastrously. Like Ibn Shabbetai, Juan Ruiz makes the act of mediation and the mediator's crucial role in the attainment of desire the central concern of his work.

Good Love: Identity, Authority, and Cultural Heritage

Beyond what the text itself tells us, little is known of the author of the *LBA*. Of the three surviving manuscripts (and Portuguese fragments) only one, a late-fourteenth-century copy housed in Salamanca, gives the author's name as Johanne Ruiz, and even that may be spurious.[3] Though most critics agree that the work was composed sometime between 1330 and 1343, this too has been called into question.[4] The work itself, a frame tale that narrates the erotic adventures of a roguish archpriest, further complicates a facile reading or classification of the text according to a particular period or genre.

The pseudo-autobiographic narration, a defining characteristic of the Iberian *maqāmāt* discussed in chapters 2 and 3, allows the narrator to play with the multiple meanings of the frame and the diegetic material.[5] In the *LBA*, the narrative thread, held together by the first-person narration, is counter woven by the presence of Trotaconventos, the go-between, who enters and leaves the narrative at key points. Her presence or absence—the use or lack of a successful mediator—determines the erotic and textual success of the narrator. In those episodes in which she is not present—when the narrator foolishly tries to use another go-between, a Ferrán García for example, or when he himself trots without the assistance of his mediator—things turn out disastrously. Trotaconventos may not be the only go-between of the *LBA*, but she is the mediator who successfully procures a widow and a nun for the archpriest, and the one whose assistance the narrator, Juan Ruiz, extols in the final lament. The go-between of the *LBA* uses the new courtly and church discourses of the nascent Castilian vernacular to represent the desire of the narrator-protagonist. The go-between allows the narrator to successfully subvert these official discourses, which often take the form of the *exempla* and *mester de clerecía*, by making them a vehicle for his own erotic narrative and by using them for his own immoral ends (seduction). In fourteenth-century Castile, didactic fiction was used in the royal courts to confirm and support the regent's legitimacy and in the church to prove the legitimacy of Christianity over all other religions, and in the *LBA mester de clerecía* and *exempla* become additional tools with which Trotaconventos attempts to convince the beloveds of the archpriest's erotic legitimacy and with which the author-narrator attempts to convince the reader of his authority.

Juan Ruiz, however, is far from a reliable narrator, and the *LBA* throws his authority into question at every turn.[6] His first-person diegetic narration is destabilized by contradictions and by unexplained shifts in voice (e.g., to the first-person perspective of the book in stanza 70 and to the third-person narration of don Melón's adventures with Endrina), recalling similar shifts and destabilization of the narrator's authority in the Andalusi and Judeo-Iberian *maqāmāt* discussed in chapters 2 and 3. Américo Castro was one of the first critics to seriously propose that the episodic structure of the *LBA* and its pseudo-autobiographic narration were based on Andalusi Arabic models.[7] In 1954 Castro proposed Ibn Hazm's *The Dove's Neck Ring*, a work that had become available in translation for the first time (since the Middle Ages) only some seventeen years before, as a model for the *LBA*.[8] The textual similarities Castro found between Ibn Hazm's and Juan Ruiz's treatment of love further strengthened his belief that he had found the model for the *LBA*. Opponents of Castro's thesis vehemently attacked the idea of Arabic influence in the *LBA*. His harshest critic, Claudio Sánchez

Albornoz, claimed that the predominantly conflictive relationship between Christians and Muslims in medieval Iberia precluded cultural exchange to the extent advocated by Castro, and the English critic G.B. Gybbon-Monypenny claimed Castro had simply ignored the "possibility of European literary influences on the structure of the *LBA*."[9] Beyond the specifics of their arguments is a basic rejection of Arabic influence in this foundational work of Castilian literature.[10] The next critic to take up Castro's approach was Lida de Malkiel, who asserted it was not the Arabic literary tradition that served as model for Juan Ruiz, but the Hebrew *maqāmāt* of medieval Iberia, specifically Ibn Zabarra's *Book of Delights*.[11] Again, critical rebuttals of Lida de Malkiel's thesis were forthcoming.[12] Francisco Márquez Villanueva (1993) and Leyla Rouhi (1999) interrogate the go-between's indebtedness to Arabic culture and include discussions of the *LBA*, but their main focus is the late-fifteenth-century *Celestina*.[13] Current *LBA* scholarship, however, has seen a revival of the tendency to deny the work's Arabic or Jewish intellectual roots.[14] However, as this chapter will show, the work's indebtedness to the Andalusi erotic tradition, as formulated in both Hebrew and Arabic texts of medieval Iberia examined in the preceding chapters, reveals itself in both the work's formal characteristics and thematic content.

The content of the *LBA* reveals that its author was familiar with the diverse population of medieval Iberia. In addition to being familiar with Jewish customs, including the guarding of the Torah scrolls (stanza 78) and their dietary restrictions (1183), Juan Ruiz also shows he is knowledgeable of vernacular Arabic (1508–1512) and includes a detailed discussion on Arab musical instruments and musical styles (1228–1234). In the episode of the *mora* (discussed in detail below), Juan Ruiz shows that he knows Andalusi Arabic, which would have been the main language of popular Iberian *maqāmāt* by the late thirteenth to early fourteenth century. The similarities between both the structure and content of the *LBA* and the *maqāmāt* suggest a connection. In the rest of the Arab-speaking world the *maqāmāt* were most often performed orally in public, and a large corpus of *maqāmāt* composed in dialectical Arabic is documented from this period.[15] Though his dialectical Arabic would have allowed him access to these performances, since no popular Iberian *maqāmāt* survive we cannot say with any certainty how much the popular forms were modeled on the Classical *maqāmāt* that have survived.[16] As in the rest of the medieval Muslim world, in medieval al-Andalus the *maqāmāt* were also performed at court and had important social functions, "[C]omposition of occasional *maqāmāt* became part of Andalusi epistolary practice in the courts of the party kings and their Berber successors. . .[T]hey were usually composed to celebrate social occasions or promote courtly interactions and interests."[17] Given the different social contexts and functions of the *maqāmāt* as popular drama and court performance, one can imagine the amount of *maqāmāt* designed for popular performance that would have still been performed for Arabic-speaking audiences in fourteenth-century Castile, but that have been lost, leaving no textual legacy.

The author of the *LBA* reveals an awareness of the different literary and linguistic cultures of the Peninsula, including not only details about the ritual habits of Castilian Jews and the language of Andalusi Arabs, but also an awareness of internal differences within the Iberian Christian community—encompassing not only northern Iberian Romance-speaking Christians, but also Arabized Christians or Mozarabs (as discussed in detail below). In addition to representing these various cultures, the *LBA* is also a witness to extra-Pyrenean vernacular and Latin literary trends. The peculiar perspective of the *LBA*, one that simultaneously reveals intimate knowledge of the customs of Christians, Jews, and Muslims, as well as familiarity with the canonical genres and works of Latin scholasticism and the Castilian court makes the work uniquely Iberian.

In the next section I review the sociocultural landscape of early-fourteenth-century Castile and the literary workshops where these new vernacular texts were created and developed. The different ethnic, linguistic, and religious groups living together in this nascent kingdom-nation had only recently begun to be defined as a comprehensive group known as Castilians. In the mid-thirteenth century, under the supervision of Alfonso el Sabio, official court literature projects a pluralistic, fundamentally secular image of Castilian identity. The official nationalist discourse of the court though, in the latter part of the thirteenth century begins to accommodate the ecclesiastical point of view and to shape the representation of the ideal Castilian in a Christian mold. Courtly culture and literary representations did not, of course, always faithfully reflect what was happening in other sectors of society. Even as clerics came to play a much more instrumental role in the official court culture during the reigns of Sancho IV (1284–1295), Fernando IV (1295–1312), and Alfonso XI (1312–1350), there continued to exist minority voices within the church. This was the case for Mozarab clerics. Other minority viewpoints, for example those of Jews and others advocating a more pluralistic tolerant image of Castilian identity, were either silenced or simply did not find representation in the official discourse of the court. To understand the way in which the *LBA*, like the earlier Iberian *maqāmāt*, subverts dominant discourses and exclusionary constructions of identity, a detailed overview of official Castilian discourses, as well as a review of those groups excluded from them, is required.

Cultural Context: Changing Attitudes in Fourteenth-Century Castile

The geographic names mentioned in the *LBA*—among them, Hita, Alcalá, Burgos, Castro de Urdiales, Calatrava, and the Duero—locate the work within medieval Castile in the environs of Toledo. These lands, although conquered by Hispano-Roman Christians at the end of the eleventh century were still home to a diverse and often contentious society. As Castilian Christian monarchs solidified their power over and increased their territorial expansion into the Muslim controlled lands of the Peninsula, their policy toward Muslims and Jews gradually shifted from one of tolerance to one of intolerance. During the first generation of the Reconquest, Castilian monarchs such as Alfonso VI (1065–1109), Fernando III (1217–1252), and Alfonso X (1252–1284) adopted certain of the Arabized customs of the local populace and guaranteed certain rights to their Muslim and Jewish subjects.[18] The Andalusi-style culture of the Muslim, Jewish, and Mozarabs of medieval Iberia was privileged over that of Christian Europe in these monarchs' courts.[19] However, changing demographics and dynastic crisis in late-thirteenth-century and early-fourteenth-century Castile, combined with the growing influence of the Western European Church and its crusading zeal, precipitated a marked shift toward intolerance of Muslims, Jews, and Andalusi-style plurality among the official legal, religious, and courtly discourses of Castile.[20]

The status and fate of the Arabized Christian minority known as Mozarabs proved to be a bellwether for the changing official attitude toward Andalusi-style plurality.[21] The fate of these Iberians during the Reconquest reflects the fate of Arabized Andalusi learning in medieval Hispano-Roman Castile. By the time Juan Ruiz composes the *LBA* these Iberians had been subjected to over two centuries of assimilatory pressure from the Hispano-Roman Christians of northern Iberia and France. The *LBA*, whether the author was a Mozarab or not, reflects the same hybridity that characterized the culturally Arabized Iberian Christians who had lived for centuries under Muslim rule in al-Andalus. Like the Mozarabs, those Arabized Christians with cultural roots in both the Arabic "East" and the Christian "West," the *LBA* functions in the cultural space of both the Arabo-Iberian street and the Latin scholastic tradition. Theirs is an identity in flux and, much like the *LBA*, one difficult to categorize given the fact that it flies in the face of much of the self-defined religious-ethnic constructions of the period. They were not Arabs or Muslims, but they knew Arabic and were familiar with Muslim customs. To the Hispano-Roman and Frankish Christians, the Mozarabs' clothing, food, and everyday life would have been barely distinguishable from that of their Andalusi Muslim and Jewish neighbors. The *LBA*'s representation of Arab and Jewish Andalusi cultural and literary traditions suggests that the author's frame of reference may have been that of a Mozarab—a Christian familiar with both traditions—Latin and Arabo-Andalusi. In the fourteenth century, the town of Hita, supposed birthplace of the author named in stanza 575 in the Salamanca manuscript, was part of the province of Toledo and was clearly an important frontier town with a diverse populace that included Muslims, Jews, and Mozarab Christians.[22]

Though they had been an important and powerful Christian minority population of the *taifa* kingdom of Toledo, and then the majority as the city's Muslims fled south ahead of advancing northern Christians, Mozarabs ended up a segregated Arabized minority under Hispano-Roman rule.[23] To the majority of Mozarabs the Christians from the north were invaders and occupiers.[24] As Reyna Pastor de Togneri points out, it may have only taken seven years for the Christians to take Toledo, but it took at least one hundred and thirty more to Hispanicize (*hispanizar*) it.[25] The process was one of forced assimilation, brought about by the impoverishment and subjection of the Mozarabs by the Hispano-Roman dominated church and court. Despite Alfonso VI's acknowledgment of the Mozarabs' decisive help in taking Toledo from the Muslims and the appointment of a Mozarab governor in 1086, the Castilian monarch nevertheless stripped them of their cultural power by approving the appointment of the Frenchman Bernard de Sédirac as archbishop of Toledo. Bernard replaced the Visigothic Mozarab rite with the Roman one, dashing Mozarab hopes for the restoration of their culture in post-Reconquest Castile.[26] What had once distinguished and united Mozarabs as Christians in Muslim-dominated al-Andalus—their ancestral Visigothic rite—although preserved by a few rich, educated Mozarab families, became, under Christian rule, identified with their language (vernacular Arabic) and Arabized customs, and further isolated them from the larger Hispano-Roman community.[27] In 1099 Alfonso VI dealt the Mozarabs of Toledo another blow by giving Santa María de Alficén, the "Mozarabs' social center as well as their place of worship," to the monastery of San Servando, which was administered by the abbot of Saint-Victor de Marseille.[28] Mozarabs and Mozarabic culture in Toledo did not fare well after the Reconquest, "[w]ith the collaboration of a king willing to acquiesce in the destruction of their cult and culture, [and] a French archbishop, whose own mentor the abbot of Cluny had described them as a barbaric people, [and] treated the Mozarabs as legally dead."[29]

A minority of powerful, rich Mozarab families, along with a handful of influential Jewish families, however, did band together, and continued to wield political and social influence, and further their own economic and cultural agendas, well into the thirteenth century.[30] There is some evidence of a Mozarabic resistance movement and a twelfth-century revival of the Mozarabic rite and concomitant script.[31] In the eleventh century Hispano-Roman and French opposition to, and intolerance of Mozarab political and social power, took the form of what Pastor de Togneri calls "Occidentalism"—an ideological privileging of Latin Christendom as better and more civilized than Mozarab culture.[32] This form of imperialism/ colonialism becomes, in the twelfth and thirteenth centuries, nascent Castilian nationalism, which by the end of thirteenth century, under Sancho IV, is articulated in the official ideology of the royal court and the church (*molinismo*). This ideology does not make the distinctions or recognize the nuances in identity, culture, and language that had marked the earliest period of Castilian culture, and in its essentializing tendencies— framing the world as Hispano-Roman (Latin) Christian or non-Christian—hybrid cultures and traditions like those of Iberian Arabized Muslims, Christians, and Jews became a threat to Christian Castilian identity.

Like their Mozarab neighbors, Iberian Muslims and Jews also experienced growing disenfranchisement under Hispano-Roman Christian rule. During the first decades of the Reconquest, Hispano-Roman Castilians still needed non-Christians to fill key positions in their administration and keep things running, as well as to pay much needed taxes. These considerations were reflected in the relatively tolerant treatment of minority groups. Peter Linehan points out that in the first century of Reconquest such practical concerns prevailed over a more intolerant aggressive form of Christianity, "'Aggressive religiosity' was marked for export only. Especially in frontier areas, it could lead to nothing but trouble unless and until a full-scale-breeding programme of the sort favored by Alfonso X had been implemented and the Christians enjoyed something like numerical equality with their non-Christian neighbors."[33] As northern Iberian Christians became established on Castilian soil and their numbers increased, however, their initial leniency toward non-Westernized and non-Christian subjects changed to one of growing intolerance.[34]

By the late twelfth century, the northern Iberian Church had established firm ties to the French Church and looked to Western Europe as a cultural model. Although early Castilian monarchs avoided aggressive religiosity for political reasons, the church adopted a more aggressive missionary zeal that sought to "convince its non-Christianizing neighbors and subjects of the incontrovertible truth of the Christian vision." This new religious agenda involved the use of new polemical and literary forms and an "argumentation that was based entirely on reason alone."[35] As Robert Chazan points out, the thrust of this argumentation, as evidenced by the works of Alfonso de Valladolid and his Jewish polemicists, was aimed at convincing Jews of the superiority of Christianity by offering a reasonable and sound exegesis of certain key passages of the Book of Daniel proving that traditional Rabbinic interpretations were false.[36] The privileging of the use of logical argumentation and political allegiance to encourage conversion also characterizes Western European Christian approaches to Muslims in the thirteenth century.[37] By the fourteenth century, when Juan Ruiz was composing the *LBA*, however, attempts to dialogue with or persuade Jews or Muslims of the merits of Christianity gave way to a more pessimistic approach to non-Christian Others.[38] Until the late thirteenth century, the growing missionary (and fundamentally anti-Semitic) movement in church ideology is kept at bay in medieval Castile by Castilian monarchs such as Alfonso X, who preferred to cultivate a secular court modeled on Andalusi models. With the accession of Sancho IV to the Castilian throne this changed though, and the distinctions between royal and church ideology were blurred as the Castilian monarch welcomed the clergy into his court.

Sancho IV's courtly ideology, discussed in detail below, marks a conscious break with the courtly ideals of his father, Alfonso X (1221–1284), known as El Sabio (The Learned), who is often championed as the ideal of medieval Iberian coexistence.[39] Alfonso's cultural model was built upon the systematic and extensive use of translations of Arabic works. The central role of translation, as both process and product, in the Alfonsine conception of the state has its origins in earlier Castilian attitudes toward and uses for translation.[40] During the twelfth century the archbishop of Toledo, Raimundo (1126–1152), had established in Toledo the so-called School of Translators—a group of scholars that produced Arabic-Latin translations, using Hebrew and Romance as intermediary languages.[41] When Alfonso X initiates the next great period of official translation activity in the thirteenth century, the target language becomes the nascent Castilian vernacular. Alfonso's translation activities were designed to replace both Arabic and Latin as the language of learning and prestige for scholars across Europe, not just Iberia.[42] Alfonso aspired to become the Holy Roman Emperor, a title he had claim to on his mother's side, and he utilized translation as a propagandistic tool for furthering that goal. By translating Arab works into Romance, Alfonso is forcing Western European Christian scholars to read them in Castilian instead of in the pan-European language of medieval Christianity, Latin. Mozarabs and, to a greater extent, Jews played important roles in the translation process, given their linguistic abilities in Arabic and/or Hebrew and the vernacular.[43] Well aware of the power translation wields in the formation of cultural identities and of its importance in "constructing representations of foreign cultures," Alfonso makes the translation activities of his court the literary arm of his imperial agenda.[44]

By and large the majority of Alfonsine translations into Romance are prose works—philosophy, science, practical treatises on hunting, chess, medicine—precisely those works that would appeal to Latin scholastics. Alfonsine translators translate a large number of Arabic works, but they do not translate poetry, the most esteemed and privileged mode of Arabo-Andalusi literature and society.[45] The image of Arab literature and learning conveyed in the Alfonsine translations disadvantages poetry and rhymed prose—the gem of Arabic letters in al-Andalus—which remain wholly absent from his translation activity.[46] Since poetry was the discourse of political power in al-Andalus, Alfonso may have been consciously avoiding panegyrics of Muslim rulers, or poetry that legitimates Muslim rule.[47] Similarly, the *maqāmāt*, traditionally used to critique and question the official discourses of power by parodying the ruling elite, the institutions of government, and the courtiers in public office would not have been well-suited to Alfonso's imperial agenda and are absent from the Alfonsine translations. Instead, in Alfonso's court, history becomes the new discourse of political legitimacy for the Castilian king.[48] The great encyclopedic histories compiled under Alfonso's supervision by teams of translators in Toledo, the *Estoria de España* and the *General Estoria*, portray Alfonso as the legitimate and ultimate ruler of not only Castile, but the Holy Roman Empire. In these histories the past of mankind, from Creation, through the Greeks, Romans, Carthaginians, Vandals, Visigoths, Arabs, to the thirteenth century has led inevitably to the ascension of Alfonso as emperor—the legitimate leader of Visigothic and Hispano-Roman Christendom.[49] These histories draw upon both Arabic and Latin sources.

Discourses of Dominance in Medieval Castile

Alfonso X's cultural model was fundamentally a secular enterprise cultivated at the expense of, and often in opposition to, the church. Alfonso X sought to structure and maintain a secular nation through the codification and implementation of the national and local law codes, the *Siete Partidas* and the *Fuero general*, that he had composed and recorded in Castilian. In addition he created a nascent Castilian courtly reality through the translation of scientific treatises and Eastern narratives.[50] *Calila et Dimna*, the first collection of Eastern stories known to have been translated from Arabic into the Castilian vernacular, is translated at the behest of Alfonso X in the mid-thirteenth century. And in it we find his new cultural agenda laid out. The series of *exempla* from which the story is composed points to the secular literary tradition that will serve as the basis of the new Castilian courtly codes of behavior in the Alfonsine court. The narrative frames into which these *exempla* are woven, first that of the Indian courtier Berzebuey who brings home to Persia ancient Indian story collections (deemed more valuable even than the secret of immortality) and then that of Ibn al-Muqaffa who further translates the Persian material at the request of the 'Abbasid caliph Harun al-Rashid, not only privilege the translator and the act of translation and mediation as the most vital of stages in the attainment of knowledge, but also implicitly compare Alfonso to these great Eastern rulers.[51]

The translation/adaptation of *Calila* was a key part of Alfonso's cultural model, and in it we find represented the hermeneutics of the coexistence he hoped to establish in his own realm. In it the great kings of the past employ learned philosophers and revere knowledge in and of itself, whether it be acquired through translation from another language or culture or not. Other cultures have valuable and important traditions from which one can learn important lessons. The lessons of the work are taught in dialogue and by example—not by force—and focus on the role of the courtier and the sovereign he serves, both of whom recognize wisdom and good advice as their mutual goal.[52] The work serves not only as a *regimine principium*, but also as a manual for courtiers, in which the latter learns a series of strategies by which he can adapt to ever-changing moral or doctrinal conditions in order to carry out his office.[53] It is the king's duty to see through malicious courtiers and choose the sage advice of the loyal servant. The secular, courtly nature of this text reveals the concerns of Alfonso X who was intent on building a secular cultural model based on previous Andalusi examples, in which the sovereign and his court, not the church as in other parts of Western Europe, were the loci of power and culture. He strategically privileges the frame tale structure and the prose of the *regimine principium* over the erotic imagery of lyric poetry, which had been the form favored by Arabo-Andalusi sovereigns to legitimate their royal ambitions.

Alfonso X's imperial schemes involved the creation of a society in which his Arab, Jewish, and Christian subjects could coexist. In Alfonso's court the ideal courtier was the one most capable of dialoguing across these various cultures and groups, and the ideal king was the wise man informed by Muslim, Jewish, and Christian advisors. With the accession of his son Sancho to the thrown, however, the Castilian ideal changes. Sancho IV and his successors, Fernando IV and Alfonso XI, continued Alfonso's translation activities and also maintained multiethnic and religiously diverse courts, although they consciously tried to break with Alfonso's secular courtly ideal. From the moment Sancho IV was crowned in Toledo in an ecclesiastical ceremony, he cultivated a close connection with the Castilian Church in an effort to legitimize his reign and his marriage. The Castilian Church, with its see in Toledo, had long been upset by Alfonso el Sabio's disregard and, after throwing its weight behind Sancho in the dynastic upheaval of the 1280s, was rewarded with increasing power and influence at court.[54] Gonzalo Pérez Gudiel, archbishop of Toledo in 1280 and cardinal by 1299, becomes the driving force behind this renewed ecclesiastical presence at the royal court in Toledo.[55] By the 1290s Pérez Gudiel and his followers, the elite clergy of Castile, dominate the administration of the kingdom.[56]

Under Sancho IV, his queen, María de Molino, and Gonzalo Pérez Gudiel with his group of courtiers drawn from the cathedral school of Toledo, the courtly ideal and the Castilian courtier class is transformed by a new political agenda that seeks to reinscribe Castile into Western Christendom, which was itself undergoing a period of reactionary reform.[57] Sancho's early political activities (including rebellion against the legitimate king of Castile, his father, Alfonso X, the murder of one of his most loyal supporters and subjects, Lope Díaz de Haro, and marriage to his own cousin, María de Molina) were ample cause for the church, his own subjects, and the neighboring European nations of France, Aragón and Portugal, with whom his father had engaged in various political and military relations, to renounce his claim to the throne.[58] Recasting Castile as a pious Catholic crusading nation and its courtly ideal as that of a devout follower of (Hispano-Roman) Christian tradition brought it more in line with the cultures of France and the other European nations of Western Christendom.

Gómez Redondo terms the new courtly ideal opposed to the tolerance and secularism of Alfonso el Sabio's court *molinismo* after María de Molina, the queen and facilitator/protector of the clergy's new role in Sancho's royal court. Gonzalo Pérez Gudiel and his cohorts were the chief proponent of the *molinista* ideology. Its rejection of the Alfonsine courtly model entails steering away from the pursuit of the natural sciences and the scientific model that had been the subject of so many of the Alfonsine translations. Instead of the search for universal knowledge (available in all traditions— Arabic, Jewish, and Christian alike) that had characterized Alfonso's court, Sancho's courtly model favors the inherited opinions of Christian authorities that served as the basis of Latin scholasticism. Defense of Christianity becomes a major literary theme in the literature of Sancho's court.[59]

Not surprisingly, wisdom literature, including the most common forms used by the clergy in their proselytizing and sermons, becomes the major form for the expression of the conservative ideology of *molinismo* in the court of Sancho IV. The major works produced in Sancho's court, including the *Libro del tesoro*, the *Libro de los castigos*, and the *Lucidario*, although seemingly of the same encyclopedic and scientific vein as Alfonso's productions are recast in a religious mode that emphasizes the theological over the rational.[60] According to Gómez Redondo the most important and representative of the works produced in Sancho's court is the *Libro del consejo e de los consejeros*. This work best exemplifies how *molinismo* shaped the doctrinal treatise that was the traditional vehicle of wisdom literature into its preferred form for expressing/representing its new cultural and political agenda.[61] The work is designed to educate the courtier in the ideal forms of behavior and ways of thinking. Unlike the Alfonsine doctrinal treatises like *Calila wa Dimna*, whose aim was to guide the courtier to an inquisitive and ultimately independent pursuit of knowledge (to learn how to think), this treatise presents him/her with a series of inherited clerical authorities (Innocent III, Cato, Saint Paul, Albertano, and Solomon) and *sententia*.[62] In the *Libro del consejo*, as in the *Castigos* and the *Lucidario*, the wise man (courtier, philosopher, or king) no longer seeks wisdom and universal truth, but instead becomes a teller of *exemplos*. The reader learns "how to correctly use these brief narratives in a clear demonstration of the scholastic system from which this methodology originates."[63] In Sancho's court a courtier must not only recount *exemplos*, but, more importantly, learn how to listen to them—interpret them in order to illicit from them appropriate models of behavior.[64]

The emphasis on *exempla* and didactic forms of literature in the late-thirteenth-century court of Sancho IV corresponds to similar literary trends among the Castilian clergy. Already in the first years of the twelfth century, the converted Jew, Petrus Alfonso, had compiled a collection of *exempla* translated into Latin from Eastern, primarily Arabic sources. By the thirteenth century, the Iberian clergy's increasing use of *exempla* for preaching led to the composition of exemplars organized alphabetically or by tale type to facilitate fast and easy consultation. The *exempla* in these collections were complemented by a variety of other material, including fables, historical anecdotes, allegories, bestiaries, and other folkloric material and *sententiae*.[65] One of the best-known works of thirteenth-century Castilian literature, Gonzalo de Berceo's *Milagros de Nuestra Señora*, is a collection of twenty-five Marian tales. José Romera Castillo classifies the Marian tale as a specialized variant of the *exemplum*.[66] Just as the court literature under Sancho IV uses the *exempla* in the elaboration of a Christian courtly ideal, in both the exemplars used as preaching aids and in the Marian tales, the *exempla* in fourteenth-century clerical literature are used as tools for the promulgation of Hispano-Roman Christian proselytizing.

There is little evidence that the courtly ideal developed under Sancho IV changed much during the reigns of his successors Fernando IV and Alfonso XI, and the presence of María de Molino as a guiding force in all three courts lends support to the idea that the courtly ideal of *molinismo* remained the dominant cultural model in Castile well into the fourteenth century.[67] María de Molina and her courtly milieu, including the high clergy in positions of critical importance in the governing of Castile, provided some much needed consistency during this quick succession of kings in the early years of the fourteenth century—the years just before or during the composition of the *Libro de buen amor*. The reigns of Fernando IV and Alfonso XI are marked by civil disorder bordering on chaos. Both kings' courts proved to be treacherous, often deadly sites of power.[68] The instability and court intrigue of Fernando IV's court is reflected in the *Caballero Zifar*, which, according to Gómez Redondo, is the basic work of *molinista* ideology and the clearest articulation of María de Molina's conception of courtliness. In this work the religious courtliness developed in the wisdom literature of Sancho's court—in the *Castigos* and *Libro del consejo*—projects those values into a fictional world to explore how the religious knight (ideal courtier) deals with an arrogant and rebellious nobility. The work also shows the tools the knight uses to restore royal authority.[69] One of the tools the author of the *Zifar* uses to develop this courtly fiction is the *exemplum*.[70] Alfonso XI's court, even after the death of his grandmother, María de Molina, continues to be dominated by ecclesiastical courtiers, including Pedro Gómez Barroso, *Notario mayor* of Toledo and future cardinal of Pope Clement VI as well as possible author of *El Libro de los consejos y consejeros*; Juan del Campo, bishop of Cuenca, Oviedo, and Leon; and Gil de Albornoz, archbishop of Toledo, mentioned in stanza 1691 in the Salamanca MS of the *LBA*. All had close personal and influential relationships with the king.[71]

It is the noble courtier, Juan Manuel, tutor of the young Alfonso XI and contemporary of the author of the *LBA*, who, in reaction to the strong ecclesiastical presence at court, stepped in to develop an alternative Castilian ideological-cultural model. In the *Crónica abreviada*, the *Libro del cavallero et del escudero*, the *Libro de los estados*, and the *Libro del conde Lucanor*, a work almost exactly contemporary with the *Libro de buen amor*, Juan Manuel articulates a version of the ideal courtier and ruler that stresses above all his nobility—his inherent status acquired not from his quest for knowledge or Christian character but from his inherited family name and blood line.[72] Despite Juan Manuel's assertion of the aristocratic noble as the ideal courtier, his former pupil Alfonso XI systematically routed the power of the Castilian nobility, and in the later part of his reign, Juan Manuel became one of his major opponents. Though Juan Manuel attempted to recast the *molinista* image of the Christian Castilian as secular noble, he continued to use the *exemplum* form that had been privileged in the literature produced in Sancho's court.[73]

The Form of the Other: *Mester de clerecía* as Counter-Discourse in the *LBA*

Juan Manuel used *exempla* to create a slightly modified, even more restrictive version of the ideal Castilian. His contemporary, Juan Ruiz, however, used this form, which by 1330 was overwhelmingly associated with official courtly and clerical discourses, not to represent Christian Castilian values, but to deconstruct the *molinista* ideology and to reinscribe the secular Andalusi erotic into Castilian letters.[74] The preceding overview of official Castilian ideology and literature allows us to see that the author of the *LBA*, in addition to being an inheritor of the rich and varied Iberian traditions— Andalusi Arabic and Hebrew poetic and *maqāmāt* traditions—was also familiar with the literary and ideological trends cultivated in the fourteenth-century Castilian court and Church. In contrast to the official chronicles produced at court and the clearly propagandistic work of thirteenth- and fourteenth-century Castilian clergy (such as Berceo's *Milagros* in which, using the commonplaces of Latin scholasticism, Jews are unequivocally represented as demonic, Christian haters), the *LBA* offers a more nuanced and ambiguous representation of Castile, its inhabitants, and literary traditions. In the *LBA* Juan Ruiz constructs around the figure of the go-between a counter model to Castilian identity as shaped by the official discourse of *molinismo*.

Just as official definitions of Castilian identity proved ill-suited to the religious, ethnic, and linguistic diversity and overlap that had long characterized the Iberian population, the *LBA* has also defied traditionally defined generic classification in Western criticism. Central to the *LBA*'s hybridity are the generic forms and courtly discourses adapted and transformed by both narrator and go-between: "The LBA belongs to those perverse narratives of early vernacular literary production characterized by permeability of generic boundaries and intertextual relationships that cross discrete genres, satirizing and mixing generic conventions. The text comprises a range of materials, representing many subliterary and literary generic forms, from Aesopic tales, fabliaux, proverbs, riddles, and exempla to an Ovidian *ars amandi*, a *comedia Latina*, a carnivalesque mock-epic battle of Flesh and Lent, and heterogeneous examples of medical, legal, and particularly religious discourse... Juan Ruiz turns all inherited discourse topsy-turvy, in a carnivalesque response to the high seriousness of canonized literature and particularly of the clerical *cuaderna vía* form."[75]

As Louise Vasvári points out, the *LBA* masterfully combines and subverts a variety of canonical discourses. Particularly salient with respect to fourteenth-century Castilian courtly literature is the masterful way in which Juan Ruiz combines the courtly *exempla* with the rhymed prose form that had become the discourse of ecclesiastical legitimacy in the nascent Castilian dialect, the *mester de clerecía* or *cuaderna vía*. The description of *mester de clerecía* given in the earliest work composed using this form, the *Libro de Alexandre*, defines it as a novel mode of narrative poetry distinguished by formal virtuosity and a strict Alexandrine syllable count (fourteen syllables per line in the Castilian literary tradition).[76] The *mester de clerecía*, the closest form Castilian has to a rhymed prose, was particularly suited for adaptation to the *LBA*'s *maqāma*-like narrative.[77] Before the appearance of Castilian fiction in prose, the *mester de clerecía* was used to compose narrative works that in later centuries would become the domain of prose: Byzantine proto-chivalresque novels of a marked Christian morality such as the *Libro de Alexandre* and *Apolonio*, as well as the didactic fiction of Gonzalo de Berceo and the Castilian foundational epic, the *Poema de Fernán González*. By adapting this preferred ecclesiastical form for mostly didactic narrative fiction to his book on good love, Juan Ruiz further destabilizes the serious morality with which it was associated in medieval Castilian letters.[78]

In Juan Ruiz's *mester de clerecía* narrative it is not the fourteenth-century clerical ideal of Christian morality that is given voice, but the secular erotic. Juan Ruiz, as did his Iberian predecessors, uses the erotic to explore Iberian identity and its construction in the official discourses of power. In the *LBA* the vehicle for this erotic discourse is no longer the traditional Arabic *qasīda* or love poem or the *maqāmāt*, but the Castilian *mester de clerecía* and the *exemplos* it is used to relate. Poetry, the discourse used to legitimate Andalusi royal authority for both the Umayyad caliphs and the *taifa* kings, has given way to the sapiential literature and forms of the Castilian court and Church.[79] The rhymed prose of the *mester de clerecía* proves to be the most successful vehicle for the erotic discourse of the *LBA* and is used in both the seduction of Endrina and Garoza (discussed in detail below). These two successful affairs are mediated via *exempla* and narrated solely in *cuaderna vía*. Whereas earlier *maqāma* authors exposed the erotic discourse of the court as bankrupt by means of a final revelatory scene in which the lies of seductive erotic poetry are exposed, Juan Ruiz subverts the *exempla*—the courtly vehicle for the church's anti-Muslim, anti-rationalist doctrine as well as for the king's political ideology of Reconquest and intolerance—by recontextualizing and appropriating it by putting it into the mouth of the rogue, the go-between, and the beloveds.[80] In the *LBA* the *exempla* are used not by a sovereign to create unity and national sentiment by exploiting religious or ideological differences, but by beloveds who unsuccessfully attempt to defend themselves by appealing to Christian moral values, and by the mediator, who successfully overcomes those religious and ideological objections and convinces her audience to succumb to desire. The go-between is there again to facilitate/mediate the translation and transformation of the narrative in order to accommodate and subvert the new cultural and literary styles of fourteenth-century Castile.

As was the case in the Iberian *maqāmāt*—those of al-Saraqustī, Ibn Shabbetai, and al-Harīzī—the go-between is privileged as mediator of the various genres and discourses of the *LBA*. Mediation and the mediator are the only effective means of overcoming the diverse discourses pulling the

LBA in many directions at once. The book itself is given voice as mediator between reader and author, and within its pages the procuress, Trotaconventos, gives voice to a series of discourses that range from the street slang of Andalusi Arabic to the refined *exempla* of the Castilian court and Church. The work is not only a representation of that other tradition of the Iberian Peninsula, that is, the Andalusi *maqāmāt*, but itself shows how to construct/represent the various Others that inhabit its pages—the Moorish woman, the Christian (Mozarab?) nun, the ambiguously Eastern go-between, the Jewish singers—in the nascent Castilian vernacular. In the *LBA*, as in the works of al-Harīzī, al-Saraqustī, and Ibn Hazm, the go-between mediates between foreign and domestic discourses and is a key component in the author's goal of creating a Castilian literary form distinct from its models.

The Hermeneutics of Mediation

The diverse genres included in the *LBA* are held together by both the pseudo-autobiographic narration and the presence of the go-between figure, although both the narrative voice and the figure of the go-between tend to shift unexpectedly, leaving the reader on unsteady ground from which to attempt an understanding of the work. The *LBA* begins with the author-narrator informing the reader of the work's purpose and providing instructions on how it should be read. In manuscript S the reader first confronts a prose introduction presented in the form of a gloss on Psalm 31 in which the author-narrator presents the reader with a series of ambiguous statements regarding the work's intent.[81] After this gloss, there follows a series of equally ambiguous episodes whose purpose, according to the narrator, is to instruct the reader on the proper way to interpret the work. These episodes are found in all of the manuscripts. The first episode, the *exemplum* of the Greeks and Romans, undermines the notion of authority and calls into question the validity of exegesis or glossing of authoritative texts. The episode thus deconstructs the gloss of Psalm 31 that the author himself has just finished (at least in the case of manuscript S), as well as calls into question the authority of all inherited discourses and their use as authoritative texts by subsequent generations. The debate between the Greeks and the Romans, designed to prove whether the Romans "understand" and deserve Greek laws (i.e., Classical knowledge, the wisdom of mankind acquired and accumulated over centuries), must be carried out using gestures since the Romans cannot understand the language of the Greeks.[82] The gestures used by the learned Greek philosopher and the Roman thug are interpreted by each group as having radically different meanings.[83] The Greeks and Romans lack both understanding of the other's language and culture as well as a competent mediator/translator—someone who understands both languages and cultures and who could effectively mediate their dispute. The reader of the *LBA* is similarly confronted with an ambiguous text that also offers contradictory readings. By comparing himself to the Greek doctor in stanza 46, Juan Ruiz shows that his narration and his interpretation of events is fundamentally flawed, just as the Greek's theological interpretation of the Romans' bellicose threats is flawed. The reader is shown that he or she cannot rely on the author-narrator for effective translation/mediation of the work's intent. In fact, its meaning is hidden and the reader, apparently without assistance, must decipher it from a purposefully deceptive narrative: "The utterances (*rrazones*) of good love are veiled: strive to find their true meanings. . .Where you think it is telling lies, it is speaking the greatest truth; in the bright colored stanzas (*coplas pintadas*) is where great ugliness lies (*falssedat*)" (68ab, 69ab).

The narrator's instability is further underscored immediately following the episode of the Greeks and Romans by the arbitrary shift from the first-person narration of the author-narrator, to the first person of the book itself in stanza 70. In this stanza the book compares itself to a musical instrument that will give different sounds according to who plays it. "I, this book, am akin to all instruments: according as you play/punctuate (*puntares*) well or badly, so, most assuredly, will I speak" (70ab).[84] The book speaks to the reader informing him/her of the very ambiguity of its message. There can be no clearer anti-model to the moralizing didacticism so prevalent in contemporary court and church literature. With the metaphor of the book as instrument, the author of the *LBA* focuses the deconstructive impulse of the Greeks and Romans from authoritative discourse in general, to the specific work being read, and to the act of reading in process. Like the gestures of the Greek and Roman, the *LBA* can produce radically different meanings according to the perspective and understanding of the reader.

As these introductory passages show us, the foundation of the *LBA*'s narrative structure, the narrative voice, can shift at any time without warning, and the reader cannot rely on the authoritative perspective of the narrator. The reader must become the mediator/translator/interpreter of the text—a text whose meaning and structure is entirely subjective and changeable. The reader becomes interpreter and translator who, should he/she choose, can be like the Greek and Roman and refuse to see past the limits of their own particular cultural, linguistic, and historical circumstances and, in the process, pervert the truth to conform to their limited perspective. The other option elaborated in the text is the antithesis, the ideal reader who seeks an understanding of both sides—of multiple cultures, languages, points of view. With the help of a shrewd and reliable mediator, the reader, like the archpriest, can succeed in his/her endeavor to understand (*entender* in both its meanings as understanding and loving *entendederas*) others. The book, like its characters, lies, and to discover when it is being intentionally deceptive, the careful reader must attempt to discern its agenda, an effort that requires the reader to put him/herself into the subject positions of the various characters and narrators of the work.

The Failures of Mediation

From these overt warnings to the reader—both in the words of the author and the book itself, as well as in the popular and accepted form of the *exemplum*— the *LBA* passes to the next level of fictional narrative, the story of the archpriest's first love affair. Now that we as readers are prepared and have been made aware of the deceptive narration and forms of the work, we can put into practice what the author has asked us to do, "understand"/interpret and mediate the fictions out of which the work is constructed. This episode, like the other attempted love affairs of the archpriest, embodies in miniature the text-interpretation dialectic established in the preliminary passages of the *LBA*. In this episode we shift from being direct readers/ interpreters of the *exemplum* and commentary to being witnesses of another reader/recipient of texts, as we pass from the extradiegetic level of the frame to the embedded narratives of seduction. We witness as the lover and beloved receive one another's texts. The author-narrator makes sure to tell us he sent erotic verses to his beloved by way of the go-between, "I sent her this love song, which is written below, by the hand of my messenger woman, who was under my instructions" (80ab). This erotic poetry, which is not included in the text, takes second stage to the *exempla*.[85] Instead of being the passive recipient of the archpriest's poems, which are designed to seduce and win her over to fulfilling his desire, the intelligent woman (*dueña cuerda*), takes control of the situation by countering his advances with a series of *exempla*, proverbs, and authoritative citations. In the first *exemplum*, the beloved compares the old go-between, who still has not spoken, to the deceitful fox (81d). The beloved then recounts the *exemplum* of the wounded lion.[86] She ends the tale by threatening the go-between, "So I tell you, old woman but no friend of mine, don't ever come to me or speak such wicked words, or I will show you how the lion gives his blessing" (89abc). Once news of the archpriest's advances get out the woman is sequestered. She asks that the archpriest compose some sad verses for her to sing, which he does: "To fulfill the request of my lady, I wrote a song as sad as this melancholy love affair; the lady sang it, I believe with sorrow; she might have been the composer of it even better than I (*podría ser dello trobador*)" (92). Once again the courtly lyric is evoked when the narrator describes himself as a *trovador*, but the actual verses are not included in the text. Instead, the woman grows exasperated with the archpriest and his false promises, using an *exemplum* to chastise and mock him. In it, she compares the archpriest's promises to the earth that began to bellow and shake, but that, instead of producing a great serpent or beast, produced only a little mole (98–101).

The juxtaposition between erotic lyric and erudite *exempla* in this episode underscores not only the contrasting motives of the archpriest (seduction) and the beloved (defense), but also the incompetence of the go-between that the archpriest uses in this encounter. She cannot effectively counter the arguments, presented in the form of *exempla*, of this beloved. The author-narrator is at great pains to tell us the beloved is a learned, erudite woman, characteristics he identifies with the use of *exempla*: "Since the good lady was highly educated (*letrada*), and understanding (*entendida*), wise and well-spoken (*bien mesurada*), she told my old woman, whom I sent to her, this appropriate fable taken from Aesop" (96). This woman knows how to interpret the archpriest's poetry and desire and to defend herself from it through the skillful use of *exempla*. She is an example of someone with the knowledge and understanding to correctly read and manipulate texts (and thus conforms to the ideal courtier defined in Sancho IV's *Castigos*). Juan Ruiz and his go-between are no match for this refined intelligent woman, and neither properly manipulates/dominates the discourses of desire or performs their role in the erotic exchange. In fact, this go-between, designated only as *mensajera*, does not speak in this episode. It is only after he has enlisted the services of Trotaconventos some six hundred stanzas later that Juan Ruiz will find a go-between capable of mediating between the erotic discourse of the archpriest and the courtly/ecclesiastical/sapiential discourse that the objects of his affection use to defend themselves. Before that he is destined to more humiliation and failure at the hands of incompetent and deceptive go-betweens.

The next go-between Juan Ruiz uses proves even worse than the first. Ferrán García, a gluttonous scholar (*escolar goloso*) (122a), decides to keep the woman the archpriest has sent him to seduce, Cruz the baker girl, for himself and leaves the archpriest salivating (118). Despite this misadventure, the author-narrator claims he was born under the sign of Venus (153), and as such is fated to be a lover. He then attempts to seduce a new beloved (167–179). Instead of sending her jewelry or clothes, he sends her poetry (*trobas e cantares* and *cantigas*). However, the woman rebuffs his advances. There is no mention of a go-between, only the woman's response instructing that his verses be returned and that he be reprimanded for the cheapness of his gifts (172). The identity and actions of the go-between have been completely elided in this failed erotic encounter.

Andalusi Ideals and the Iberian Go-Between

Following these three encounters in which Juan Ruiz and his different go-betweens prove less than satisfactory in the art of seduction, the archpriest has a dream vision in which love personified, don Amor "Sir Love," visits him offering advice about women and seduction. Amor describes for the archpriest the perfect woman to love and the perfect go-between to assist him in seducing her. Amor's role as picaresque erotic authority recalls al-Sadūsī's role in al-Saraqustī's "*Maqāma 9.*" Like al-Sadūsī, don Amor appears just when the narrator-protagonist requires his assistance in matters of love. He imparts to the protagonist the basics of the discourse of Andalusi erotics as formulated in *The Dove's Neck Ring* and in the poetry of the East and al-Andalus. His lessons contain the kernel of Ibn Hazm's advice in *The Dove's Neck Ring* distilled down and presented as the authoritative wisdom of Ovid. Whereas Ibn Hazm attempted to earnestly present his own advice on love from the authority of his position as learned courtier, Juan Ruiz, like the other *maqāmāt* authors whose work we have examined in the previous chapters, subverts this position—in this case making don Amor, the learned intellectual, an ironic dream authority.[87]

Once Juan Ruiz finishes chastising and berating Amor, which he does via a series of *exempla*, a discourse on the deadly sins and a mock gloss of the psalms (all of which would be part and parcel of the intellectual work of the cleric and thus establish Juan Ruiz's clerical authority and learning), Amor is finally given the opportunity to address the archpriest (423). Whereas Juan Ruiz's long diatribe contains the elements of clerical discourse—*exempla*, proverbs, glosses—Amor and his discourse are presented as courtly and refined. He is a refined courtier, "Then Love replied in measured tones (*con mesura*)" (423a) and, in contrast with the stupidity of the archpriest's diatribe (*baldón*) (425a), his discourse is *mesurado* and reasonable, "Listen to moderation (*la mesura*)...you listen to me (*mi rrazón*)" (425a,c). Amor tells the archpriest to listen to his *castigos* (427), recalling one of the foundational texts of Sancho IV's courtly ideology, the *Castigos e documentos* in which the king advises his son on how to lead a moral life. Amor tells the narrator-protagonist that if he reads Ovid, whom Amor claims as his own pupil, he will find the lessons of Amor ("If you read the words of Ovid, who was my servant, / there you will find the things I taught him," 429ab). Amor reveals that Pamphilus and Nason were also his students (429d). The citation of these scholastic authorities locates Amor's discourse not only in the Andalusi court, but also in the Latin tradition of the West and the Castilian court. Just after alluding to Ovid, Pamphilus, and Nason, however, Amor clarifies that his *castigos*, unlike those of Sancho IV, which were designed to impart moral and spiritual lessons, are designed to seduce women, "If you want to have a lady to love or any other woman, you must first learn a great many things" (430ab).

Amor makes his objective perfectly clear. It is not the spiritual or moral betterment of his trainee, but the latter's sexual gratification. He then lists the physical attributes of the ideal woman and describes the rhetorical skills and peripatetic lifestyle of the ideal go-between. Whether the description of the ideal woman conforms to Western European or Arabic poetic norms has been the subject of much critical debate.[88] The woman's wide hips (*ancheta de caderas*) (432d), darkened eyes (*pintados*) (433a), long neck (*cuello alto*) (433d), small (*menudiellos*), sharp (*agudillos*), well-separated teeth (*eguales e bien blancos; un poco apartadillos*) and thin lips (*angostillos*) (434) all mark this description as deriving just as much from the Andalusi poetic canon as from Western European models. Juan Ruiz is aware that the Iberian (male) reader is defined as much by what/who he desires as by the constructions of Castilian male (Christian) behavior in battle or at court developed in thirteenth- and fourteenth-century Castilian prose. Here he provides the reader (just as Amor provides the author-narrator) with an Iberian model of beauty—redefining the object of desire along Iberian, and not strictly Western European, models.

Immediately following the description of the ideal woman is the description of the go-between, which derives, even more so than the details of the beloved's beauty, from the Andalusi and Judeo-Iberian tradition.[89] The ideal go-between can be found among the old women who know every alley way (438) and who "roam everywhere, through public squares and enclosed lands" (439b). Amor instructs the archpriest to take an Andalusi style *alcahueta*: "Take one of those old crones who pretend to be herb-healers; they go from house to house proclaiming themselves as midwives; with powders and cosmetics and with vials of eye makeup they cast their spells on girls and blind them indeed" (440). Not only the object of desire, but also the means of attaining it, is framed in the *LBA* within the Andalusi cultural model. The most important characteristic required of the old woman is that she be, like the book itself (as described in stanzas 68–69), subtle, well reasoned, and a liar: "Strive as far as you can to find a messenger / who is discreet (*bien rrasonada*), subtle and patient, / knowing how to bend the truth (*mentir fermoso*) and persevere to the end (*siga la carrera*)" (437abc).

Amor then adapts Andalusi erotic motifs to the typical representational modes of the fourteenth-century cleric and courtier. He illustrates his points with two *exempla*. Whereas the use of the *exempla* form locates his discourse in the learned milieu of the court and church, their content and context betrays a subversion of the didactic purposes for which these literary forms were commonly used in scholastic discourse. Instead of conveying higher moral truths, both these *exempla* are bawdy and scandalous in nature. The first is about two lazy men who want to marry the same woman (457–471) and the second about Pitas Payas (474–489), the painter who leaves his wife for ten years.[90] The author includes several proverbs to elucidate the moral of the first *exemplum*, citing a troubadour as authority (472–473). The lesson of both *exempla* is that lovers must be attentive and serve their beloveds. The salacious and bawdy elements of both tales, however, work to undermine this supposedly earnest and courtly lesson. From the secular court model of the troubadour, Amor moves to the ecclesiastical court of the pope, relating a personal anecdote describing his experiences at the papal court in Rome (493–507).[91] Amor's familiarity and use of these learned models and his personal experiences in the papal court betray him as learned cleric. However, his privileging of the Andalusi erotic model reveals that he is an Iberian (Mozarab? *converso*? of Muslim descent? Or any combination thereof?) cleric.

Don Amor's subversive use of canonical Castilian courtly genres recalls the way al-Sadūsī, Kozbi, and Sitnah similarly manipulate the *topoi* and formal modes of courtly Andalusi erotic poetry to their own ends. These picaresque figures, like don Amor and the author-narrator Juan Ruiz, transform and expose the discourse of the court—the discourse used to further political (and religious) ideologies—to further personal desire. Just as Juan Ruiz plays with assertions of authority and knowledge in the preceding material (the prose prologue, the episode of the Greeks and Romans, and Amor's own allusions to Ovid, Pamphilus, and Nason), here he (Juan Ruiz) uses the *maqāmāt* technique of placing the discourse of legitimacy in the mouth of a deceptive rogue, transforming it from a trope designed to educate a prince in the ways of ruling and being a Christian soldier, into a tool with which the lover can satisfy his desire. Amor utilizes these allusions, *exempla*, and proverbs, not to help mold a Castilian knight, but to make Juan Ruiz into an Andalusi-style lover.

Juan Ruiz uses the figure of Amor to open up a space in the text and in the discourse of Castilian legitimacy/nationalism for the Andalusi, for the Arab and the "Eastern," precisely that which *molinismo* as an ideological construction had pushed to the margins. Juan Ruiz brings the conventions of Andalusi erotics (as discussed in chapter 1) into the realm of Castilian canonical discourse, and the effect is a complete destabilization of that discourse's ideology. Whereas *molinismo* was interested in forging a fundamentally Christian Castilian identity, the *LBA* works to expose Iberian culture and literature as a complex fabric of Romance, Arabic, and Hebrew cultures and literatures. In the episode of don Amor, as in the subsequent episode, that of doña Endrina and don Melón, the author of the *LBA* opens up the Western European Latin tradition to accommodate the

Andalusi erotic, creating a hybrid literary and cultural space that reflects the sociocultural landscape of fourteenth-century Iberia. In so doing, the author of the *LBA* destabilizes those courtly and ecclesiastical discourses that sought to exclude the Andalusi (Arab, Jewish, and Mozarab) from participating in the fundamentally Western European Christian model of Castilian identity being propagated by the royal court and at the cathedral school of Toledo.

Pamphilus Undone

After don Amor cedes the word to his wife, doña Venus, in stanza 585, Juan Ruiz introduces material adapted from the pseudo-Ovidian *Pamphilus*.[92] Doña Venus reiterates her husband's advice on finding the ideal woman and the perfect intermediary. Amor's detailed description of the ideal go-between elaborated in stanzas 436–443 is echoed by Venus, who, however, limits her discussion of the go-between to one verse. This corresponds to the similarly brief mention of the go-between in the *Pamphilus*. The much more developed portrait of the go-between Amor has just provided Juan Ruiz in stanzas 436–441 (to which Venus refers in 645) transforms the Ovidian material of the *Pamphilus*. Juan Ruiz uses the brief description of the go-between in the *Pamphilus* as a narrative opening within which he inscribes the much more developed Judeo-Arabic go-between as developed in the literature of medieval Iberia.[93] The introduction of the go-between of the *maqāmāt* and the Andalusi erotic discourse she represents into the heart of the *Pamphilus* material has the same destabilizing effect as did Amor's destabilization of the *exempla* and proverb by including salacious content and by using it in the context of the erotic conquest.

Doña Endrina and the pseudo-Ovidian narrative *Pamphilus* upon which Juan Ruiz constructs his tale of seduction (653–891) become yet another of the many transformed Others in the text. In this case the foreign material adapted to the Iberian context of the *LBA* is the Western scholastic erotic tradition. Juan Ruiz transforms one of the most ubiquitous and well-read texts of medieval Christian Europe, the *Pamphilus*, into a vehicle for the Iberian intermediary. Juan Ruiz's *translatio* of the Latin tale is neither seamless nor apolitical. The transition from "yo" (I) to Melón and back is abrupt and jarring. The abrupt shift from the "yo" (I) of the protagonist-narrator to the "él" (he) of don Melón is underscored in stanza 909. Here final emphasis is given to the otherness of the Endrina episode, distinguishing it from the frame, "Place the right interpretation on (*entiende bien*) my story about the daughter of the Sloe-thorn (Endrina); I told it in order to give you a parable, and not because it really happened to me: be on guard against false old women and the speech of a wicked neighbor; don't trust yourself alone with a man nor press up too close against the thorn." This is the only episode of the *LBA* that the narrator-protagonist specifies as not having occurred to him, and for which the testimonial eyewitness account is not valid. This conscious distancing of the Endrina narrative is echoed in stanza 891 where the narrative voice transitions back to that of the narrator-protagonist, Juan Ruiz, who immediately disavows the tale's content, "Lady Sloe and Sir Melon have now been joined together in marriage; their guests make merry at the feast, quite rightly. If I have said anything offensive, please let me have your pardon, since what is unseemly in the story was told by Pamphilus and Ovid."[94] This particularly strong desire and emphasis on distinguishing the Endrina episode from the other episodes of the *LBA* reveals the author's particular uneasiness with this foreign scholastic material.[95]

Juan Ruiz strategically modifies the *Pamphilus* material in order to adapt it to the Andalusi erotic of the *LBA* and to the Iberian context of his readership. These modifications revolve around the figure of the go-between. The brief sketch and limited dialogue given the go-between in the *Pamphilus* is greatly expanded in the *LBA*. The portrait of the go-between already developed along Andalusi lines by Amor is further elaborated with details recalling the description of the go-between in Ibn Hazm's *The Dove's Neck Ring*, and the number of lines given to the go-between is increased substantially. In her expanded dialogues, Trotaconventos proves an able master of the courtly *exempla*, a form entirely absent from the Latin text.

As negotiator and composer of fiction, Trotaconventos owes more to the *maqāmāt* of Ibn Shabbetai or al-Saraqustī than to the medieval Latin comedy. Precisely when Trotaconventos is introduced in stanza 697, "I searched for a go-between (trotaconventos) as Love instructed," do we find material added by Juan Ruiz (what Gybon-Monypenny describes as an "interpolation")—one of the many points when Juan Ruiz inscribes the Semitic into the Latin frame.[96] With the help of God and fortune, the narrator finds just the mediator he is looking for; she is artful, shrewd, and wise ("cunning and skillful and very knowledgeable," 698b), a street vendor who sells jewelry while laying traps to ensnare lovers, "She was an old peddler, of the kind who sell jewels: these are the ones who set the snare, these are the ones who dig the pitfalls; there are no experts like these wicked old bawds (*viejas troyas*); these are the ones who strike the fatal blow: Lady, if you have ears, listen!" (699). These elaborate descriptions of the go-between are not found in the *Pamphilus*. They are original material that Juan Ruiz takes from his own knowledge of the Andalusi go-between tradition and incorporates into the Latin tale. Juan Ruiz breaks the narrative frame to call the reader's attention to the go-between and her craft—underscoring his unique contribution/transformation of the *Pamphilus* material.

Juan Ruiz continues to interrupt and destabilize the *Pamphilus* narrative, opening up spaces in which to inscribe the go-between and her voice, which increasingly dominate the episode. The next so-called interpolation is the inclusion of Trotaconvento's direct speech in which she interrupts Melón and promises to be a faithful servant, "Said the old woman: 'Well, speak up and trust me. Speak out your heart's desire to me with assurance; I will do all I can for you, I will be faithful to you'" (703d–704b). She continues to explain the importance of secrecy and the details of her office. Gybbon-Monypenny points out that in the Latin *Pamphilus* the protagonist is not interrupted by the go-between. These interpolations continue, becoming longer and longer, as Trotaconventos speaks again and again, appropriating her voice and taking over the episode. In stanzas 709–712, Trotaconventos describes how she will go to Endrina's house and bewitch her, thus curing Melón's lovesickness with her medicine, recalling similar imagery used by Umm 'Amr and Kozbi. In this addition to the *Pamphilus* material we also learn that not only is Endrina an old acquaintance of Trotaconventos, but also a widow.[97]

Trotaconventos's mention of Endrina's widowhood serves an important narrative function: it allows the old go-between to introduce a series of proverbs and sapiential wisdom on the theme of sexual experience. Endrina, like the women procured by Andalusi go-betweens, is familiar with sex and sensuality, and because of that experience, she is eager for more. Trotaconventos relates no less than three proverbs on this theme: "there is no pack mule that will refuse to carry a saddlebag" (710d); "Wax that is very hard and stiff and cold, once it is between one's hands and gets kneaded, can soon, with the slight warmth be bent a hundred times" (711abc); and "the first to reach the mill gets his grain ground first" (712b).[98] These are followed by two proverbs encouraging Melón to act.[99] Trotaconventos is a master of manipulating proverbial sapiential wisdom to her own ends. She uses these proverbs, "what is often said (*lo que dezir se suele*)" (712a) to peak Melón's interest by describing Endrina's eagerness for sex, and then to pressure him into contracting her skills as mediator—which include casting spells (*escantar*) and speedily delivering messages.

In the following material emended by Juan Ruiz to the *Pamphilus* material (723–725), the activities and office of the go-between is described, and we learn she is an Ibn Hazm style door-to-door saleswoman who rings bells to call attention to the wares she is hawking, including jewels, rings, pins, and fabric. From 737 to 782—some forty-five stanzas—Juan Ruiz introduces material not found in the *Pamphilus*. This material ruptures the *Pamphilus* narrative, tearing it apart in the center. This interpolated section consists of a long exchange of *exempla* between Endrina and Trotaconventos, in which Trotaconventos tries to convince Endrina to accept Melón as her lover. The *exempla* and debate form here subverted by Juan Ruiz underscore the shift in letters from Iberian poetry to sapiential literature as court discourse. Trotaconventos does not inscribe the lover and beloved in the erotic universe of Andalusi poetry. She does not depict them as the gazelles, hinds, or the luscious fruit of Andalusi poetry.[100] Instead the old go-between engages the lovers' intellect, trying to convince Endrina of the logic of taking a lover, and Melón of her abilities as the best possible go-between. Like Amor, Trotaconventos manipulates the preferred vehicle for the Castilian discourse of power, the *exempla*, to seduce the protagonist's neighbor, the widow Endrina.[101]

In a large section of material composed by Juan Ruiz and added to the *Pamphilus* material (stanzas 737–782), he elaborates an extensive scholastic style debate between Endrina and Trotaconventos in which each defends their position and attacks the other by employing *exempla*.[102] In the first *exemplum* recounted in this episode, Trotaconventos tells Endrina not to be like the bustard that ignored the swallow's warnings about the hunter, otherwise she will fall prey to those seeking to take advantage of her (746–755). Endrina responds with a *fábula* or *exempla* of her own about the wolf who passes up several opportunities for food for the promise of even better victuals—only to be left empty-handed in the end. The exchange of *exempla* is interrupted by two significant breaks in the text, both *lacunae* in the manuscripts.[103] Much of the missing material was probably further development of *exempla* in the debate between Endrina and Trotaconventos. After the interpolated exempla of the debate, Juan Ruiz returns to the *Pamphilus* version of the go-between tale, including additions and other transformations of the pseudo-Ovidian material. Again the interpolations greatly expand the role of Trotaconventos, amplifying her parts of the dialogue with Melón (808–812) and Endrina (832–833, 865–866) and including an invented dialogue between Trotaconventos and Endrina's mother, doña Rama (824–829). After the final *lacuna* of this episode—the one presumably narrating the rape of Endrina in Trotaconventos's house (between 877 and 878)—the *LBA* again significantly diverges from the *Pamphilus*. As Gybbon-Monypenny points out, the text resumes in stanza 878 with Trotaconventos blaming Endrina for the rape. In the *Pamphilus*, the protagonist intervenes in the dialogue, cutting the go-between off. Not so in the *LBA* where Melón remains silent and Trotaconventos continues to speak for four stanzas.[104] Melón and Endrina are married (891), a resolution to the tale not found in the Latin version or in other vernacular adaptations of the *Pamphilus*, which end with the go-between merely suggesting the two marry.[105]

Juan Ruiz's intervention and transformation of the *Pamphilus* material is almost wholly devoted to expanding and developing the go-between's role. Central to this process is the development of the go-between's voice.

Juan Ruiz substantially increases the number of lines given to the go-between of the *Pamphilus*, and makes her not just a skillful intermediary, but also an author of *exempla*, the very form dominating both courtly and clerical literature in the fourteenth-century.[106] The text itself implicitly links Trotaconventos's discourse with Castilian Church practice in stanza 740, when Endrina tells Trotaconventos to stop preaching to her, "Callad ese predicar." By using the *exempla* as a vehicle for the Andalusi go-between inscribed within a Latin rape tale, Juan Ruiz strips the *exemplum* form of its supposed didactic Christian value, showing that it does not impart, in and of itself, universal truths, but that it, like other forms of literature, can be used to manipulate people for amoral purposes.

Juan Ruiz uses the pseudo-Ovidian material of the *Pamphilus* to introduce the Iberian go-between tale of the Arabic and Hebrew *maqāmāt* of the eleventh to the thirteenth centuries into the larger Western European tradition, just as the anonymous author of *De Vetula* had introduced similar material into Latin Europe over a hundred years before. Juan Ruiz transforms the pseudo-Ovidian tale by creating an active, speaking go-between character modeled on the Andalusi courtier. This character is capable of manipulating the discourses of high culture and of imposing a model of mutual benefit (no matter how unbalanced or uncomfortable) on both parties. The forced/coerced marriage of Melón and Endrina is a further echo of the uneasy combination of Semitic and Latin elements in the *LBA*. The relocation of the medieval Latin tale within the vernacular Castilian narrative based on Arab and Jewish models does not fit comfortably in its new home. This tale destabilizes and ruptures the narrative frame of both the *Pamphilus* and the *LBA* itself, introducing another protagonist and a concomitant shift to third-person narration (diegesis)—the only such shift in the *LBA*. The self-consciousness with which Juan Ruiz adapts and transforms the Latin *Pamphilus* marks it as a foreign text—foreign to the *LBA* and to the Iberian go-between tradition. Juan Ruiz, however, mediates the work's foreignness by inscribing within it the Iberian go-between of the *maqāmāt*. He performs the ultimate appropriation—wrenching apart the heart of the Latin tale and inscribing within it that Other Iberian go-between of the Semitic tale to whom he then gives a voice. Trotaconventos then becomes not simply negotiator, but author who composes and manipulates the courtly discourse of the *exempla* and wisdom literature to seduce Endrina.

"Buen Amor"

Following the Endrina episode, Juan Ruiz addresses his audience with an *exemplum* designed to warn women (the *dueñas* to whom the author-narrator addresses himself in stanza 892) away from the *loco amor* that befell Endrina.

However, he then immediately relates yet another attempted seduction, in which he uses his loyal *alcahueta* to seduce a secluded woman. Having learned his lesson he does not choose as mediator another Ferrán García, but a "loyal old woman" like Trotaconventos (914a). The go-between proves an able mediator and seductress, who takes both the author-narrator's songs and gifts to the woman, "Right at the start I composed these songs, the old woman took them to my lady along with other love charms (*adamares*)" (915ab). Just when it seems Juan Ruiz is about to succeed, he carelessly insults the go-between. After disparaging her he provides the reader with a lengthy list of comic and insulting names one should never use when referring to a go-between (924–927). The episode shows the power of the mediator to determine ultimately both lover and beloved's fate. The old woman sabotages the affair in an act of revenge, proclaiming the archpriest's intentions in the streets and publicly exposing the affair. Seriously injured by love and feeling like a lost sheep, the archpriest tries to make amends with the go-between. In turn, she gives him a lesson emphasizing how much he needs her and how she should be treated. She stresses her power over him, "Never let it happen with you again; and I will give the lie completely to what I said, I'll bet, and will demolish it altogether, just as mud is squashed under one's feet: I will cap your whole affair with success and get it moving as though on wheels" (931). She warns him of the power of language: "Never utter a bad name or an ugly one; call me 'Good Love' (*Buen Amor*) and I will be loyal to you, for everyone around takes pleasure in good words: nice speech costs no more than senseless words" (932).

The go-between forces the author-narrator to reframe the way he re/presents her. Instead of denigrating her, he must, in his own self-interest, treat her respectfully. He clearly understands and internalizes this lesson, choosing to name the entire book for her: "For love of the old woman and to speak the truth, I named this book 'Good Love' and her too from this time on; once I started taking good care of her she gave me many a present: there is no sin without punishment, nor good deed without reward" (933). The book, like the go-between, can be designated in different ways, but the names the speaker chooses will affect his own well-being. This lesson on the effects of different ways of naming/framing, echoes the lesson of the Greeks and Romans. It is a lesson about how dominant discourses and the people in power manipulate language and literature to marginalize others. This episode underscores the power not only of discourse, but also of the go-between figure. Juan Ruiz may adopt exclusionary discourses such as those of the court and church that denigrate non-Christians (Jews, Muslims, and even go-betweens in the case of Alfonso X's *Siete partidas*), but these non-Christians, like the secular Andalusi go-between, can take revenge. In this case the go-between refuses to be marginalized, she insists on remaining and on keeping her power to speak back. She transforms the insult into an opportunity as she encourages the archpriest to reframe the argument and to open up a space for her to operate, convincing him that ultimately everyone will benefit from this.

Once the archpriest has witnessed how Trotaconventos redeems him and the affair by convincing the town she had gone crazy and her previous exposure of the affair was merely nonsense, he sings her praises: "I never placed a better kiss than this on any old woman's hand" (935d); "whoever has an old helper like this should cherish her like his own soul" (936d). The power dynamic is inverted with the male archpriest kissing the hand of the old go-between. After successfully opening up a space for the Iberian erotic, Juan Ruiz then elevates it to the status of the discourse of power. Trotaconventos, mediator from the Andalusi *maqāmāt*, and historical trope of conjunction, again brings together two competing systems. As in the Hebrew *maqāmāt* this figure privileges the secular discourse of the Andalusi erotic lyric over that of the Christian ethics of Western Europe. What Juan Ruiz values above all else, though, is not one discourse or the other, but the mediator (the go-between and the book). The mediator's activity of bringing discourses and people together is what he celebrates in the *LBA*. Such conjuncture had no place in official fourteenth-century Castilian literature and ideology, which instead represents the non-Christian communities of medieval Iberia as Others, that is, as not part of the ideal Castilian community (and often as bent on its destruction).[107] The go-between is a counter model to this official representation of Others.

If there is any doubt lurking in the reader's mind as to this go-between's Andalusi origins after the Endrina and secuestered maiden episode, Juan Ruiz puts them to rest in his detailed portrait of her in stanzas 937–942. Like Ibn Hazm's ideal messenger, Juan Ruiz's also sells jewelry from house to house, "She disguised herself as a vendor (*corredora*), one of those who sell jewels" (937a); "I also told you that these old peddlers go from house to house selling many gift articles" (938ab). Like Kozbi she digs pits to entrap her victims, "I have already told you that it is these women who dig the traps and pitfalls" (937b). The parallels with Kozbi continue as Juan Ruiz portrays the way she bewitches the beloved with a series of pharmocopics deriving from the Andalusi erotological tradition, "Whether she bewitched my lady or gave her borax (*atincar*) to swallow, or whether she gave her *raynela* or gave her *mohalinar*, or whether she gave her poison or some love charm, she managed to drive her out of her mind very quickly" (941). Francisco Márquez-Villanueva and James T. Monroe have shown that these previously unidentified terms, *atincar*, *rainela*, and *mohalinar*, come to Castilian from Arabic and refer to herb wine and a kind of marmelade.[108]

The tools the old go-between uses and the vocabulary used to describe them again reveal Andalusi origins.

The Castilian Sierra: Rape and Exploitation

After the woman the go-between has bewitched with these various pharmocopic potions dies unexpectedly, the author-narrator decides to go alone to the Sierra. Having learned the lessons of the preceding episodes, we readers realize that, without his go-between, he is doomed to failure. Yet, like the typical *maqāmāt* protagonist, Juan Ruiz seems never to learn this lesson. In his trip to the mountains, Juan Ruiz will leave Andalusi courtly desire behind in favor of Western European erotic discourse in the form of the *pastourelle*.[109] This transition from Andalusi to European material is marked by an allusion to the Christian scholastic authority Paul ("To try all things the apostle commands us," 950a)[110] used here to justify an absurd and personal proposition on the part of the archpriest, "I went to make a trial of the mountains, and I went on a fool's errand (*loca demanda*)" (950ab). In case the reader had forgotten, the archpriest narrator again reminds us that he is a purposefully subversive interpreter of texts and authoritative sources, and therefore completely unreliable as a narrator. In the Sierra he meets a series of rustic mountain women or *serranas*. The *serranas* are natural companions to the pseudo-Ovidian material of the Endrina episode because they too, as foreign elements, destabilize the text.[111] As he did with the Latin material in the Endrina episode, Juan Ruiz marks the Western European *pastourelle* by creating a rift in the fabric of the narrative. He leaves the springtime of the city for the cold and sleet of the mountains, he disrupts the *mester de clerecía* by the inclusion of lyric poetry (which, at least in two of the cases, offers a different version of events than that narrated in the *mester de clerecía*), and as protagonist he becomes the victim of the women's sexual advances.

In the traditional vernacular *pastourelle*, the victim is the innocent, beautiful rustic woman seduced by the passing courtly knight, but in this case it is Juan Ruiz who is raped by brutish *serranas*. As Juan Ruiz leaves the comfort of the city and confronts his first *serrana* he recognizes he is ill prepared for the climate, as well as for this different sociocultural milieu, "Seeing myself in distress, stiff with cold, ill-treated: 'My dear,' I said, 'a dog prepares fallow ground (i.e. does farm labor) against his will. Let me through, my dear and I will give you some mountain-girl jewelry; if you please, tell me what kinds are worn hereabouts'" (954cd, 955ab).[112] In this new northern landscape, the narrator-protagonist is completely out of his element. Faced with possible death, either from the frigid weather or at the hands of the bellicose maidens, he chooses to succumb to their desires. The author-narrator repeatedly tells us he is lost in this rural northern Castilian landscape, "I'm done for (Só perdida), if God does not help me" (1007d). Without his mediator he is helpless. He does not know what these wild mountain women want or how to deal with them. After the archpriest promises her mountain jewelry, la Chata throws him over her shoulder and takes him to her hut for food and warmth. The narrator informs the reader that what happened next he recorded in a poem, "Out of what happened there, I composed the verses written below" (958d). In this *cántica de sierra* we discover that he was forced to have sex with her, "She grabbed me by the wrist; / I had to do what she wanted. / Believe me, I made a good bargain (*buen barato*)" (971efg).

The hostile landscape and maiden offer a clear counterpoint to the refined urban Andalusi women of the city whom he tries to seduce with poetry and the help of the go-between. His adoption of the cultural norms of the mountains—the bad food, horrid wine, primitive clothing, and shelter—is undertaken out of absolute necessity. The *serrana* episodes of the *LBA* illustrate the cultural interaction and differences between Iberians and Western Europeans. The author shows how unsuitable Western European erotic lyric and culture is for a refined and learned Iberian formed in the Andalusi cultural model. Whereas it was the secular Andalusi lifestyle, as epitomized in the Arabized Andalusi lyric of both Muslim and Jewish courtiers, that embodied the threat of cultural assimilation in the Hebrew *maqāmāt* discussed in chapter 3 and *De Vetula* of chapter 4, in the *LBA* it is the unrefined Western European erotic lyric that represents the threat to Iberian identity.

As in the Endrina episode, these episodes in the Sierra narrate rape, but in this case it is Juan Ruiz who is the victim. In this world turned upside down, the narrator-author who, thanks to Amor, is now skilled in the refined culture of Al-Andalus is raped and victimized by rude, rustic Castilians, who address him in the language of goatherds. The first, La Chata, is described as an aggressive brute who subdues him with her sling shot and then throws him over her shoulder and takes him home. "That devilish yokel girl (*La Chata endiablada*)/—St. Julian confound her!—/ threw her shepherd's crook at me / and whirled her sling at me, / aiming the stone-pouch; / 'By the true Father, / today you'll pay me the tax!" (963), and the fourth, the most hideous of all, is described as worse than the figure of the Apocalypse. She is as big as a mare, with a large head, short, stubbly black hair, red eyes, ears larger than a donkey's, and the large, wide teeth of an ass. The archpriest claims her big hairy wrist is larger than his entire hand and that her breasts are so long and saggy that she keeps them tucked into her belt (1010–1021). Like al-Harīzī, who when confronted with his horrible exchanged bride immediately seeks relief by composing poetry (see chapter 3), Juan Ruiz cannot help but describe the hideousness of this *serrana*, "Her limbs and her figure are not to be passed over in silence" (1010a). He claims to have composed three entire *cantigas* on the theme of her ugliness (1021). Whereas in the Hebrew *maqāmāt* the go-between, as a co-agent in the seduction and acculturation of narrator-protagonist, constructs the object of desire on the secular Andalusi model, in the *LBA* the go-between is conspicuously absent from these episodes in the Sierra. This absence is explained not only by her absence from the Western European *pastourelle* and from the Castilian countryside, but also because in the *LBA* the go-between becomes the agent for redefining Castilian identity as one encompassing pluralism and hybridity. The identification of the go-between with the secular erotic tradition of al-Andalus is threatening in the Hebrew *maqāmāt*, but in the *LBA* the go-between as agent of mediation and hybridity is offered as a counter model to Western European and new Castilian courtly models of intolerance. The Castilian *serranas*, like the ugly philistines of the Hebrew *maqāmāt*, are oblivious to the author-narrator's refined discourse of love. Like Ritzpah in the *Offering*, these *serranas* are concerned exclusively with material items of immediate utility, not the love tokens of the city women, and the author-narrator's refined culture and literary skills are lost on them. The go-between as vehicle of this refined erotic culture would have no effect on these women. Whereas the exchange of poetry and *exempla* prove vital components of the other seductions of the book, with the ignorant *serranas* such exchanges/mediation are impossible.

In the context of the Iberian *maqāmāt*, these monstrous *serranas* recall the grotesque women that the deceptive go-betweens of the Judeo-Andalusi *maqāmāt* exchange for the beautiful hind of the Andalusi lyric. Just as the *maqāmāt* of Ibn Shabbetai and al-Harīzī call into question the Andalusi discourse of desire by transforming the hind into a hideous old hag, here Juan Ruiz similarly subverts this European discourse of desire by exposing the object of that desire, the shepherdess, not as an innocent beauty, but as a horrible monster. The *serranas* represent one of the many possible objects of desire/cultural models for the Iberian (male) reader, who is defined as much by what/who he desires as by the constructions of Castilian male (Christian) behavior in battle or at court developed in thirteenth- and fourteenth-century Castilian prose.

The author-narrator, an urban Iberian now trained in the Andalusi refinements of *adab*, comes face to face with an unsophisticated rural peasant. In this Castilian countryside (in the mountain passes outside of Segovia), the archpriest encounters the descendents of the Hispano-Roman inhabitants of Castile—just those Castilians privileged in courtly chronicle and sapiential literature. Whereas in thirteenth- to fourteenth-century Castilian chronicles such as those of Rodrigo Jímenez de Rada and López de Ayala, the noble Castilian—first of Visigothic, then of Hispano-Roman Christian origin—is portrayed as the ideal of Castilian masculinity, these rustic Castilian women belie Castile's (and Western Europe's) cultural impoverishment vis-à-vis Iberian al-Andalus.[113] These *serranas*' rustic Castilian offers a counterpoint to the refined prose of Juan Ruiz's *mester de clerecía*, and their brutish behavior is a counter model to the urban courtly erotics of the Andalusi tradition. By couching the episode in the *pastourelle* genre, the author identifies these *serranas* with the poetic styles of Western Europe (France), the very styles used as cultural models in the Castilian court and Church. Thus Juan Ruiz implicitly sets up a comparison between Andalusi style erotics (as defined by Ibn Hazm, elaborated in Arab and Hebrew court poetry, and implicit behind the erotic advice of don Amor and Juan Ruiz in the *LBA*) on the one hand and the vernacular erotic tradition of Western Europe as manifest in the *pastourelle* on the other.[114] Later Castilian authors such as the Marqués de Santillana would adapt the *pastourelle* to Castilian literature; however, the author of the *LBA* frames it as a foreign and ultimately coarse literary form in comparison with the refined erotic tradition of Andalusi Iberia.

Garoza and *limpio amor*

Juan Ruiz, happy to have survived his foray into the Sierra, offers *cantigas* to both Mary and Jesus (1046–1066) in thanksgiving. He does not, however, give up the search for pleasant company (*fenbra plazentera*) (71) mentioned at the book's opening as his prime motivation. Back at home in the city following Lent, the author-narrator sees a beautiful woman in church during the procession of St. Mark. Despite Trotaconventos's protests, he insists that she approach the woman on his behalf. Although seemingly interested in Juan Ruiz, the woman marries a knight (1329). This failure prompts Juan Ruiz to ask Trotaconventos what he should do, and she advises him to take a nun as a lover (1332). This seemingly amoral and blasphemous advice does not surprise the reader of the *LBA*, who has been prepared to see nuns as erotic (not religious) beings, by the warm reception the nuns of Castile give Amor in the preceding episode of Flesh and Lent. After Flesh roundly defeated Lent in a mock battle of epic proportions, his good friend Amor was received like an emperor by the religious orders of Castile, and entreated by the nuns to forsake the clerics and come stay with them. "'Leave them all, accept service from us,' the nuns said to him; 'Sir, you will have no comforts, they are poor wretches given to much disagreeable disorder; Lord, come with us, try out our hair shirts'" (1255). While the male members of the religious orders and the knights advise Love not to go with the nuns, claiming they are deceptive teases, "flowery little words, pretty little touches of cosmetics, with loving gestures and deceitful toying: they drive many men mad (*locos*) with their false smiles" (1257bcd), the author-narrator says that should Amor have gone with them, he would never have regretted it, "If my lord, Sir Love, had believed me, he would have accepted the invitation of the nuns; he would have enjoyed every luxury in the world, and every pleasure; if he had entered their dormitory, he never would have regretted it" (1258). This episode prepares us not only to believe Trotaconventos's assertions regarding the love of nuns, but also the archpriest's willingness to accept it. Whereas Amor decides to forgo the nuns' invitation in the preceding episode, the archpriest does decide to accept Trotaconventos' suggestion.[115]

According to Trotaconventos, a nun is an ideal match for the archpriest. In this episode Trotaconventos provides us with a long description of this ideal woman, recalling Amor's similar description in stanzas 431–435. Based on ten years of service to nuns, Trotaconventos knowingly informs Juan Ruiz that they possess all manner of pharmocopics, spices, and sweets, including many aphrodisiacs.[116] They are refined and experienced courtly lovers. They are like the finest wines; they are polite, pleasant and exceedingly beautiful (1333–1342). They welcome love, which, with them, is always refined and lasts a long time, "their love is everlasting; they are thoughtful, accomplished, and have every sort of courtesy (*toda mesura*)" (1341cd). In fact the nuns are the most expert lovers, who have refined the art of pleasure and recreation, "Every pleasure in the world and every nice love word, most sweet enjoyment and affectionate fondling: all this is to be found in nuns, more than anywhere else; try it this time and make up your mind now to be at peace" (1342). The author-narrator is thoroughly convinced by Trotaconventos's description of the merits of nuns, but does not know how he can initiate an affair, asking the old go-between how he can enter where he knows of no little door, "How can I get in, when I don't know the entrance (*tal portillo*)?" (1343b). In order to attain this ideal love, Juan Ruiz must use the services of a mediator. Unlike the episode of the *serranas* in which the author-narrator attempts to traverse the women's passes himself, in this episode Trotaconventos will be his guide, telling him, "I can walk the road (*lo andaré*) in a very short time" (1343c). The metaphor opening this affair perfectly described the liminal space within which the go-between works—she passes through the little "door" of the convent, bridging the gap between man and woman, between lover and beloved.

Before the nun is willing to entertain the idea of having the archpriest as her lover, however, Trotaconventos must break down her resolve and convince her of the archpriest's merits. Garoza is an old acquaintance of Trotaconventos, and one of her former clients. Garoza's name, the Arabo-Andalusi term for bride, marks Garoza as a hybrid Iberian subject.[117] As a nun she may be a bride of Christ, but Juan Ruiz chooses to redefine the Iberian nature of her marriage within an Andalusi-Iberian context by designating her with an Arabo-Andalusi name. While the Andalusi term does describe the metaphoric marriage of the nun and God, such a spiritual union is completely foreign and incongruous in the Arabo-Andalusi social and religious traditions, in which a bride constitutes a social and legal category and implies sexual union. The use of the Arabic term garoza (*'arūsa*) for the nun seduced by Trotaconventos only makes sense in the Iberian context. Garoza's Andalusi name gives her away not only as a hybrid Iberian subject, but also as a potential lover. Just as Juan Ruiz transforms Garoza from Christian nun to Andalusi bride, in this episode he redefines the chaste love (*limpio amor*) of the bride of Christ into the erotics of courtly secular Andalusi literature.

Garoza may be the servant of a Christian Lord, but that does not preclude her from being an expert in worldly love. She is well aware of the old go-between's nature and function in the ritual of love and asks the old bawd what she has been doing since she left the nun's service. When she hears that Trotaconventos is now serving an archpriest, Garoza realizes the purpose of the old woman's visit, which she does not welcome. She responds to Trotaconventos with an *exemplum*, comparing the old woman's words to the ungrateful and deceitful serpent that kills the orchard-keeper who saves its life, recalling Endrina's similar use of *exempla* to defend herself against the old woman's advances. Trotaconventos, not to be thwarted, again illustrates her own domination of this sapiential form, responding to Garoza with her own *exemplum* and telling Garoza not to be hostile only because the go-between has come empty-handed (i.e., not bearing presents). Trotaconventos compares herself to the old greyhound no longer capable of hunting. The women's debate continues through eight more *exempla* (to stanza 1481) firmly establishing both women's skill in the sapiential literary forms of the period.[118]

The Garoza episode is in many ways a companion piece to the episode of Endrina. Garoza, like Endrina, is not only physically beautiful, but also smart and learned. In fact, she is even more skilled at verbal defense than either Endrina or the old go-between. Garoza thwarts Trotaconventos's attempts to convince her to give the archpriest a chance and to believe the old woman's words with one last *exemplum* (of the thief who signed a pact with the Devil). Trotaconventos, as if admitting defeat in this exchange of sapiential discourse, praises Garoza's knowledge of *exempla* and proverbs, but then informs her that she has misjudged the go-between and her motives. "'Lady,' said the old woman, 'you know a great many sayings; but I am not counseling what you think, rather only that the two of you talk things over now; come to some agreement with each other as soon as you get together'" (1480). Garoza anticipates from Trotaconventos just the sort of betrayal that befell Endrina and tells the old woman that should she ever agree to meet the archpriest, the old woman would dishonor her by locking her in alone with him (1481). Trotaconventos, a skilled liar, implores the nun to trust in her, assuring Garoza that she is there to protect her.

After ably defending herself in the scholastic style debate with Trotaconventos, in which she reveals her familiarity with the go-between's motives and tricks, Garoza then begins to discuss the finer points of the courting ritual. In stanza 1483, Garoza says that the *fuero* does not say the woman should be the first to speak of love in the affair, "Old woman, it is not dictated by statute (*fuero*) that the lady should be the first to begin the love talk" (1483ab). She does not cite a scholastic authority, but a particularly Iberian civil authority, a *fuero*.[119] The *fuero* is a uniquely Iberian statute or body of laws established by local inhabitants of a town or region and based on local custom. By alluding to the *fuero*, Garoza firmly establishes herself as conscious of (and adhering to) local Iberian secular erotic conventions. Garoza, familiar with Trotaconventos and her ways, will not be fooled. She tells the old woman that the only certain mediator of the love affair is seeing the lover for herself, "it is fitting to gaze very steadily, which is a sure way of conveying our message" (1483c). Garoza exposes the false system of representation used by the old go-between to trick the young women she seduces for the archpriest. She questions the entire system of erotic mediation of which the go-between is the essential component. Though Garoza understands Trotaconventos's agenda, she is trapped by her circumstances, as the old woman points out in the next line, "a silent bird cannot utter omens" (1483d). Garoza, a nun confined to the convent, cannot meet with the archpriest, and thus see him with her own eyes in order to decide whether to pursue an affair with him. She is essentially blind, and therefore cannot make any judgment on how he looks or on his character, just as the mute bird cannot tell the future. Trotaconventos successfully conveys with this one-line proverb Garoza's dependence on her.

In this case Trotaconventos gains the upper hand, not because of her superior rhetorical skills, but simply because of the social and religious norms of sexual exclusion imposed upon nuns. Garoza acknowledges that she must rely on the old go-between because of her circumstances and asks for a true description of the archpriest. The episode of Garoza, more so than any of the archpriest's other erotic encounters, conforms to the model of the love affair developed in the earlier Andalusi go-between tale, including the physical segregation of the lovers as requisite for the go-between's mediation. As in the earlier Arabic and Hebrew *maqāmāt* (discussed in chapters 2–3), in the episode of Garoza, the lovers rely exclusively on the go-between's verbal portraits as the basis of their desire. As did al-Saraqustī, al-Harīzī, and Ibn Shabbetai, Juan Ruiz exploits the social conventions of sexual segregation to create an affair in which the go-between becomes not simply mediator, but also author of desire. Since neither lover can see the other, they are wholly reliant on Trotaconventos to be their faithful messenger and representative. Both the archpriest and Garoza accept this, and Trotaconventos, having patiently endured Garoza's Castilian didactic discourse, is free to develop the Andalusi erotic seduction of which she is the agent and master. Garoza, having dutifully defended herself with her fourteenth-century Christian literary arms of defense (*exempla* and *sententiae*), then gives in to the Iberian discourse of desire. Well aware of Trotaconventos's motives and function in the love affair, in stanza 1484 Garoza knowingly asks her for a description of the archpriest. Based on the list of physical attributes Trotaconventos provides, Garoza then decides to engage in the affair. Garoza becomes an active member in the affair—a reader and interpreter of signs (similar to Ayyala in the *Offering* and the *qiyān* described by Ibn Hazm)—distinguishing her from the often absent and/or silent women/objects of desire constructed by male authors in Western European erotic lyric. This smart, beautiful woman is well versed in the science of love and knows how to play the (Andalusi) love game. Because of this knowledge she is the ideal lover. The reader witnesses her not only dominate the genres of sapiential wisdom, the *exempla* and the proverb, to prove her familiarity with Iberian courtly and church culture, but also to scientifically interpret Trotaconventos's portrait of the archpriest, showing her knowledge of the Arabo-Andalusi science of physiognomy. Whereas Peter Dunn argues that Trotaconventos's portrait of the archpriest portrays a body ill suited for physical love, Gregory Hutcheson has called that into question.[120] Hutcheson convincingly reads the traits described by Trotaconventos as a thinly veiled description of the penis.[121] Garoza certainly responds as if convinced of Juan Ruiz's potential as a lover, telling Trotaconventos that she will consider the matter (literally "see it," "Ver me he") (1492a) and agreeing to meet him the following day. It is Garoza who dictates the conditions of the first meeting, stipulating that it be in the morning and that Juan Ruiz bring friends. She even specifies suitable topics of conversation, "speak nice words to me, not words of mockery or ribaldry; and tell him not to recite to me any of those fables of yours" (1493cd).

Like the women of the Judeo-Andalusi *maqāmāt* and medieval Latin comedy, Garoza is veiled when the archpriest finally sees her for the first time. Unlike in those *maqāma*, however, in which the beloved represents the potential threat of a foreign culture, in the *LBA*, the Iberian bride is the perfect companion for the archpriest. Under her black veil we discover not the hideous monsters Ritzpah or the she-ghoul, but a vision of beauty:

> Help me, Holy Mary! I clasp my hands!
> Who gave to a white rose a nun's habit and black veil?
> It would be better for this lovely thing to have children and a grandchild
> than a black veil like that, or a hundred nun's habits.
> Although sinning with a nun is for the wooer
> an offense against God,
> O God, how I wish I were that sinner,
> to do penance for this sin after it was consummated!
> She gazed at me with eyes that looked like flame;
> I sighed for them; my heart said: "Behold her!"
> I went to the lady, she spoke to me and I to her;
> the nun captured my heart and I captured hers. (1500–1502)

In this case, neither of the lovers has been deceived by the go-between. Both are happy and fall in love. The archpriest becomes her faithful lover: "The lady accepted me as her true paramour; I was ever her obedient and loyal lover" (1503ab). Their happy affair, however, is cut short by Garoza's untimely death two months later (1506).

Garoza proves to be an ideal lover. Unlike the affairs arranged by go-betweens in the Iberian *maqāmāt*, this one ends with both parties happy. Garoza does not represent a threat to the archpriest because, like him, she is an Iberian familiar with the Peninsula's diverse traditions. Garoza, or Juan Ruiz's depiction of her, defies the passive Western European representations of the object of desire. Nor does she conform to the image of the wicked, deceptive woman as object of desire depicted in both scholastic and Judeo-Iberian moralizing, misogynist discourses. She is a nun competent in the Western European scholastic discourses of *exempla* and proverbs, but, as the Andalusi bride Garoza, she is also familiar with the Iberian ritual of love. She is a hybrid Iberian subject, who, with the help of Trotaconventos, inscribes herself into this canonical medieval text and into the archpriest's life from the margin, from the confines of her convent. The go-between is an essential tool of this marginal Iberian subject. Just as Garoza uses the go-between to inscribe herself into the discourse of love/power, the author, Juan Ruiz, uses the go-between *cum* book to inscribe Andalusi heritage into the official courtly and church discourses of Castile and Western Europe.

La mora

Juan Ruiz's journey through the varieties of erotic and literary traditions present in fourteenth-century Castile is not complete without a final Encounter with the Arabo-Andalusi.[122] Following the death of Garoza, the archpriest, who is desirous of another affair, calls Trotaconventos. She attempts to seduce a Moorish woman, but despite the archpriest's fine present and verses, this *mora* refuses to listen to the old woman, telling her instead to be quiet and go away. The four stanzas that include the dialogue between the two women all end in Andalusi-Arabic phrases placed in final rhyme position. This encounter with the *mora* and the inclusion of Andalusi Arabic in this Castilian work further suggests that the *LBA*'s author may have been a Mozarab or member of another of the hybrid groups marginalized by Castilian Christian ideology. What this Arabic-Castilian code switching reveals of the author's knowledge of Arabic has been the focus of critics seeking to prove or disprove Juan Ruiz's possible direct familiarity with Arabic models.[123] But this episode is important in other ways. It also tells us about Juan Ruiz's audience and about the Iberian society represented in the work—both of which hear/read and understand this untranslated Arabic. The use of Arabic does not preclude the learned clergy as potential reader/author for the work, since notarial documents testify to the continued use of Arabic among the Castilian clergy whose ranks still included Mozarabs until the beginning of the fourteenth century.[124]

The introduction of this Andalusi Arabic into the learned Castilian *mester de clerecía*, a form associated with traditionally moralizing Christian authors such as Gonzalo de Berceo, is yet another instance in which Juan Ruiz destabilizes/deconstructs the very forms of Castilian literature being used by contemporaries to construct an exclusionary model of Castilian identity. In this episode he makes this Castilian literary form, so closely associated in contemporary literature with the Castilian clergy and the Reconquest, and makes it a vehicle not just for the go-between, but for the voice of the Moorish woman—perhaps the most marginalized of Iberian subjects. In the *LBA* the Moorish woman's brief responses to Trotaconventos are privileged by their line and stanza final position.

Juan Ruiz would be happy to court this Arabic-speaking Moorish woman, but she has no interest in him or his representative. Trotaconventos gives up and Juan Ruiz composes some songs for Jewish and Moorish women, "and for ladies in love" (1513b). As readers we have witnessed Juan Ruiz's attempts at seducing women as jealously guarded as the Torah, Moorish women, and women like Endrina and Garoza who did eventually become his lovers. The women he attempts to seduce, represent, as do the imagined audience for this narrative, the plurality of Iberian society. The Moorish woman rounds out the narrative journey through the variety of discourses, literary forms, and identities that make up the fourteenth-century Castilian linguistic and cultural landscape.

The Death of Love

After the attempted seduction of the Moorish woman, Trotaconventos, Juan Ruiz's loyal go-between and the mediator who has successfully negotiated the culturally diverse landscape of Iberia in his service, dies. Few details are given regarding the cause of her death, simply that she died serving the archpriest: "She died serving me, which makes me disconsolate" (1519b). Despite his claim at being at a loss for words, he goes on for over fifty stanzas decrying the horrors of death (1521–1574), concluding with an epithet composed for Trotaconventos's tombstone.

Juan Ruiz claims to be so affected by Trotaconventos's death that he cannot put one more drop of ink on paper. "[A]nd I, from great grief, cannot say a thing [a drop], because Convent-trotter no longer walks or trots" (1518cd). With Trotaconventos's death, the book that bears her name also comes to a close. She will no longer run or trot or help lovers. Without his go-between, the archpriest cannot envision further erotic adventures. Facing life without his go-between, the archpriest suddenly finds himself at a loss for words:

> It's come to pass—sad fate!—that my old crone is now no more.
> She died while in my service, which afflicts me with great pain.
> I don't know how to say it, but a very good old door
> Has now been closed to me, which used to be wide open before. (1519)

Despite the death of one beloved after another, Juan Ruiz could continue his erotic adventures, but without Trotaconventos he finds closed doors. The spatial metaphor is key in this stanza. Juan Ruiz has described his affairs as passages through physical spaces—mountain passes or, in the case of Garoza, small little doors. Without Trotaconventos, expert at traversing these liminal areas and closing the distance between lovers, that which lies behind the door—good love—is inaccessible to him.

The go-between, representative of the secular erotic Andalusi discourse of desire, passes from the Iberian stage, at least for the next century and a half.[125] Juan Ruiz recognizes that with her disappearance, the modes of love—the refined Andalusi erotics of Ibn Hazm—also disappear. The growing influence of Western European Christianity on both the royal court and the Church of medieval Castile, had, by the fourteenth century, when Juan Ruiz is composing his book of good love, taken its toll on the previously predominantly secular discourses of power and love originating from those sites of power. The potential channels of communication that defined the go-between and her office become closed doors, just as increasingly narrow-minded scholastic morality comes to dominate official Iberian discourses. With the *LBA*, Juan Ruiz presents a sense of what it is to be a fourteenth-century Iberian. As he does this he holds up genres and ideologies used in the construction of the ideal Christian Castilian developed in the late thirteenth to early fourteenth centuries as a counterpoint to a more inclusive, cosmopolitan Iberian identity. Iberians are not just Christian sinners, they are also lovers, Muslims, and Jews, who live together in urban spaces and who share food, wine, and their bodies. The moral ethics of Western scholasticism fit this Iberian ideal poorly, and the *LBA* is a renunciation of these perceived "foreign" values. Though the go-between and the Andalusi erotics she represents may die at the tale's end, just as the Ibero-Andalusi culture of prestige was giving way to new Christian-dominated, Western European cultural models in fourteenth-century Castile, Juan Ruiz's inscription of the go-between and the Andalusi discourse of love into this seminal work of Castilian fiction assured that both the Ibero-Andalusi go-between and cultural model would continue to speak up and out, and to assert its position within Iberian Romance-speaking literature and culture for centuries to come.

CONCLUSION

> *Three ingredients, then, are necessary to make Europe: Rome, Greece and Christianity*
>
> —Rémi Brague, *Eccentric Culture*

Rémi Brague's provocative assertion that the only traditions that contributed to the formation of contemporary Europe are Western ones reflects contemporary critical views of European identity and history.[1] The Iberian Peninsula, as both birthplace of the authors whose works we have examined in this book and as imaginary locus of those same authors' identities, was the "home" to which these intellectuals longed to return, or against which they sought to redefine themselves, be it the culture of the secular court, or the physical spaces of the cities in whose streets and palaces they spent their youth. This Iberia is a part of a different historical Europe than that conceived of today and reveals moments and loci in which the urge to define European identity, and more specifically Iberian identity, was constructed upon Arab secular, rational ideals, and an Arabo-Andalusi imaginary. The Andalusi go-between narrative, whose death is announced in the *LBA*, is one of the lost constructions of identity—one of the possible models of identity subsequent Europeans did not take up. As medieval readers and authors cleansed the go-between of her Arabo-Andalusi origins and incorporated her into the Roman/Greek/Christian construction of identity being formulated by medieval scholastics (discussed in chapters 4 and 5), the go-between passed from the Andalusi into the Roman/Greek/Christian construction of European identity. In this book we have explored the Arab/Andalusi/Jewish behind the Roman/Greek/Christian and also investigated why Iberian courtiers and intellectuals chose to return repeatedly to the Andalusi version of the go-between.

Although early-thirteenth-century scholastics cleansed the Andalusi go-between of her Arab origins by making her Ovid's *vetula*, and Juan Ruiz announced her death in the middle of the fourteenth century, the go-between continued to enjoy a rich life in Spanish letters—she continued to allow the Andalusi courtly discourse of love in by the side door to wreck havoc among the discourses of Castilian Catholic power. However, she continued to function as a tool of mediation and reflection not in the official discourse of courtly power, namely *cancionero* poetry, but in the theater. She found a new home in this emergent genre that would come to dominate sixteenth-century Spanish literature and that, importantly for the go-between and her authors, responded to a wider public of Iberians and their interests than to the more exclusive systems of courtly power in which she had originated some five hundred years before. It is the *converso* author Fernando de Rojas that would again take up the go-between to address his own role as a *converso* intellectual in the increasingly Catholic and Spanish Iberia of the Catholic monarchs, Isabel and Ferdinand. The late-fifteenth-century work, the *Celestina*, stands as a testament to the resilience of the Andalusi go-between narrative and to its continued ability to address the complexity of Iberian identity, even as that complexity was coming under ever-increasing attack by sociopolitical forces such as the Inquisition and the end of the Reconquest.[2] Fernando de Rojas is not a courtier, and in late fifteenth century Spain, *conversos* such as Rojas found themselves officially excluded from public offices. He uses the go-between tale not to address the in-between spaces of official Spanish cultural identity, but the impossibility of reconciling his own Iberian cultural identities with official models of what it is to be a Spaniard. Not only the *Celestina*, but also a slew of works inspired by it, will reach the Americas with the first generation of Spanish colonizers. There, far from the Iberian courts where she originated, she will find fertile new ground for her narrative of desire, longing, and exile. Though a detailed examination of the *Celestina* and her brood is beyond the scope of this book, their existence and continued ability to signify well beyond the Mediterranean boundaries explored in this book further testify to the continued relevance of the Andalusi cultural model in the history and literature of both Europe and its colonies.[3] At least in the imaginative world of fiction, these old women continue to survive and adapt because of their ability to translate and represent desires across linguistic, ethnic, religious, and class boundaries.

NOTES

Introduction: Representing Others in Medieval Iberia

1. Bhabha, *Location of Culture*, 227–228, uses the term "in-between" to refer to the spaces of diaspora, where "migrant and minority discourse" negotiate cultural difference.
2. For the sake of ease of reading, Arabic and Hebrew consonants have been transliterated by the closest Romance character. I have indicated long and short vowels in Arabic terms and proper names for which there are no accepted English transcriptions. Commonly recognized English spellings for better-known Hebrew and Arabic names and terms have been used. While I include in the text English translations of the material I am analyzing, I have included in the notes citations of all primary texts in the original Arabic, Hebrew, Latin, or Spanish.
3. Echoing the opinion of Catherine Brown, Jeffrey Jerome Cohen has pointed out that in general the "Middle Ages have been characterized too often as a field of undifferentiated otherness against which modernity (and therefore the possibility of a premodern postcoloniality) emerged." Cohen, introduction to *Postcolonial Middle Ages*, 4; see also Brown, "In the Middle." Modern critics have constructed medieval Iberia, and particularly al-Andalus, as sites of political and social otherness in order to offer an alternative to contemporary social and political attitudes of intolerance. D. Fairchild Ruggles calls for an approach to al-Andalus that recognizes it as a site of problematic cultural intermingling that anticipates more modern colonial spaces. "Mothers of a Hybrid Dynasty," 65–66. Also see note 9 below.
4. For the tenth-century nun Hroswitha's description of the Umayyad court in Cordoba as "Ornament of the World," see Menocal, *Ornament of the World*, 12.
5. "Europe North of the Pyrenees showed little interest in Islam before the first Crusade of 1095–1099." Tolan, *Saracens*, 69. On Raymond d'Aguilers and Petrus Tudebodus, see Tolan, *Saracens*, 111–118.
6. Said, *Orientalism*, 61.
7. Pre-Umayyad medieval Iberia was what Arjun Appadurai describes as a "diasporic switching point," an area to which or through which various diasporic-subjects traveled and in which they often settled for various reasons, but without the idea of renouncing their former cultures or of making it their

"homeland." *Modernity at Large*, 171. For a concise overview of the early centuries of recorded Iberian history, see Payne, *History of Spain and Portugal*, 1–14 and Barton, *A History of Spain*, 5–30.
8. Barton, *History of Spain*, 5.
9. Américo Castro coined the term *convivencia* to describe the coexistence of Jews, Muslims, and Christians in medieval Iberia. *España en su historia*, 200–209. Later historians, such as Norman Roth, have imbued the term with an extremely optimistic (in David Nirenberg's terms) reading. See Roth, *Jews, Visigoths and Muslims*, 2. Menocal, *Ornament of the World*, 9–13 also paints a more positive picture of medieval Iberian coexistence. David Nirenberg is a recent representative of the conflictive version of Iberian coexistence. See *Communities of Violence*. Other representatives of this approach include the so-called lachrymose school of Jewish historians, which includes Baer, *History of the Jews in Christian Spain*. For a summary of these positions see Nirenberg, *Communities*, 8–10 and Brann, *Power in the Portrayal*, 3–10. Other recent studies examine medieval Iberia, especially al-Andalus, as a more complex society in which different ethnic, religious, and cultural groups coexisted in an often problematic way. See, for example, Meyerson, introduction to *Christians, Muslims, and Jews*; Ray, *The Sephardic Frontier*; and Makki, "The Political History of al-Andalus," 3–87.
10. See Meyerson's recent evaluation of the problematics of studying Spanish history through the lens of mainstream European history and/or as a site of alterity, introduction to *Christians, Muslims, and Jews*, xii–xiv.
11. Makki, "The Political History of al-Andalus," 6–77, provides a detailed discussion of the political rivalry between these different ethnic groups.
12. Andalusi exiles established settlements, among other places, in North Africa—particularly in current day Tunis and Morocco. In the old city in Fes there is still an Andalusi quarter and some Moroccans still refer to themselves as Andalusis, attesting to the survival of al-Andalus even into the present.
13. The Andalusi court model is adapted from the earlier Umayyad court in Baghdad that similarly accommodated ethnically and religiously diverse courtiers from the different populations of the Umayyad Empire such as Persians, Nestorians, and Arabs. Peter Heath characterizes *adab* as a type of practical "cultural knowledge based on the body of literary traditions and cultural norms" of the Arabs. Though originally based on the tribal traditions of the pre-Islamic inhabitants of the Arabian Peninsula, as the Islamic Empire spread and as its centers of power became more urban, these traditions also changed, adapting to the changing demographics of imperial expansion. By the end of the ninth century, elements of the varying traditions (Persian, Hellenic) with which the Islamic Empire had come into contact are also incorporated into *adab*. Heath characterizes ninth-century *adab* as a "new Islamic synthesis of interrelated fields of knowledge that encompassed and combined such genres as poetry, belles lettres, grammar, genealogy, history,

biography, proverbs, ethics, wisdom and advice, and examples of behavior recognized as models worthy of emulation." Heath, "Knowledge," 107. Raymond Scheindlin also describes the "cosmopolitan intellectual life sometimes referred to as Arabic humanism" developed in the Baghdadi courts, which attracted people from diverse religious and ethnic groups. "Merchants," 335. Also see Robinson, *In Praise of Song*, 69–80, who compares the Andalusi and Baghdadi models of the ideal courtier in the context of the *majlis*, literary and drinking parties among court intimates.

14. On these terms and their usage in the courtly context see Robinson, *In Praise of Song*, 11, 70–72, 78, 103–104. Also see Monroe, *Shu'ūbiyya in al-Andalus*, 6–7 for a discussion of the growing importance of the *kātib* or courtier-secretary under 'Abd al-Rahman III.
15. For example, the tenth-century Ibn 'Abd Rabbihi, courtier to 'Abd al-Rahman III, states that the secretary-courtier should be "spotless in his dress, clean in the assembly, exhibiting manly courage, sweet of smell, keen of wit, elegant of tongue, sweet in giving hints, witty in metaphor," etc. Quoted in Monroe, *Shu'ūbiyya*, 6.
16. For more on these poets see Monroe, *Hispano-Arabic Poetry*; Robinson, *Praise*.
17. On the usage of Arabic among Andalusi Jews see Halkin, "The Medieval Jewish Attitude toward Hebrew"; Drory, "'Words beautifully put,'" 61–63; and Rabin, "Hebrew and Arabic in Medieval Jewish Philosophy."
18. The *taifa* kings that emerged after 'Amirid rule had disintegrated held power in their various realms until the invasion of the North African Almoravids in the 1080s. See Kennedy, *Muslim Spain*, 130–195; Wasserstein, *Rise and Fall of the Party Kings*.
19. Monroe, *Shu'ūbiyya*, 7–9, 24.
20. Andalusi courtiers, like the Jews of the Diaspora described by Denise McCoskey, "occupied multiple, often intersecting, positions of identification simultaneously and could find themselves activating or being categorized by only one or more of these positions, depending on the context," 400.
21. Ibn 'Abd Rabbihi claims "the secretaries of kings are their eyes that see, their ears that listen, their tongues that speak" and advises, "in them may be found the manners of kings and the modesty of subjects." Quoted in Monroe, *Shu'ūbiyya*, 6.
22. The origins and meaning of the term Mozarab is further discussed in chapter 5, n21.
23. Cohen, *Medieval Identity Machines*, xviii.
24. Bhabha uses the term "unhomely," which he adapts from Freud (*The Location of Culture*, 10), to designate the hidden that when revealed (often in intimacy) estranges.
25. See Bakhtin, *Rabelais and His World*, 303–436; Kayser, *The Grotesque*; Russo, *The Female Grotesque*.
26. Among Arabic literary scholars, and to an extent among those working in medieval Hebrew, the rhymed prose narratives studied in this book have received little critical attention compared to that given by Hispanists to the *Libro*

de buen amor. James T. Monroe's relatively new translation of al-Saraqusti's *Maqāmāt al-luzūmīyah* (which I examine in chapter 2) has been the impetus for some new critical reappraisals of al-Saraqusti's importance as an Andalusi author and of the Arabo-Iberian *maqāmāt* in general. See Young, *Rogues and Genres* and "Preachers and Poets"; Wacks, "Performativity"; and my own "'Words sweeter than honey.'" Ibn Hazm's chapter on the messenger (the subject of chapter 1) has similarly received scant contemporary attention, although it was at the heart of a disagreement between Américo Castro, G.B. Gybbon-Monypenny, and Claudio Sánchez Albornoz during the 1950s and 1960s. This debate centered, however, not on a reading of Ibn Hazm in the context of Andalusi literature, but on the extent to which it may have influenced the Spanish work, the *Libro de buen amor*. See Castro, *La realidad histórica de España*, 402–429 and *España en su historia*, 355–446; Sánchez Albornoz, *España: Un enigma histórico*, 1: 202–226; and Gybbon-Monypenny, "Autobiography in the *Libro de buen amor*," 64. Within the last twenty years, among a handful of scholars, including Matti Huss and Tova Rosen, there has been growing interest in the Hebrew work studied in chapter 3, Ibn Shabbetai's *Offering*. See Rosen, "On Tongues," "Sexual Politics," and *Unveiling Eve*; Huss, "Critical Editions of *Minhat Yehuda*"; and Fishman, "A Medieval Parody of Misogyny." Early studies on Ibn Shabbetai's *Offering* include Dishon, "The Sources of the *Maqāma*" and "Critical Examination." Studies of the other work analyzed in chapter 3, al-Harizi's Gate Six of the *Tahkemoni* include Dishon, "The Sources" and "Critical Examination"; Haberman, *Shalosh Maqamot*; and the analysis included in the newest translation and edition by Segal, *Book of the Tahkemoni*, 454–458. Hebrew poetry of the Golden Age (as opposed to the prose studied in this book) still continues to receive the lion's share of critical attention by Hebraists. The Castilian work, the *Libro de buen amor* has been and continues to be one of very few canonical Spanish medieval texts and is at the heart of some of the central debates of medieval Hispanism. For recent studies on the *Libro de buen amor* and its role in medieval Spanish studies see Robinson and Rouhi, *Under the Influence*, especially the studies by Louise Vasvári ("Perverted Proverb") and Gregory Hutcheson ("Garoza's Gaze"). Also see Haywood and Vasvári, *A Companion to the Libro de buen amor*, and Heusch, *El libro de buen amor de Juan Ruiz, Archiprêtre de Hita*.

27. Readers will recognize in the title of chapter 1 an allusion to María Rosa Menocal's second section of *The Ornament of the World* in which she considers Umayyad court life in al-Andalus.
28. "'Amirid dynasty" is the name given to the rule of al-Mansūr and his sons al-Muzzafar and Sanchuelo, who ruled al-Andalus from 981 to 1009 in the name of the Umayyad caliphs whose power they had usurped. Kennedy, *Muslim Spain*, 109–129.
29. I follow Ross Brann's usage of the term "courtier-rabbi" to describe the "elite class of Andalusian Jews" who were "fervent enthusiasts of Arabic courtly values, style, and culture," *Compunctious Poet*, 8.

NOTES

Chapter 1 Palaces of Memory: Mediation, Court Culture, and the Caliphate

1. Ibn Hazm's work, *The Dove's Neck Ring*, is one of the best-known works of Andalusi literature. It is probably one of Ibn Hazm's earliest works and was composed between periods of imprisonment. Scales, *Fall of the Caliphate of Cordoba*, 30. Ibn Hazm claims in the preface that he wrote the work at the request of a friend. See Giffen, "Ibn Hazm," 420. The work survives in only one fourteenth-century manuscript copy, but was known among medieval Andalusi scholars. Ibid., 421; García Gómez, introduction, *El collar de la paloma*, 72–73. It is available in several translations. In English there are the translations of Nykl, *The Dove's Neck Ring* and Arberry, *The Ring of the Dove*. García Gómez translated the work into Spanish as *El collar de la paloma: Tratado sobre el amor y los amantes*. Henceforth I refer to the page numbers of at-Tāhir Ahmad Makkī's Arabic edition of *Tawq al-hamāma*. All translations are from Nykl's English translation unless otherwise noted. *The Dove's Neck Ring* is familiar to many non-Arabists thanks to the studies of A.R. Nykl, Miguel Asín Palacios, Emilio García Gómez, and Américo Castro. This scholarship focuses on comparing *The Dove's Neck Ring* to Provencal poetry and later Peninsular works in Spanish. *The Dove's Neck Ring*, though, has received comparatively scant recent critical attention and little analysis of how the work fits into the social and literary trends of eleventh-century al-Andalus has been done. Asín Palacios, *Abenházam*; Castro, *La realidad histórica de España*, 406–429; *España en su historia*, 355–446; García Gómez, introduction, *El collar de la paloma*; Nykl, *Dove's Neck Ring*; and Monroe, *Hispano-Arabic Poetry*, 14–20. Several of Ibn Hazm's many other works survive and attest to his fame as a theologian and expert in jurisprudence. He was a prolific writer and, according to the twelfth-century writer al-Marrākushī, his body of work encompassed some 400 volumes—over 80,000 handwritten folios. García Gómez, introduction, *El collar de la paloma*, 41–42. The best known of his works included, in addition to *The Dove's Neck Ring*, a debate with the courtier-rabbi Samuel ibn Nagrela over which religion was better, Judaism or Islam. See Brann, *Power in the Portrayal*, 54–90.
2. For a detailed study of the *fitna* and its ethnic basis, see Scales, *Fall of the Caliphate of Cordoba*.
3. Ibn Hazm, *The Dove's Neck Ring*, 58–59.
4. Eric Ormsby discusses Ibn Hazm as an exilic writer in "Ibn Hazm," 244. García Gómez similarly interprets Ibn Hazm as a quixotic figure who constantly longed for the past as a better time. See García Gómez, introduction, *El collar de la paloma*, 5, 48–49. Also see Ormsby, "Ibn Hazm," 247–248.
5. See Menocal, *Ornament of the World*, 12.
6. The 'Amirids (al-Mansūr and his sons al-Muzzafar and Sanchuelo) controlled the Umayyad caliphate from 981 to 1009. See Wasserstein, *Rise and Fall of the Party Kings*, 41–51.

7. See for example Ibn al-Qūtiyya, *Kitāb Tarīkh Iftitāh al-Andalus* in Lewis, *Islam from the Prophet Muhammad to the Capture of Constantinople*, 1: 120–123; Ibn 'Abd al-Hakam, *Futūh Misr*, 32–36; and Ibn Buluggīn, *The Tibyān*.
8. The best-known and most thoroughly studied group of non-Muslim Andalusi courtiers were Jews, such as Samuel ha-Nagid, *vizier* in Zirid Granada, with whom Ibn Hazm debated the virtues of Islam versus Judaism. Jews, however, were not the only non-Muslims at court. There were also many courtiers of Christian and Berber origin, as discussed below.
9. See my discussion of *adab* in the introduction, especially note 13. For the mastery of *adab* as a means of entry for non-Arabs into Muslim public life, see Scheindlin, *Gazelle*, 7.
10. Al-Mansūr was from a humble family from Algeciras, far from the capital, Cordoba. Kennedy, *Muslim Spain*, 111. Unlike Ibn Hazm, he had no personal ties to the Umayyad court and came to Cordoba to study with his uncle, after which he served as a public scribe, and it was in that capacity that the *vizier* al-Mushafi brought him to the caliphal court as tutor to al-Hakam II's son. Reilly, *Medieval Spains*, 86–87. He first became director of the mint (A.D. 967), then treasurer (968), then *qādī* of Seville (969), and finally prime minister (*hājib*) (after 978). Domination of *adab* or Arab *belles lettres* and personal refinement allowed him *entrée* into the royal court and also provided the means for his further advancement. Wasserstein, *Rise and Fall*, 41–43.
11. García Gómez, introduction, *El collar de la paloma*, li–lii. Asín Palacios, *Abenházam de Córdoba*.
12. Kennedy, *Muslim Spain*, 86; Makki, "The Political History of al-Andalus," 45. A historian from eleventh-century Zirid Granada, 'Abd Allāh ibn Buluggīn, describes al-Mansūr's rationale for diversifying the military: "Since all his troops were of one race, al-Mansūr anticipated that they might engage in conspiracies calculated to undermine his power and join forces in revolt against his authority irrespective of whether his commands were to their liking or not. He therefore paid close attention to the problem and allowed himself to be guided by the view that his troops should be drawn from various tribes and diverse elements so that, should any one group think of defecting, he might subdue it with the help of the other detachments. . . . He therefore imported such Berber chieftains, champions and redoubtable warriors as were known to him for their horsemanship and skill in the arts of war." *The Tibyān*, 44.
13. Kennedy, *Muslim Spain*, 117.
14. Ibid., 120. Also see Ruggles, "Mother of a Hybrid Dynasty," 70–76.
15. After the fall of the 'Amirids and the *fitna*, smaller independent *taifa* kingdoms formed out of what had once been the Umayyad caliphate. Many of the *taifa* kings (*mulūk at-tawā'if*) and their courtiers, such as Ibn Hazm's father, had risen to high positions in the courts of al-Mansūr and his sons. Like Ibn Hazm (at least according to García Gómez), many *taifa* rulers were often not of Arab origins and could not legitimately claim to be caliphs. These *taifa* kings, however, cultivated and maintained a class of intellectual

elites formed in the court culture of the 'Amirids who, in their positions as ministers, *viziers*, and advisers, continued to control much of the politics and official culture of al-Andalus.

16. During the later *taifa* period this preference for Arabness and things Arab inspires a reactionary movement known as the Shu'ūbiyya, followers of which, in al-Andalus, protest this pro-Arab current in Andalusi thought by attacking the Arabs and their culture. One of the only surviving works of the Andalusi Shu'ūbiyya movement is an epistle by Abū 'Amir ibn García, courtier-poet to the *taifa* kings of Denia, Mujāhid al-'Amirī, a Slav, and his son 'Alī, who had been brought up in captivity in Italy until he was ransomed as a fourteen year old. For more information see Monroe, *Shu'ūbiyya*, 1–62 and the Introduction.
17. Robinson, *In Praise*, 115.
18. García Gómez, introduction, *El collar de la paloma*, 33–34.
19. Monroe, introduction, *Hispano-Arabic Poetry*, 14–18; Robinson, *Praise*, 111–116.
20. Monroe, introduction, *Hispano-Arabic Poetry*, 10.
21. For a detailed discussion of this transition see Robinson, *Praise*, 48–87. The *majlis al-uns* was a "small group with steady membership centered around a common, often intellectual, concern" and "was a versatile social and cultural institution, one which might house activities ranging from 'serious' religious, exegetical, philosophical or intellectual debate to 'frivolous' or amusing poetic recitation and composition, singing, wine-drinking and an ostentatious enjoyment of leisure in the company of witty and elegant 'beautiful people.'" Ibid., 74–75. Monroe has also addressed the difference between al-Mansūr's court and that of the Umayyads. Monroe, introduction, *Hispano-Arabic Poetry*, 10.
22. As Monroe points out, al-Mansūr was not of royal blood and "could therefore mingle more intimately with his courtiers." Monroe, introduction, *Hispano-Arabic Poetry*, 9.
23. Robinson, *Praise*, 70.
24. The cupbearer and slave women had not always formed part of the Arab poetic tradition and the social reality from which it derived. These characters are added to the stock elements of the Arabic love poetry adopted from Jāhiliyya and 'Udhrī poets in the late Umayyad and early 'Abbasid courts—by poets such as Bashshar ibn Burd and Abū Nūwās. Schippers, *Spanish Hebrew Poetry*, 146–147. This morally lax atmosphere cultivated in the 'Amirid and later *taifa* courts would be used by the religiously conservative Almoravids as justification for their invasions of the 1080s and 1090. See Reilly, *Medieval Spains*, 96–97 and chapter 2, n8.
25. Robinson, *In Praise*, 147.
26. Monroe, introduction, *Hispano-Arabic Poetry*, 7.
27. Ibid., 8.
28. Ibn Hazm, *The Dove's Neck Ring*, 17.
29. The *risāla* genre originated among the 'Abbasid courtiers of Baghdad and was perfected by al-Jāhiz (d. 869) and, arguably, by Ibn Hazm himself. See

Ormsby, "Ibn Hazm," 237. The *risāla*, or epistle form, is used to expound a thesis, normally in the first person, and usually addressed to a real or fictional correspondent. See Rubiera Mata, *Literatura hispanoárabe*, 189–90. The *risāla* becomes popular in al-Andalus in the early eleventh century, just when Ibn Hazm is writing *The Dove's Neck Ring*. In addition to being used for this work, this form was used for debates (Ibn Burd), literary criticism (Ibn Hazm's friend Ibn Shuhaid), philosophical allegory (Ibn Tufayl), and mystic works (Ibn al-'Arabī). Rubiera Mata, *Literatura hispanoárabe*, 199–204. For a detailed study of the *risāla* see de la Granja, *Maqāmas y risālas andaluzas*. Ibn Hazm adapts the relatively new genre of the *risāla* to a theme addressed by similar treatises composed at the 'Abbasid court. One of the Eastern models that Ibn Hazm alludes to in *The Dove's Neck Ring* is the *Kitāb al-zahra* by the tenth-century poet Muhammad ibn Dāwūd. Giffen, "Ibn Hazm," 422; García Gómez, introduction, *El collar de la paloma*, 67–69. Ibn Hazm alludes to Ibn Dāwūd's work in the first chapter, *The Dove's Neck Ring*, 21. The one hundred chapters of the *Kitāb al-zahra* consist of prose introductions to poems on different aspects of love. Other treatises on similar themes include al-Kharā'iti's *I'tilāl al-qulūb* and the *risāla* of the Baghdadi scholar and poet al-Washshā'. Giffen, "Ibn Hazm," 422. Ibn Hazm's treatise, like these earlier 'Abbasid models, frames love and friendship as part of an ethical system of behavior using the imagery and forms of Arabic court literature. All of these treatises combine "esoteric and philosophical concerns with literary, and particularly lyrical, ones." Robinson, *Praise*, 74–75.
30. Ibn Hazm, *The Dove's Neck Ring*, 19.
31. On the origins of Ibn Hazm's Neoplatonism see Monroe, introduction, *Hispano-Arabic Poetry*, 16–18.
32. If that beautiful form does not cover a beautiful soul, though, then its appreciation cannot lead to love but only to passion. "As regards the cause because of which love ever occurs in most cases, it is an outwardly beautiful form; because the soul is beautiful and passionately desires anything beautiful, and inclines toward perfect images: and if it sees such an image it fixes itself upon it; and if it discerns, after that, something of its nature in it, draws close to it, and true love comes to pass: and if it does not discern behind it something of its kind, its affection does not go beyond the form. Thus it is with passion. Truly, images are a wonderful vehicle of bringing about a union between parts of the souls distant from each other." Ibn Hazm, *The Dove's Neck Ring*, 24.
33. Ibn Hazm, *The Dove's Neck Ring*, 161.
34. As Monroe points out, the philosophical vocabulary Ibn Hazm uses here, as well as the opposition he creates between soul and intellect, derive from Islamic philosophy's elaboration of the concept of the active intellect found in Aristotle's *De Anime* and the relationship posited between it, the soul and divine love in the work of Plotinus. Monroe, introduction, *Hispano-Arabic Poetry*, 16–18. In Ibn Hazm's narrative we have the earliest example of a work linking this ethical vocabulary and imagery—Iblis, *hawā*, and the soul—to the Andalusi go-between.

35. Ibn Hazm, *The Dove's Neck Ring*, 164.
36. Ibid., 58.
37. For example in chapter 4, "Love from Description," we find a description of this situation. Ibn Hazm claims that those who most often fall in love simply from a description of the beloved without ever having seen them are noble women maintained in "veiled seclusion": "Among whom it occurs most is among noble ladies in castles, kept in veiled seclusion with their men relatives." Ibn Hazm, *The Dove's Neck Ring*, 38.
38. Ibn Hazm, *The Dove's Neck Ring*, 38.
39. Ibid., 52.
40. "[S]elect him, and pick him out carefully, and seek him cautiously, for he is an indication of a man's wit, and in his hand lies his life and death." Ibn Hazm, *The Dove's Neck Ring*, 58.
41. "It behooves that the messenger be ready and keen, for whom a sign is sufficient, who guesses right things hidden, is capable of doing things of his own initiative, and supplies from his own wit what the one who sent him has overlooked, and conveys to the person who sent him everything he witnesses precisely." Ibid., 58.
42. Ibn Hazm's father was a courtier to al-Mansūr, and Ibn Hazm also served as courtier first in the 'Amirid court and later in the *taifa* courts of Almería, the Baleares, and Seville.
43. The poem Ibn Hazm composed on this subject, not included in the passage above, equates the go-between with the sword: "Your messenger is a sword in your right hand, so choose / A sharp sword and do not strike with it before grinding it: / He who relies on a blunt sword, the damage (resulting to him therefrom) / Rebounds upon him who depends upon it because of his stupidity!" *The Dove's Neck Ring*, 58–59.
44. This is my own translation of the passage.
45. Love of slave women is also the impetus for several tales of cross-cultural contact in *The Dove's Neck Ring*. Ibn Hazm tells of an Andalusi who, not realizing how in love he was with his slave girl, sold her to a Berber. Afterward he goes to the Berber and explains his love and need to get the girl back. The king takes pity and eventually the two are reunited. *The Dove's Neck Ring*, 159–160. Khalaf, courtier to Hishām an-Nāsir, fled when Hishām was killed, but returned shortly thereafter to Cordoba where he was killed searching for a slave girl he had left behind. Similarly, an Andalusi *vizier*'s son went over to the Berbers' side only because a slave girl with whom he was in love had moved into the region under their control. Ibid., 174–175.
46. The anecdote in the chapter on falling in love while sleeping recounts the love that afflicted a friend who fell in love with a slave girl (*jāriya*) he saw in his sleep. Ibn Hazm, *The Dove's Neck Ring*, 36–37. In a like vein Ibn Hazm tells a series of tales about friends and their slaves: one of a friend who fell in love with a slave girl at first sight, one whose slave girl only fell in love with him after having sex with him, one who fell in love with a short slave girl, and one who fell in love with a slave girl with a wide mouth. Ibid., 41–42, 46, 47. He also tells of a friend, a former leader of the Mosque of Cordoba

(killed by the Berbers), who freed his slave girl in order to marry her, only to have her marry his brother, a future leader of the Muʿtazilites of al-Andalus. Ibid., 71–72. One account tells of a young man whose slave girl was infatuated with him although he did not realize it and another tells of one whose uncle arranged a meeting with a slave girl he loved, and yet another tells of the beautiful Abū ʿAmir, whose attractiveness apparently caused the death of many slave women who fell in love with him. Ibid., 92–93, 96, 105. Two important aristocrats Ibn Hazm knew lost their minds because their families prevented them from being with the slave girls they loved. Ibid., 138–139.
47. Goitein, *Individual*, 321. Abdelwahab Bouhdiba, however, claims slave girls (*jawārī*) were "anti-wives" whose presence in the household was problematic, often leading to jealousy and intrigues resulting from their competition with the wives for favors and attention. "The concubine was the intruder par excellence. Nor should we forget the innumerable rivalries that resulted from concubinage and which set brothers of different beds—and different condition—against one another." *Sexuality in Islam*, 106–107.
48. Ibid., 107.
49. On the popularity of Basque, Frankish, and sub-Saharan African slaves, as well as their pricing according to education level see Levi-Provençal, *España musulmana*, 116.
50. Ahmad ʿAmin as quoted in Bouhdiba, *Sexuality in Islam*, 108.
51. Excerpt from al-Tīfāshī, *Mutaʿat al-Asmāʿ fī ʿilm al-samāʿ* translated in Liu and Monroe, *Ten Hispano-Arabic Strophic Songs*, 37–38.
52. Of the slaves that figure prominently in *The Dove's Neck Ring*, many are depicted as singers and master musicians, recalling al-Tīfāshī's description. Ibn Hazm tells us that as an adolescent he fell in love with a beautiful sixteen-year-old slave girl who sang the verses of al-ʿAbbās ibn al-Ahnaf for him. Ibn Hazm, *The Dove's Neck Ring*, 64–65. In chapter 8, "About Allusion in Speech" a slave woman who is clearly a *qiyān*, a singer, rebukes her lover for wanting a relation that was "not quite proper" in a song performed in front of a large and important royal party. She uses the commonplaces of Andalusi love poetry, the gazelle, the full moon, and the beautiful bough. Ibid., 52–53. Ibn Hazm also tells of a loyal slave girl who refused to have sex and pretended not to know how to sing after the death of her owner. Her new owner beats her daily for failing to fulfill her obligations, both sexual and social. The language of love, including the vocabulary and tropes of Arabic love poetry, was the common idiom of both courtiers and slave girls, who, as we see in these examples from *The Dove's Neck Ring*, found that it had become part of their identity in eleventh-century Andalusi court culture.

Chapter 2 "Many a Zayd and ʿAmr": Mediation and Representation in al-Andalus

1. Monroe, preliminary study to *al-Maqāmāt*, 35.
2. Robinson, *Praise*, 49.

NOTES

3. Monroe, preliminary study to *al-Maqāmāt*, 23.
4. Though I focus on al-Saraqustī's text as an Andalusi one, it clearly also addresses issues of larger concern in the Islamic Empire. Al-Saraqustī's combination of local, indigenous elements with literary genres and *topoi* popular across the Islamic Empire reveals a unique Andalusi perspective. Four of al-Saraqustī's *maqāmāt* are set in al-Andalus, and the rest are set in locales across the Islamic Empire, from China to the Maghreb. See Monroe, preliminary study to *al-Maqāmāt*, 46. Al-Saraqustī not only uses local poetic forms, (the *zajal*), but also forms popular in the Islamic East.
5. Ibn Hazm, *The Dove's Neck Ring*, 164.
6. See Guichard, *Al-Andalus*, 37–51.
7. See Robinson, *Praise*, 20. Also see Reilly, *Medieval Spains*, 96–97.
8. On Almoravid views of Andalusi moral laxity, see Kennedy, *Muslim Spain*, 164 and Wasserstein, *Rise and Fall*, 285–291.
9. The Almoravids would stay in al-Andalus until 1147. They seem to have been welcomed by the non-Arab Andalusis. 'Abd Allāh Bullugīn, *taifa* king of Granada, describes in his memoirs how the different members of court, particularly the Berber courtiers, welcomed the Almoravids, Hugh Kennedy describes it in the following way: "When the invaders approached Granada itself, 'Abd Allāh knew that there was no hope of resistance and he gives us an analysis of why all classes would welcome the new regime, the Berber troops because they 'rejoiced at the arrival of their kinsman,' the merchants because they simply wanted to do business, the common people because they would only be required to pay alms tax and tithe. The Maghrebi courtiers (whom he describes as the mainstay of his regime) were the first to welcome his enemies. Slaves, Slavs, women and eunuchs, all were prepared to listen to the blandishments of the Almoravids. In the end the unfortunate king was deserted by all except his aged mother. The evidence is less full for other areas, but it suggests that the Kingdom of Granada was not unique." *Muslim Spain*, 169.
10. Monroe, preliminary study to *al-Maqāmāt*, 11.
11. Ibid., 12, 43–44. His continued presence at court suggests al-Saraqustī was a career courtier. Abū Bakr Muhammad ibn Hayr (d. 1179), a historian and contemporary who claimed to have personally known al-Saraqustī, refers to him as a courtier or secretary, *kātib*. Monroe, however, thinks Ibn Hayr's depiction of al-Saraqustī as a *kātib* is an unjustified assumption. Instead Monroe characterizes al-Saraqustī as a private citizen who probably supported himself by teaching. Even if he was the type of intellectual free agent described by Monroe, al-Saraqustī was someone who shared the courtiers' educational formation and who participated and moved at times in their world. See Monroe, preliminary study to *al-Maqāmāt*, 27, 12, 35.
12. Monroe, "Al-Saraqustī," 1–7.
13. Ibid., 27, n64.
14. Reilly, *Medieval Spains*, 122–123.
15. In twelfth-century al-Andalus, al-Hamadhānī "remained a symbol of stylistic sophistication in Andalusi culture." Drory, "The *Maqāma*" 192–193.

Al-Harīrī's *maqāmāt* also quickly became known in al-Andalus. Several leading Andalusi intellectuals were actually present in the public readings officiated by al-Harīrī in Baghdad. Once back in al-Andalus these intellectuals transmitted and recorded al-Hamadhānī's and al-Harīrī's *maqāmāt*. See Monroe, preliminary study to *al-Maqāmāt*, 41. While al-Saraqustī, whose *maqāmāt* are the focus of this chapter, is the most outstanding of the Andalusi *maqāmāt* writers inspired by al-Harīrī, he was by no means the only one. Other Andalusis writing in the Haririan tradition include Abū ʿAbd Allāh ibn Abī al-Khisāl, Lisān al-Dīn ibn al-Khatīb, and al-Fath ibn Khāqān, whose *Maqāmāt al-qurtubiyya* attacked a leading Andalusi intellectual, al-Batalyūsī, thus sparking a series of literary debates among the Andalusi literati. See Nemah, "Andalusian *Maqāmāt*," 85–88.
16. Drory, "The *Maqāma*," 194. Monroe points out that al-Saraqustī composes his *maqāmāt* only some 25–30 years after the introduction of al-Harīrī's collection into al-Andalus. Monroe, preliminary study to *al-Maqāmāt*, 43.
17. Drory, "The *Maqāma*," 192. Al-Harīrī had an "unequalled mastery of the Arabic language and a perfect command of its inexhaustible vocabulary," and his followers regarded him as the "most perfect representative of the genre." See *Encyclopaedia of Islam*, s.v. "Al Harīrī."
18. Al-Saraqustī, *Maqāmāt*, 17. As we will see in chapter 3, al-Harīrī's influence extended beyond the limits of Arabic literature and had a profound impact on Judeo-Andalusi literature in Hebrew as well.
19. He addresses the relations between Berbers and Andalusis in "*Maqāma* 41," and the Muslim–Christian relations of Iberia in "*Maqāma* 19."
20. The *maqāmāt* are a valuable source of information regarding contemporary literary genres and fields of knowledge. Monroe talks about the relationship of the *maqāmāt* to other literary genres in the preliminary study to the *Maqāmāt al-luzūmīyah*, 1–18. Young, *Rogues and Genres*, 21–67, discusses in detail the relationship of the *maqāmāt* to several contemporary genres, including the sermon, hadith, poetry, and even the Quran. "*Maqāma* 34 (*The Horse*)" of the *Maqāmāt al-luzūmīyah* reveals al-Saraqustī's familiarity with Arab horse manuals and the science of equine physiognomy, 355–362.
21. There are many instances in which mediation is central to the plot of the *maqāma*, as for example in "*Maqāma* 28," in which al-Sadūsī acts as both a mediator and a courtier/secretary by insinuating himself into the court of a local potentate. See al-Saraqustī, *Maqāmāt*, 296–301. Similarly in "*Maqāma* 25," al-Sadūsī is a judge, mediating disputes in the Iranian region of Rayy. The corruption of the courtier/court lifestyle is central in this *maqāma*, where al-Sadūsī's own corrupt secretary/courtier berates him for his debauchery and fraudulent lifestyle. Ibid., 277–284.
22. Olivia Remie Constable also includes details of a historical scam similar to the one represented in this *maqāma*. "Medieval Spain," 265, 270–271. On relations with slaves and free women also see Goitein, "Sexual Mores," 47.
23. Al-Saraqustī, *Maqāmāt*, 122–123.
24. "A girl like the full moon, to win whom, maternal and paternal uncles would have been sacrificed at once; a girl who, when she smiled, displayed

NOTES

a gap between her teeth, which were as fair as hailstones, and who swayed with a figure like the sword fashioned by an incomparable swordsmith." Al-Saraqustī, Maqāmāt, 122.
25. Al-Saraqustī, Maqāmāt, 122.
26. See for example the scene in Ibn Shuhaid's Risālat al-tawābiʿ, 79–80, in which the author meets al-Hamadhānī's *jinnī* in the literary otherworld and asks the *jinnī* to give him a theme upon which he can improvise. The *jinnī* tells him to compose the description of a slave woman. "Maqāma 34" has another type of conventionalized description that will also make its way into subsequent go-between tales, that of the hideously ugly object of desire. In "Maqāma 34" the object of desire is not a woman, but a horse.
27. In his treatise on the specialized, singing slave woman, Risālat al-Qiyān, Abū ʿUthmān ʿAmr ibn Bahr al-Jāhiz (ninth century) reveals that slave owners must have been criticized as pimps, for in their defense we are given a description of how the slave owners actually did behave as go-betweens, using their slaves to negotiate sexual unions with others. See al-Jāhiz, *Epistle on Singing-Girls*, 37–38. This type of negotiation does not seem to have been uncommon, for, as Beeston points out, such slave women often were sources of income for their owner, often in less than legitimate exchanges such as the one depicted in this *maqāma*. See Beeston, introduction to *Epistle on Singing-Girls*, 2.
28. Al-Saraqustī, Maqāmāt, 86–87.
29. Ibn Hazm, *The Dove's Neck Ring*, 164.
30. Al-Saraqustī, Maqāmāt, 87.
31. Al-Sāʾib's encounter is similar to that described in chapter 5 of *The Dove's Neck Ring*, "About Love at First Sight," which tells of the man who "falls in passionate love with an image without knowing what she is, and does not know her name, or her permanent abode." Ibn Hazm, *The Dove's Neck Ring*, 40–41.
32. Ibid., 41.
33. Al-Saraqustī, Maqāmāt, 87.
34. Ibid., 88.
35. Ibid., 89–90.
36. See Sells, "Love," 133; Roth, "Care and Feeding of Gazelles," 96–118.
37. See Ibn Hazm, *The Dove's Neck Ring*, 98–99.
38. Al-Saraqustī parodies the courtly love tradition of Arabic poetry in other *maqāmāt* in this collection. See for example, "Maqāma 25." Maqāmāt, 284.
39. Al-Saraqustī, Maqāmāt, 90.
40. Ibid., 90.
41. Manzalaoui, "'I Follow the Religion of Love,'" 122–123.
42. Al-Saraqustī, Maqāmāt, 91.
43. Ibid., 92.
44. Ibid., 92–93.
45. Ibid., 89.
46. Drory, "The Maqāma," 195.
47. Ibid., 196.

Chapter 3 Translating Desire: The Violence of Memory in the Judeo-Iberian *maqāmāt*

1. For the Hebrew original of "The Poem of Two Exiles," see Ibn Ezra, *Shire ha-Hol*, Poem 20, 1: 24–27.
2. Before the arrival of the Almoravids, in al-Andalus, as throughout the Muslim world, Jews and Christians were considered *ahl al-dhimma*, people of the book, and received the right to practice their own religion. In general, and especially true of the elite members of the Jewish community, Jews in the medieval Muslim world were "prosperous, little subject to persecution, economically well integrated with the environment, and self-confident." Despite this prosperity, Jews were, however, what we would consider second-class citizens since they had to pay for this right and to submit to other regulations such as restrictions on clothing and proselytizing, Scheindlin, "Merchants," 317, 323. On the Almoravids see chapter 2, esp. notes 8 and 9; Kennedy, *Muslim Spain*, 154–188; and Wasserstein, *Rise and Fall*, 290.
3. Studies of the theme of exile among the literature of Andalusi Jews include Navarro Peiro, "Moshe ibn Ezra: El poema de los dos exilios"; Alfonso, "Uses of Exile"; Decter, "A Myrtle in the Forest"; and Anidjar, *Our Place in al-Andalus*.
4. Diane Lobel characterizes both Ibn Gabirol and Ibn Paqūdā as Jewish philosophical mystics, 24. In her study, *A Sufi-Jewish Dialogue*, Lobel focuses on the ways in which both these Judeo-Iberian authors use contemporary philosophical and mystical vocabulary and imagery in their better-known works (the *Crown of the King* in the case of Ibn Gabirol, and particulalry chapters 1–3, 5, 8, and 10 of the *Duties of the Heart* in the case of Ibn Paqūdā). She considers both authors within the larger Muslim mystic and philosophic traditions of the Middle Ages. In contrast, I focus on how both Ibn Gabirol and Ibn Paqūdā develop specific religio-philosophic images within the context of contemporary sociohistorical events in the Judeo-Iberian community, specifically those alluded to in Ibn Gabirol's poem, "Leaving Saragossa" and the allusions and parables relating to the Judeo-Andalusi courtier-lifestyle in chapters 7 and 9 of Ibn Paqūdā's *Duties of the Heart*; texts that Lobel does not engage.
5. "Merchants," 377.
6. Other early Judeo-Iberian *maqāmāt* include those of Solomon ibn Saqbel and Joseph ibn Zabara. See Scheindlin, "Merchants," 329, 333; Drory, "*Maqāma*," 199–200. Al-Ḥarīzī's *Taḥkemoni* and Ibn Shabbetai's *Offering* are examples of the two different forms of the Hebrew *maqāmāt* in Iberia. According to Judith Dishon, al-Ḥarīzī's collection of fifty *maqāmāt* is the unique exemplar of the classical Hebrew *maqāma*, which she defines as modeled upon the great Arabic *maqāmāt* collections of al-Hamadhānī and al-Harīrī. Ibn Shabbetai's *Offering* is representative of the other form of Iberian *maqāmāt* in Hebrew that Dishon terms the "Spanish *maqāma*." This second type, instead of being a collection of several *maqāmāt*, usually consists of a single *maqāma* or narrative, expanded to include a much more developed

plot. "Hebrew *Maqāma*," 66–67. Scheindlin, on the other hand, simply characterizes al-Harīzī's collection of *maqāmāt* as an exception to the general type of Judeo-Iberian Hebrew narrative prose. "Merchants," 380.
7. *Models*, 165–177.
8. J.M. Millás Vallicrosa asserts that al-Harīzī was from Toledo and that he died sometime in the 1230s. *Literatura hebraicoespañola*, 77. Al-Harīzī did live for some time in Provence and traveled extensively in Egypt, Palestine, Syria, and Iraq. Navarro Peiro, *Narrativa hispanohebrea*, 322. Ibn Shabbetai's work, especially the "Writ of Excommunication," locates him in Saragossa. Talya Fishman maintains that Ibn Shabbetai also lived in either Toledo or Burgos, based on the fact that his patrons Abraham al-Fakhkhār and Todros Halevi Abulafia were located in these cities. See "Medieval Parody," 103, n2. On Ibn Shabbetai's life also see Huss, "Critical Editions," 1: 183–188.
9. The fact that al-Harīzī composed both his collection of original Hebrew *maqāmāt*, the *Tahkemoni*, and an Arabic *maqāma* (the only such Arabic *maqāma* known to have been composed by a Jewish author), in the Muslim East, however, complicates this picture. The differing prefatory dedications of the *Tahkemoni* (most in Hebrew, but one in Arabic), discussed by Drory, *Models*, 218–230, suggests that the choice of language was dictated by the needs and wants of the potential patron, al-Harīzī's own desire to "prompt Eastern Jews to be interested in Hebrew," as well as by convention. Drory, "*Maqāma*," 206.
10. Drory, *Models*, 230.
11. Until recently the scholarly consensus was that al-Harīzī's original collection of *maqāmāt*, the *Tahkemoni* was composed while the author traveled through the East. However, based on the introduction to a now lost Hebrew *maqāma* of al-Harīzī, Joseph Blau and Joseph Yahalom suggest that material composed before he left Iberia or Provence was incorporated into the *Tahkemoni* at a later date. See Blau and Yahalom, "Poetic Flowers," 5–20 and *Wanderings of Judah al-Harīzī*. According to Carlos del Valle Rodríguez, al-Harīzī made two trips through the East, including stops in Egypt, Palestine, Syria, and Mesopotamia, but Drory (based on Habermann) thinks he made only one trip between 1205 and 1216. See Valle Rodríguez, prologue to *Las asambleas de los sabios*, 12 and Drory, *Models*, 217.
12. Fragments of the *Tahkemoni* are included in a thirteenth-century Italian copy of a Sephardic manuscript now housed in the Toledo Cathedral Library (Z-86-25). See Malachi Beit-Arié, "Collection," 314–316. Other manuscripts of Sephardic provenance include Bodlein MS 1270 and Jewish Theological Seminary MS 8935. See Beit-Arié, *Supplement*, 208–209; and Zotenberg, *Catalogues des Manuscrits Hébreux*, 231.
13. Scheindlin, "Merchants," 334. On the use of and attitudes toward Hebrew among medieval Jewish communities, see Halkin, "Medieval Jewish Attitude toward Hebrew."
14. Henceforth I refer to Ibn Shabbetai's *maqāma* as the *Offering* and al-Harīzī's sixth *maqāma* or gate as the "*Maqāma* of Marriage." Al-Harīzī divided his

maqāmāt into gates (bāb plural abwāb) following the Arabic denomination of chapters as gates.

15. Huss maintains that Ibn Shabbetai revised the 1208 version in 1228. See Huss, "Critical Editions," 1: 207–221; Rosen, *Unveiling Eve*, 227, n3.
16. Drory, "Al-Harīzī's *Maqāmāt*," 68.
17. See Dishon, "Critical Examination," 102–103; "Sources."
18. All citations from the *Offering* give the line numbers of Matti Huss's edition of the 1208 version. See Huss, "Critical Editions," 2: 1–35. When possible I have used the English translation of Scheindlin, "The Misogynist," 269–294. When I have used material not included in Scheindlin's partial translation, the English translation is my own as indicated in the notes.
19. Ibn Shabbetai's patron, Abraham al-Fakhkhār, is a member of the Judeo-Andalusi aristocracy and the brother-in-law of the famous medieval Talmudic scholar Meir Ha-Levi Abulafia (ca. 1165–1244), known as Ramah. See Septimus, *Hispano-Jewish Culture*, 3. Also see Rosen *Unveiling Eve*, 115 and Huss, "Critical Editions," 1: 263–273. The patron for another of Ibn Shabbetai's works (the *Debate between Wisdom and Wealth*) was Ramah's father, Todros Halevi Abulafia, who had been elevated to a high political office by Alfonso VIII of Castile. Septimus, *Hispano-Jewish Culture*, 5–6.
20. See Rosen, *Unveiling Eve*, 104 and "Sexual" 159.
21. Later examples include the debates in France over the *Roman de la Rose* and *cancionero* debates on the same theme in fifteenth-century Spain. Matti Huss argues that Ibn Shabbetai is playing with the illogical realm of the world turned upside down and the work's polyvalence prevents one definitive reading. For Huss the work lampoons both men and women. *Critical Editions*, 1: 100. Rosen, on the other hand, points out the inherent misogyny of the representations of women in the *Offering*, and that contemporary readers also read it as antifeminist. *Unveiling Eve*, 118.
22. Davidson, *Parody in Jewish Literature*, 12–15. This ban survives in only one manuscript copy, Bodleian 1980. See Neubauer, *Catalogue*, 669–670. Also see Dishon, "Critical Study," 48. The publicly condemned work has not survived.
23. Davidson, *Parody in Jewish Literature*, 14. Also see Dishon, "Critical Study."
24. See Baer, *History of the Jews*, 94.
25. Ibn Shabbetai, *Offering*, lines 35–100.
26. Lines 120–125.
27. Among the women reviled are Eve, Rachel, Dinah, and the Medianite woman of Numbers 31:15–16. For a discussion of this list, which Tova Rosen claims to be the first of its type in Hebrew literature, see *Unveiling Eve*, 106.
28. The *Duties of the Heart* is Ibn Paqūdā's only surviving work, and was one of the most important and widely read of Judeo-Iberian treatises and undoubtedly would have been known by both Ibn Shabbetai and his audience. It was the Andalusi translator relocated to Provence, Shlomo ibn Tibbon, who translated both Bahyā ibn Paqūdā's treatise and Maimonides's *Guide of the Perplexed* (ca. 1180) from Arabic to Hebrew, thus making them accessible

NOTES

to the Provencal and Northern European Jewish communities. Millás Vallicrosa, *Literatura hebraicoespañola*, 142. Henceforth I refer to the work as *Duties*. All English translations are those of Menahem Mansoor.

29. Ibn Gabirol's Neoplatonism is developed in the *Fountain of Life*, and the moral treatise, *The Improvement of the Moral Qualities*. See Gottheil and Wise, "Ibn Gabirol," 527. Lobel suggests that Ibn Paqūdā's *Duties* is heavily influenced by the latter work. *Sufi-Jewish Dialogue*, 3–4.

30. Ibn Paqūdā's *Duties* attacks the *adab*-style education and courtly lifestyle at length. See Safran, "Bahyā ibn Paqūdā's Attitude." This will be discussed in detail below. Ibn Gabirol similarly attacks Judeo-Andalusi courtiers' worldliness and use of Arabic in his poetry. See Ibn Gabirol, *Poesía Secular*, 37–42.

31. Line 20. For the entire poem in Hebrew, see Ibn Gabirol, *Shire ha-Hol*. 67–68. For a Spanish translation accompanied by the Hebrew original, see Ibn Gabirol, *Poesía Secular*, 37–42. Line 20 can be found on page 39.

32. After leaving Saragossa, Ibn Gabirol wandered in Muslim-controlled al-Andalus. Ibn Shabbetai's fate after exile is unknown, although given the changed political landscape of the Peninsula in the thirteenth century he probably stayed in Christian lands.

33. See Pagis, introduction to *Poesía secular*, xxxvi–xxxvii.

34. Ibn Gabirol declares that he will use his tongue/language as a weapon (a *kilshoni*, winnowing fork) to destroy them, complaining, "If their ears are closed to me [if they choose not to hear me] how can my message reach them?" See line 28. *Poesía secular*, 38–39.

35. Ibn Paqūdā, *Duties*, 278.

36. For a detailed summary of Ibn Paqūdā's *Duties* and of the system of spirituality he develops in it, see Lobel, *Sufi-Jewish Dialogue*, 9–22. "For Bahyā, the soul is a spiritual substance, a light from the divine whose task is to serve God. According to Bahyā, the soul is given a sojourn in the material world; our test is to see if we can manage the desires and needs of the body and harness them to serve God. When we forget our purpose and get distracted by the needs of the body, it is reason (*'aql*) that comes as a guide to remind us of our task." Lobel, 9. Ibn Paqūdā's portrayal of the relationship between the soul and reason/intellect is reminiscent of Neoplatonic thought as we explore below in the section on al-Harīzī's intoductory *maqāma*.

37. See the Arabic original of the *Duties*, *Al-Hidāya*, 233. Ibn Paqūdā, although critiquing Andalusi learning, adopts the vocabulary of the Andalusi courtly discourse, including *hawā*. On *hawā* in the Andalusi context, see my discussion of Andalusi love and lovers, chapter 1, and al-Saraqustī's use of the term in his "*Maqāma 9*" in chapter 2. Steven Harvey briefly discusses Ibn Paqūdā's use of erotic vocabulary, although focusing on his use of *al-mahabbah* to designate the love of God. "Meaning of Terms Designating Love," 179–180.

38. Lobel points out that for Ibn Paqūdā, "it is the light of the intellect (*nūr al 'aql*) that awakens the soul," 33.

39. *Duties*, 405.

40. See *Duties*, 377, 378.

41. Ibid., 282–283.
42. See Wolfson, "Eunuchs Who Keep the Sabbath," 153–154.
43. Asceticism is found among kabbalists, but Ibn Paqūdā's treatise anticipates by over one hundred years the first recognized kabbalistic texts (those of Isaac the Blind, 1160–1235). However, in the thirteenth-century *Zohar*, a foundational text of the Kabbalah, the ideal Jewish scholar, like Zerah, studies the Torah with a group of fellow scholars and on Friday nights, when other Jews are performing their religious duty to copulate with their wives, they instead come together to study. Elliot Wolfson describes this intellectual displacement of the sexual as an "upward displacement of the phallic energy from the genitals to the brain." "Eunuchs Who Keep the Sabbath," 162. Wolfson discusses in detail the tension between asceticism and sex in the Kabbalah, 151–185. It seems likely that Ibn Shabbetai's work may also have been designed as a critique of this nascent group of Provencal and Iberian kabbalists just beginning to emerge onto the Judeo-Andalusi landscape during Ibn Shabbetai's lifetime. The kabbalists' beliefs regarding abstinence also seem to have been informed by Ibn Paqūdā's *Duties*.
44. Lobel, *Sufi-Jewish Dialogue*, 2–3, 15–17, 162–191. See also, Allan Lazaroff, "Bahyā's Asceticism Against its Rabbinic and Islamic Background." Mansoor also points out that celibacy is a tenet of a variety of mystical currents, including Mu'tazila and Sufism, with which Ibn Paqūdā was familiar. Introduction to *Duties*, 36–37.
45. See Rosenblatt, introduction to *Book of Beliefs*, xxiii. The Rabbinic Judaism of medieval Ashkenazim was based on both Palestinian and Babylonian traditions in which abstinence was not unusual for Torah scholars. See Diamond, *Holy Men*, 33–54. See also Biale, *Eros and the Jews*, 34–36. In the introduction of the *Duties*, Bahyā tells the reader that he went to the writings of great Talmudic scholars of the Babylonian tradition because their "devotion to the duties involving their own souls was much stronger and deeper" than that of Iberian Jews. Ibn Paqūdā, *Duties*, 96. Mansoor calls attention to the fact that Ibn Paqūdā himself suggests a concrete source for his ascetic views, an "Ethical Will:" "An excellent literary piece on asceticism has come to my notice, brother. It was composed by one of the pietists as his last testament, addressed to his son. It pleased me so much that I have set down here as I found it, to serve as the conclusion to the treatise, instead of concluding with my own exhortation and instruction to you." Ibn Paqūdā in Mansoor, introduction to *Duties*, 37. This genre of Jewish ethical treatises originates and flourishes among Ashkenazi Rabbinic scholars; the earliest known "Ethical Will" being that of the German Tosafist Eleazar, son of Isaac of Worms (ca. 1080). See Abrahams, *Ethical Wills*. This allusion to an unknown ethical will suggests that one source of Ibn Paqūdā's abstinence may be, in addition to Neoplatonism, Muslim mysticism and Second Temple behavior, a Rabbinic tradition of Northern Europe.
46. Ibn Paqūdā, *Duties*, 406.
47. Kozbi and Zimri also figure in later works that deal with Jewish identity and acculturation. In 1305 the Rabbi of Barcelona, Solomon ibn Adret

NOTES

(1235–1310), publicly banned the study of Greek and Arabic philosophy, claiming that Jewish scholars who followed the Arabized Judeo-Andalusi tradition were like Zimri, who abandoned his people to consort with Kozbi. Not only does he use the same biblical allusion to compare philosophical study and idolatry, Ibn Adret also employs the same literary form as Ibn Shabbetai—a rhymed prose laden with biblical references: "Woe to mankind because of the insult to the Torah! For they have strayed far from it. / Every man with his censer in his hand offers incense / Before the Greeks and Arabs. / Like Zimri they publicly consort with the Midianitess / And revel in their own filth! / They do not prefer the older Jewish teachings / But surrender to the newer Greek learning the prerogatives due their Jewish birthright." "Ban of Solomon Ben Adret," 190.

48. Ibn Shabbeati's reimaginings of both the allegory of the battle against Folly and the episode of Zimri indicates to the reader that this *maqāmā* will address the Judeo-Andalusi courtier's lifestyle. The fact that Ibn Shabbatai adapts his go-between, Kozbi, from the latter also indicates that he was reading Ibn Paqūdā in the Arabic since those parts referring to Zimri, Phinehas, and Arabized *adab* learning that Ibn Shabbatai alludes to (as discussed below) are not included in Ibn Tibbon's Hebrew translation of the *Duties*. See Mansoor, *Duties*, 282, n6. This helps to confirm that Ibn Shabbatai knew Arabic and that he was trained in the Arabized Judeo-Andalusi model.

49. Lines 302–304.

50. In the *Duties*, 283, Ibn Paqūdā describes necromancy as one of the customs of the Gentiles that Judeo-Andalusi courtiers sought to learn. Quoting both Deuteronomy and Numbers, Ibn Paqūdā describes the customs of the Gentiles, who "hearken unto soothsayers" and use divination, enchanters and sorcerers. Ibn Shabbatai complicates Ibn Paqūdā's identification of sorcery and astrology as Gentile sciences by attributing both to the women of Israel and their representative, Kozbi. He presents the women's pursuit of necromancy as a last resort, taken only after they find themselves shunned by their own community. As the *Offering* will show, the women's use of this Gentile science, the necromancy of Kozbi, actually restores the community in the end.

51. Line 284. We must acknowledge, as Tova Rosen, *Unveiling Eve*, 119 points out, that the register these women use is purely that of an educated Jewish male and not that which would have been spoken by real medieval Judeo-Iberian women; nevertheless, the inclusion of the women's voice and of their reaction to Zerah's version of Ibn Paqūdā's advised abstinence destabilizes the latter's moralistic discourse. By including the perspective of the women of Israel, Ibn Shabbatai points out how particularly unsuitable Ibn Paqūdā-style abstinence is for the Jewish community as a whole.

52. Lines 293–297. My translation.

53. Isaiah 38:17. See Scheindlin, Misogynist, 291n34.

54. Psalm 104:3. See Scheindlin, Misogynist, 291n35.

55. Lines 374–377. My translation.

56. Lines 776–777. He uses *'am* (people) in the sense of the people of Israel.

57. Lines 310–316. My translation.
58. See Moses ibn Ezra's poem, "Fire Whose Flame No Man Hath Kindled," lines 59–77.
59. Lines 367–68. My translation.
60. See Scheindlin, *Wine*, 81–82 for a discussion of the descriptive love poem and a list of words from the same semantic field as hind (fawn, gazelle, mountain goat, deer, doe, buck) being used as code words in Andalusi poetry. Such stock descriptions are designed, not to distinguish the beloved as unique but on the contrary, to establish him or her as the archetypal beautiful beloved. Scheindlin stresses the fact that the beloved has no name in this poetry, and is, instead, referred to by epithets such as fawn and gazelle further underscoring her/his universal nature. Also see Roth, "Care and Feeding of Gazelles," and Sells, "Love," 133. The lover of the Song of Songs is described as a roe and hart (2:9). Many Judeo-Andalusi poets went to the Hebrew of the Song of Songs and its metaphors for the language of their profane love poems. A contemporary audience would read such images as biblical material filtered through the erotic Andalusi tradition. Scheindlin, *Wine*, 100, 112, 145.
61. 1: 127. See Brann, *Compunctious Poet*, 72–73, for analysis of Ibn Ezra's use of this phrase. For a detailed discussion of Moses ibn Ezra and other contemporary poets' attitude toward poetry as false see Rosen, *Unveiling Eve*, 66–68, 74–79. In the Muslim religious tradition, poetry is sometimes stigmatized as false. See Surah 26, "The Poets," 192–227. The truth of Muhammed's teachings is contrasted to the false flattery of poets, whose verses only lead to evil (verse 224).
62. Maimonides, *Words of Logic*, cited in Rosen *Unveiling Eve*, 77. Also see Brann, *Compunctious Poet*, 73.
63. An allusion to the Song of Songs 6:11. My translation.
64. Lines 468–480. My translation.
65. The epithet Ibn Shabbetai uses to describe Ayyala, "the hind let loose from the garden of Eden," is also significant in the Judeo-Andalusi literary tradition, and, as Raymond Scheindlin has shown, is an allusion to Deuteronomy where the term refers to non-Jewish women taken as war captives. See Scheindlin, *Wine*, 94. This description of Ayyala would have particularly resonated within the Jewish communities of medieval Iberia, many of whose members had adopted and maintained the sexual mores of al-Andalus, including the possession of singing slave women, even after the Reconquest and while living among the Christians of Iberia.
66. Prominent Jews played an important part in its existence, being central in the sexual slave trade, exporting Muslim boys and girls to the north, and Christian boys and girls to the south to satisfy the sexual appetites of the kingdoms within which they lived. Assis, "Sexual Behaviour" 37–38; and Eisenberg, "Juan Ruiz's Heterosexual 'Good Love,'" 257–259.
67. Lines 488–489.
68. Examples from Arab poems include those of Bakr ibn Nattāh, "As if she were a splendid day; as if [her hair] were on her a night," and of Yūsuf ibn

Harūn, "you hair is dark like the night; your face is like a dawn." Similarly the Judeo-Andalusi poet Samuel ha-Nagid tells his beloved, "you hit hearts with the light of your face and with hair like darkness." For these and many more examples, see Schippers, *Spanish Hebrew Poetry* 176–178. See also Judah Halevi's poem, "The night the gazelle displayed to me her cheek—the sun—beneath its veil of hair," in Scheindlin, *Wine*, 119.

69. For the "mosaic-style" of medieval Hebrew poetry and prose see Cole, introduction to *Selected Poems*, 13; Hamilton, "*Libro de buen amor*," 20–21.
70. Lines 492–493. The images used in this exchange are commonplaces in medieval Hebrew and Arabic poetry. For Moses ibn Ezra and other examples in Arabic and Hebrew of arrow-shooting eyes see Schippers, *Spanish Hebrew Poetry*, 173–175.
71. Lines 501–502.
72. Lines 504–505.
73. Lines 522–523. My translation. For another example of the long neck see Ibn Gabirol, *Poesía Secular*, 470–471.
74. Lines 525–528.
75. *Wine*, 81.
76. Fuery, *Theories of Desire*, 16. On Lacan's construction of desire see *Ethics of Psychoanalysis*, 12–14.
77. Genesis 2:23.
78. Lines 481–485. My translation.
79. Line 483–484. Ayyala is, like Kozbi, a woman of inheritance (*yerusha*). Zerah claims she has inherited beauty (*yofi*) and intelligence (*sekhel*). See also Tova Rosen's discussion of lady Wisdom (*hokma*) in ben Eleazar's *maqāma* (1233 A.D.). Rosen links female wisdom with the European conception of philosophy: "Wisdom is the Hebrew equivalent of Sophia, the allegorical embodiment of philosophy, the medium through which the human intellect can elevate itself to the impersonal level of the cosmic intellect." *Unveiling Eve*, 99.
80. In this book I am analyzing a particular cultural construction of the bedtrick—the Andalusi—in a select number of literary and social contexts, including the Andalusi, the Iberian, and the Western European. For a comparatist study of the bedtrick from ancient Indian mythology to contemporary American cinema (without, however, a consideration of the Andalusi), see Doniger, *The Bedtrick*.
81. Lines 583–585. My translation.
82. Russo, *Female Grotesque*, 63.
83. Bakhtin, *Rabelais and His World*, 27.
84. Russo, *Female Grotesque*, 8.
85. Lines 630–631. Ritzpah conforms to the prosaic, demanding image of the wife that Rosen compares to the idealized image of the bride in medieval Hebrew poetry and prose. "The wife is not mute as is the courtly lady, nor is her voice comely as is the bride's. The wife's mouth is ceaselessly open—gulping food; demanding money, maids, house utensils" etc. See *Unveiling Eve*, 11.

86. Lines 608–618. My translation.
87. Lines 641–642.
88. See Brann, *Compunctious Poet*, 64–68.
89. The image is from Exodus 21:6. See Scheindlin, "Misogynist," 293, n57.
90. Lines 608–626. The image of Israel being ruled by slaves was not uncommon in Judeo-Andalusi religious poetry. Ibn Gabirol uses a similar image in his *piyyut*. See *Shire ha-Qodesh*, 2:456; and Roth, "Polemic," 162.
91. Ibn Shabbetai's rupture of the narrative frame and inscription of himself as character in his own work also merits special attention in the history of literature as it anticipates literary techniques associated with the sensibilities and techniques considered by literary historians as explicitly modern and reflective of the fractured identity of modern life.
92. Lines 784–785.
93. Vasvári, "Perverted Proverb," 175.
94. See Dishon, "The Sources," 57–73 and "Critical Examination," 99. Dishon points out that al-Harīzī fails to cite many of the authors whose work he used. Despite the fact that he did not acknowledge the *Offering* as a source for the "*Maqāma* of Marriage," al-Harīzī was aware of Ibn Shabbetai and his writings. They may have met in Barcelona, and al-Harīzī referred to Ibn Shabbetai as *Meyan ha-melitzot*, "The Fount of Figurative Language." See Dishon, "Critical Examination," 99.
95. Ezrahite is a patronym for the name Zerah—both are derived from the same Hebrew root, z.r.h.
96. See Segal, "Analysis of the Introduction," 418–421.
97. For a detailed study of al-Harīzī's translation activities see Drory, *Models*, 227–232.
98. Al-Harīzī's translation of al-Harīrī's *Maqāmāt* includes several significant changes of the Arabic text, changes that make the work more understandable in a Jewish cultural context. For a detailed comparison of al-Harīrī's original and al-Harīzī's translation see Lavi, "Comparative Study."
99. "Writing in Hebrew was accompanied by ideological declarations which assigned to Hebrew writing the role of marking a particular collective or ethnic identity, that could be called 'national.'" Drory, *Models*, 231. Other advocates of Hebrew over Arabic include Saadiah Gaon, Maimonides, and Judah Halevi. See Sigel, "Analysis of Introduction," 420–421.
100. Drory, *Models*, 230.
101. This preface is actually the first Hebrew dedication of the work. Drory, *Models*, 218–219. It is this preface that has been included as the introduction in the editions of Reichert and Segal.
102. Al-Harīzī, *Tahkemoni*, 14–15. Two English translations of al-Harīzī's *Tahkemoni* exist: Semha Segal's 2001 English translation, *The Book of Tahkemoni*, and Reichert's 1965 edition. Page numbers given are from Toporovsky's Hebrew edition. Unless otherwise noted translations are Reichert's.
103. Al-Harīzī, *Tahkemoni*, 8.
104. Ibid., 21.

105. Ibid.
106. Ibid., 22.
107. Ibid.
108. Ibid.
109. Among subsequent thirteenth-century Judeo-Andalusi poets in Christian Spain, the comparison of poetry to a beautiful, sexual woman will become commonplace. See Rosen, *Unveiling Eve*, 73–74.
110. Al-Harīzī, *Tahkemoni*, 9–10.
111. Ibid., 8–9.
112. Ibid., 9. Al-Harīzī, Maimonides, and Moses ibn Ezra are working from a set of shared tropes. Moses ibn Ezra, *al-Muḥāḍara*, 1: 243, contrasts eloquent, ornate poetry (*al-biyān*) to naked "stammering" (*al-'ayy*). From a letter of Maimonides addressed to Ibn Tibbon: "Be assured that, when I saw the beauty of your style and remarked the depth of your intellect and that your lips utter knowledge clearly, I greatly rejoiced. I was the more surprised that such should be the talents, such the thirst for knowledge, such the acquaintance with Arabic (which I believe to be a partially corrupt dialect of Hebrew) displayed by one who has been born among 'stammerers.' I also admired your being so well versed in the niceties of that language in abstruse subjects; this is, indeed, like 'a tender plant springing out of a dry ground.'" Maimonides here refers to non-Arab speakers as stammerers. See "Translation of an Epistle," 1: 221. A contemporary of al-Harīzī, Judah Halevi, also calls non-Hebrew speakers "stammerers and stutterers." *Shire ha-Qodesh*, II: 413; Roth, "Polemic," 172.
113. Al-Harīzī, *Tahkemoni*, 9–10.
114. Ibid., 9.
115. Ibid., 11.
116. Ibid., 10.
117. Ibid., 11. Al-Harīzī here takes parts of the biblical text of the Song of Songs in order to describe this erotic encounter. As in the Song of Songs, Hebrew has milk and honey under her tongue, and is a spring of fresh water for her lover (4:11). The honey and milk are also, however, an allusion to Moses ibn Ezra's treatise on Arabized Hebrew poetry, *Kitāb Zahr al-Riyāḍ* (*Sefer ha-Anaq*), in which he "considers poetry as the honey of intelligence and the milk of wisdom." Because they are composed in Hebrew (like the Song of Songs) the author's poems are beautiful. *Sefer ha-Anaq*, chapter 10, poem 5. *Shire ha-Hol*, 1: 395; Schippers, *Spanish Hebrew Poetry*, 302. This is one of several allusions in the *Tahkemoni* to *Sefer ha-Anaq*.
118. Moses ibn Ezra similarly compares poetry to "the beautiful vestments woven by the weavers of poetry" and to jewels, gold, and necklaces. See *Sefer ha-Anaq*, chapter 10, poems 32, 37, 47, *Shire ha-Hol*, 1: 399, 401. Also see Schippers, *Spanish Hebrew Poetry*, 302. Moses ibn Ezra takes this metaphor from the common image of poetry as a necklace in both Judeo-Andalusi poetry and the Arabic tradition where the term *nazm*, meaning "the arrangement of pearls in a necklace" was the same term used to designate the composition of poetry. *Encyclopaedia Islam*, s.v. "*Shi'r*." Rosen,

Unveiling Eve, 66, also discusses Hebrew poets' attitude that the poem must be beautifully decorated with rhetorical ornaments, which they compare to garments and jewels. On poems being given as necklaces and jewels to adorn patrons see Schippers, *Spanish Hebrew Poets*, 303.

119. Al-Harīzī, *Tahkemoni*, 75.
120. The relation between the go-between and the Devil is also found in the Arabic tradition. The late-fourteenth- to early-fifteenth-century Tunisian author, Sheikh al-Nafzawī, whose chapter on procuration (known now only from a translation of a lost original) draws upon a wealth of earlier sources, credits the Devil himself with inventing the profession: "The art of procuration was first revealed to man by the Devil, who—God curse him for it!—is a great seducer of women." See al-Nafzawī, *Glory*, 75, 87–88.
121. Al-Harīzī, *Tahkemoni*, 76.
122. Rosen, *Unveiling Eve*, 14. Moses ibn Ezra, in speaking of the power of poetry to benefit the wise and harm the foolish describes it as a mixture of honey and venom. *Sefer ha-Anaq*, chapter 10, poem 29, and Schippers, *Spanish Hebrew Poetry*, 302.
123. For a discussion of Tevel (Mother Earth) in Judeo-Andalusi poetry see Rosen, *Unveiling Eve*, 14–17. Also see Gate Two of the *Tahkemoni*, in which al-Harīzī includes a lengthy description of Tevel, the "World" whose real name he claims is "Pollution" and who appears as a "bride that adorns herself with jewels," and whose "men of understanding are confused." Al-Harīzī, *Tahkemoni*, 32.
124. Al-Harīzī, *Tahkemoni*, 10–11.
125. Ibid., 75–76.
126. See Schippers, *Spanish Hebrew Poetry*, 80–81, 88–89, 152 for a detailed study of Moses ibn Ezra's *Kitāb Zahr al-Riyād* (*Sefer ha-Anaq*) and its Arabic models.
127. See Schippers, *Spanish Hebrew Poetry*, 153.
128. The image of the fawn breasts is also found in the Song of Songs (7:3), but the fact that since it was later used by Judeo-Andalusi poets and figures in Moses ibn Ezra's treatise on Arabized Hebrew poetry leads me to believe the audience would have recognized it in this context as an allusion to secular Andalusi poetry.
129. Al-Harīzī, *Tahkemoni*, 10.
130. See note 61 above.
131. For the Arabic thinker al-Fārābī, Sitnah's type of rhetorical skill is a base form of argument to be used only "in shaping the theological opinions of the masses." Brann, *Compunctious Poet*, 73.
132. Al-Harīzī, *Tahkemoni*, 76.
133. Ibid., 77–78.
134. Ibid., 78.
135. See Rosen, *Unveiling Eve*, 12–13, who focuses on how this description functions as antithesis of the formulaic description of the ideal bride's beauty.
136. On the usage of Ham among medieval Jewish and Arab authorities see Schorsch, *Jews and Blacks*, 17–35. Several Judeo-Andalusi intellectuals thought

that the curse of Noah fell upon Ham and all his offspring, who were marked by having black skin, supposedly recalling the burning of Ham's skin upon seeing Noah naked. According to this view their skin color reflects the blackness of their souls that "chase after their desires" and "lust for the material" world. Ibid., 27.

137. Al-Harīzī, *Tahkemoni*, 79.
138. Ibid., 80–81.
139. Ibid., 81.
140. *Sefer ha-Anaq*. Chapter 10, poem 1. See Schippers, *Spanish Hebrew Poetry*, 302.
141. Rosen, *Unveiling Eve*, 13.

Chapter 4 Turning Tricks: The Go-Between in Western Europe

1. Translated in Davis, "The Colonial Subject," 263.
2. Hexter, *Ovid and Medieval Schooling*, 2–3. The term *Aetas Ovidiana* (Age of Ovid) was coined by the German classicist Ludwig Traube to designate the twelfth century. In present usage it designates roughly the two centuries, from the middle of the eleventh through the first part of the thirteenth century, during which Ovidian and pseudo-Ovidian works were incorporated into German, French, and English school curriculums. Allen, *Art of Love*, 47; Hexter, "Ovid's Body," 327–328; and Burkard, *Archpriest of Hita*, 13.
3. Among the earliest allusions to *De vetula* are those found in Bacon, *Opus Maius* (1266); Matheolus, *Lamentations* (1295–1301); de Bury, *Philobiblon* (1344); Bradwardine (1290–1349), *De Causa Dei*; and Petrarch, *Epistolae Seniles* (1361). Based on the allusion to the Byzantine ruler Vatatze in the preface, Robathan dates the work to 1250. See Robathan, introduction to *Pseudo-Ovidian* De Vetula, 1–2, 8. Hexter dates the work to sometime between 1222 and 1268. "Ovid in the Middle Ages," 439, n56. For more on the dating of the *De vetula* see Klopsch, *Pseudo-Ovidius*, 78–99.
4. For a summary of the three books of *De Vetula*, see Hexter, "Ovid in the Middle Ages," 441–442.
5. By making this pseudo-Ovid a proto-Christian, the author of *De Vetula* circumvents the admonitions of early church fathers such as Tertullian against the study of pagan authors. See Stroumsa, "Tertullian on Idolatry and the Limits of Tolerance," on Tertullian and later Christian intolerance.
6. See chapter 5 for a more detailed account of Castilian translation movements during the thirteenth century. For evidence of Arabo-Andalusi learning on the European scholastic model see Roy, "Medieval Latin Scholasticism," 22–26; Fakhry, *Averroes*, 129–164 and Hamilton, "*Libro de buen amor*," 25.
7. See chapter 3, n20.

8. The fourteenth-century French translator of the *De Vetula*, Jean le Fèvre, names Richard de Fournival as author. Richard de Fournival was the son of King Philip Augustus's personal physician and was himself trained in medicine. In addition he wrote both lyric poetry and treatises on courtly love, and, after a "dissolute" adolescence, joined the clergy and became chancellor of the cathedral of Amiens. His knowledge of Hebrew literature is not documented; however, what little is known of Richard de Fournival suggests that his lifestyle and educational training in Latin was comparable to that of the Andalusi courtiers in Arabic to the south. See Robathan, introduction to *Pseudo-Ovidian* De Vetula, 7.
9. Ibid.
10. Ibid., 6–10. Klopsch, *Pseudo-Ovidius*, 78–99, also thinks that it is doubtful Fournival is the author.
11. Fournival, *La Biblionomia*, 531–535.
12. Hexter, "Ovid," 416.
13. His patrons included M. Valerius Messalla Corvinus (64 B.C.–A.D. 8), and he married three socially connected women. White, "Ovid," 2–8.
14. Hexter, "Ovid," 416–417.
15. Lines 2: 200–201, 3: 1–18. All citations are to line numbers in Robathan's edition of the Latin original. No English translation of all three books of *De vetula* is currently available. Translation of passages from book 2, lines 202–728, are those of Burkard, *Archpriest of Hita*, 173–186. All other translations are my own. I would like to thank Clinton J. Armstrong for his assistance with the translation of the Latin text.
16. Lines 1: 758–765. This section is also alluded to by the high chancellor and treasurer of England, Richard de Bury in *Philobiblum* (see note 5 above). See Bury, *Love of Books*, 67–68. See Thomas, preface to *Love of Books*, ix–xi, for more on Richard de Bury.
17. Reynolds, "Emergence of Professional Law," discusses the training of lawyers in northern France, as well as prevalent hostility toward them.
18. Lines 1: 780–785.
19. For a discussion of Western European ideas linking Arabic language and knowledge to alchemy see Moran, *Distilling knowledge*; Patai, *Jewish Alchemists*, 98–158; and Vernet, *Lo que Europa debe al Islam*, 264–270.
20. Lines 2: 14–43.
21. Twelfth-century French theologians and thinkers such as Alain de Lille, Gilles de Corbeil, Gautier de Châtillon, and Gautier de Coincy framed their attack of homosexuality in similar grammatical metaphors. See Baldwin, *Language*, 45–46.
22. In this section (lines 20–195) the anonymous author locates *De Vetula* in a thirteenth-century theological-philosophical debate precipitated by the introduction of Aristotle's theories of natural science into Western Europe. Aristotle's single-seed theory ("that only the male emits sperm whereas the female produces no sperm but merely menstrual blood for the formation of the embryo") as translated in the commentaries of Avicenna came into conflict with the Galenic-Hippocratic two-seed theory (that both man and

woman contributed seed to the "generation of the embryo") as expressed in the Latin *Prose Salernitan Questions*. See Baldwin, *Language*, 94. This debate spread among physicians and theologians in early-thirteenth-century England and France and offers one example of how Western sciences and beliefs responded to the new material and ideas being translated from Arabic into Latin. John Baldwin points out that the one- or two-seed debate had great consequences for the larger question of how the West chose to gender the "body into the male and female sex." "Artistotle's one-seed theory opened a radical division between the sexes and proposed the ultimate superiority of the male." Ibid., 94–96. Also see Cadden, *Meanings of Sex Difference*, 13–54. Much of the Aristotelian material reached Europe via Iberia, and Judeo-Andalusi Jews had instrumental roles in this translation activity as discussed in chapter 3. See Vernet, *Lo que Europa debe al Islam*, 170–176.

23. Central among this would be those commentators on that famous eleventh-century *eunuch* or *semiviros*, Peter Abelard. See Ferroul, "Abelard's Blissful Castration," 134–137.
24. Line 2: 36–37.
25. Ibn Shabbetai, *Offering*, lines 374–377. Kozbi's prayer is included in chapter 3.
26. In lines 120–128 the pseudo-Ovid discusses the fact that *spadons* cannot said to be chaste, for chasteness requires suffering and choice, but the *spadons* have no urge so their lack of activity is not a virtue.
27. Lines 2: 112–113.
28. On eunuchs as part of the Mediterranean slave trade see Kathleen Biddick, who points out that, "adult males exchanged from Slavic regions into al-Andalus and the eastern Mediterranean were commonly castrated at port of entry." "Translating," 203.
29. Similarly Peter Abelard recalled that according to the Bible (Leviticus 22:24, Deuteronomy 23:1) eunuchs are "forbidden to enter a church." Ferroul, "Abelard's Castration," 136.
30. Lines 2: 135–139.
31. The comment about investigating the nature of God is particularly striking within the context of twelfth- and thirteenth-century scholastic debates that were beginning to engage with Aristotelian rationalism, as commented by the Andalusi, Ibn Rushd (Averroes), whose theories were banned by the bishop of Paris, Etienne Tempier, during the period of *De Vetula*'s popularity. Fakhry, *Averroes*, 134.
32. Gerson Cohen, "Esau as Symbol," 19–48.
33. Zeitlin, "Origin of the Term Edom," 262–263. Rashi, in fact, takes us back to Kozbi's narrative, Numbers (24:19), interpreting Edom as Rome. In his commentary on Deuteronomy (32:21), he compares Esau to nonbelievers and reads the chapter as a parable for the treatment of the Jews in exile. Rashi, *Torah*. Contemporary Judeo-Andalusi poets also identified Esau/Edom with Christians. In a metaphor for Christian and Arab persecution of Jews, Levi ibn al-Tabbān depicts both Esau and Ishmael as thorns in his side. *Shire Levi ibn al-Tabbān*, 62. And Judah Halevi claims that "Edom has

become a resident in my palace / and the hands of the Arab and Esau reign / And there rules over me." *Shire ha-Qodesh*, II: 352; Roth, "Polemic," 162–164.
34. Lines 2: 196–201.
35. Lines 2: 202–228.
36. Ibid., 238.
37. "You would think that lilies were engaged in a struggle with roses: the rose red and the snow white combine to form one color, but in such a way that the red is overcome by the white." Lines 2: 281–283.
38. Ibid., 243–306.
39. The discussion of *spadons* that segues into the go-between tale with its uber-heterosexual paradigm were part of a larger French scholastic debate on homosexuality in the thirteenth century (See Baldwin, *Language*, 45–46) and suggest that the *De Vetula* author not only wants to guide clerics away from the path of lawyers and eunuchs, but also the unmentioned Sodomite that seems to be lurking behind this text (just as it seems to be hiding in the idyllic homosocial Eden of Zerah in the *Offering*).
40. She has a forehead whiter than ivory like the countenance of the bride promised to Heber, which was described as so brilliant that it could light the way at night. Like Ayyala in the *Offering*, this woman's brows are curved. This woman has bright eyes, recalling the Christian-cupbearer's eyes that ignited a conflagration in al-Saraqusti's "*Maqāma* 9," as well as the exciting gazelle eyes of Ayyala and Heber's would be bride. This woman's cheeks are compared to red roses and white lilies and her lips are said to resemble cherries. These metaphors recall those of the *Offering* in which Ayyala and Zerah's cheeks are described as *shoshanim*, the Hebrew term used for both lilies and roses. Ayyala also comments on Zerah's scarlet, bloodstained cheeks and lips. In *De Vetula* the woman's teeth are described as small, straight, well ordered, and brighter than silver, which recalls Sitnah's description of the ideal woman, who has rows of teeth like sapphires, as well as the slave woman in "*Maqāma* 12," who has teeth "fair as hailstones." Lastly this woman's white, unblemished neck recalls Ayyala's, described as the neck of the graceful gazelle, "like an ivory column" that Zerah is afraid of blemishing.
41. See Vinsauf, *Poetria Nova*, 36–38. Also see Baldwin, *Language*, 98–99. For a discussion of the important slippages between *De Vetula* and French and Latin rhetorical models as well as a discussion of parallel Arabic poetic manuals and descriptive canons see Hamilton, "Rereading the Widow."
42. Lines 2: 318–328.
43. This woman has small, firm, curvaceous breasts: the slave woman groped by al-Sā'ib had breasts like apples. Here her torso is slender: the slave woman had a narrow, taught waist. This woman has full, graceful loins and a modest, but ample rump: the slave woman's rear was "broad as spreading sand-dunes" and flanks that "swayed from side to side."
44. Lines 2: 500–514.
45. On concubinage, see Brundage, *Law, Sex and Christian Society*, 145–150. The reform of clerical practices goes back at least two centuries before the

NOTES 177

Fourth Lateran Council of 1215 and is a major concern of eleventh-century reformers such as Bishop Ivo of Chartres (1091–1116) who sought to abolish clerical marriage and concubinage. Ibid., 175–183. The Fourth Lateran Council was the culmination of a series of previous councils and decrees attacking clerical marriage and concubinage issued over the course of the twelfth century. Ibid., 220–221.

46. Parallels in the descriptions of the exchanged old women in the three works include: the skin bag, which in *De Vetula* is used to describe the woman's breast (line 505) and in the *Offering* Ritzpah's swollen lips; hard legs, which in Gate Six describe the legs of the old woman which are compared to tree stumps and in *De Vetula* to diamonds; and the hard, wrinkled stomach that for the she-ghoul is a pit and cave, and for the old woman of *De Vetula* is like land furrowed by a plow.

47. Lines 2: 530–547.

48. For more on Petrus Alfonsi see Menocal, *Ornament of the World*, 147–157; Lacarra, *Pedro Alfonso*. On Alfonso de Valladolid see Chazan, "Undermining the Jewish Sense of Future," 186–189; Baer, *History of the Jews*, 1: 327–354.

49. Foucault, *History of Sexuality*, 24–27, posits the eighteenth century as the period during which the need to classify and categorize sex and gender became institutionalized in the West; whereas *De Vetula* reveals that already in the thirteenth century ecclesiastical culture is attempting to categorize Andalusi desire and the sexual behaviors to which it leads as Other. In the Andalusi and Arab courts both men and women were suitable objects of desire, and theoretically there is no distinction between hetero- and homosexual desires. In Ibn Hazm's treatise, *The Dove's Neck Ring*, there are numerous examples of same-sex male love. *De Vetula* reveals an anxiety about homosexual desire, a desire only hinted at in Ibn Shabbetai's thirteenth-century narrative, but which is underscored as part of the go-between and protagonist's way of life in *De Vetula*.

50. Line 3: 15.

51. See Hutcheson, "Sodomitic Moor"; Boswell, *Christianity*, 198–199.

Chapter 5   Representing Others in the *Libro de buen amor*

1. Subsequently I refer to the *Libro de buen amor* with the abbreviation *LBA*. I have chosen to retain the title given to the work by Ramón Menéndez Pidal, based on the author-narrator's claim in stanza 933b to have given the work this title out of love for his go-between. See "Título que el Arcipreste de Hita dio al libro de sus poesías," 139–145.

2. Translations (except where noted) are those of Raymond S. Willis, *Libro de buen amor*. Stanza numbers correspond to G.B. Gybbon-Monnypenny's edition of the *Libro de buen amor*. The epigraph includes a slightly modified version of Saralyn Daly's translation of stanza 1519, *Book of Good Love*.

3. The series of studies on the author of the *LBA* over the last thirty years has yet to prove beyond the shadow of a doubt the identity of Juan Ruiz.

The possible candidates include Juan Ruiz de Cisneros, any one of a number of Juan Ruizes professionally active between 1380 and 1382 found in archival sources by Ansgar Kelley, "Juan Ruiz Directory" and "Juan Ruiz and Archpriests: Novel Reports," and the *madrileño* named Juan Ruiz who served as witness to a 1330 document found by Francisco Hernández, "Juan Ruiz" and "Venerable." On Juan Ruiz de Cisneros, see Emilio Sáez and José Trenchs, "Juan Ruiz de Cisneros," and Francisco Márquez Villanueva, "Nueva biografía." Because the name Juan Ruiz "is embedded in the work in rhyme position," Louise Vasvári considers it a joke. See "Non ha mala palabra," 173, n2. For a detailed discussion of the critical debate concerning the authorship of the *LBA* see Haywood, "Juan Ruiz," 24–25.
4. Ansgar Kelley favors a later date, sometime in the 1380s. See "Juan Ruiz Directory." For a detailed discussion of the critical debate regarding the date of the *LBA* see Haywood, "Juan Ruiz," 22–24.
5. Louise M. Haywood also includes a detailed discussion of the major theoretical approaches to the autobiography of the *LBA*, including: Américo Castro and María Rosa Lida de Malkiel's assertion that it derives from the Semitic *maqāmāt*; Gybbon-Monypenny's assertion that it pertains to the pan-European genre of erotic autobiography; and Michael Gerli, Marina Brownlee, and André Michalski's that the autobiography of the *LBA* derives from Augustine's *Confessions*. See Haywood, "Juan Ruiz," 26–29. For a detailed comparison of the Castro-Lida de Malkiel theory and the Augustine theories of Gerli, Brownlee, and Michalski see Hamilton, "*Libro de buen amor*," 20–25.
6. James T. Monroe compares the unreliable narration of the *LBA* with that of the Arab *maqāmāt* in *Art of Badi' az-Zamān al-Hamadhānī*, 20, 40–46.
7. Castro, *España en su historia*, 355–446. Castro designates the *LBA*'s indebtedness to Andalusi literary and cultural models as *mudejarismo*. He again addresses Arabic influence on the *LBA* in 1954 with *La realidad histórica de España*. The influence of the Arabic *maqāmāt* on the *LBA* was first suggested by the Arabist Francisco Fernández y González in 1894. Other studies relating the *LBA* and the Andalusi traditions of Iberia include, Juan Martínez Ruiz, "La tradición hispano-árabe en el *Libro de buen amor*," and Joaquina Albarracín Navarro, "El vestido y adorno hispanoárabes," 488–494.
8. See Castro, *España en su historia*, 370. A.R. Nykl's edition and translation of *Tawq al-hamāma* came out in 1931.
9. Sánchez Albornoz, *España: Un enigma histórico*, 1: 202–226 and Gybbon-Monypenny, "Autobiography in the *LBA*," 64.
10. For a comparison of Sánchez Albornoz and Castro's approaches to Spanish history see Glick, *Islamic and Christian Spain*, 7–8 and Hillgarth, "Spanish Historiography," 23–37.
11. See Lida de Malkiel, *Two Spanish Masterpieces* and "Nuevas notas para la interpretación del *Libro de buen amor*."
12. See, for example, Rico, "Sobre el origen," 302, n2.
13. Márquez Villanueva, *Orígenes y sociología del tema celestinesco*, 88–104 and Rouhi, *Mediation and Love*.

NOTES

14. See recent studies by Burkard, *Archpriest of Hita*; Morros, "La comedia elegiaca"; and Montaner Frutos, "Las señales non çiertas." For further discussion of the recent tendency away from the Arabic and Hebrew roots of the *LBA*, see Hamilton, "Rereading the Widow."
15. See Drory, "*Maqāma*," 191–195, and Moreh, *Live Theatre*, 108–109.
16. In all likelihood the *maqāmāt* originate in early medieval Arabic *hikāya* ("a play performed by actors, sometimes dressed in accordance with the requirements of the 'dramatis personae' and sometimes using props as well"). The *maqāmāt* are, in fact, the cousin of the popular medieval shadow drama, works composed in dialectical Arabic whose existence in medieval Iberia is testified to by Ibn Hazm, but of which no actual text remains. Moreh, *Live Theater*, 124.
17. Drory, "*Maqāma*," 190.
18. For a history of scholarship on the Reconquest see O'Callaghan, *Reconquest and Crusade* and Linehan, *History and the Historians*, 205–208. Linehan favors a traditional interpretation of the Reconquest as a "religious quest for national unity," 205. Also see Payne, *History of Spain*, 1: 55–75, 134–137, who compares the Reconquest and the crusades of Western Europe and who reviews scholarship through 1973. Payne claims, "Almost from the beginning, Leonese-Castilian society was marked by a degree of religious identification unknown in France or Italy, but the impulse to reconquest by Christian society was not synonymous with a crusading desire either to convert or to exterminate the infidel," 136. Despite the possible religious motivations/pretexts for the Reconquest, Castilian monarchs did adopt Andalusi-style customs. Alfonso VI, "king of the three religions," was the first of many Castilian kings to prefer Arab-style garments and to take Arabized lovers. Ibid., 1: 136–137. Whether because they personally admired the Andalusi lifestyle or were simply catering to their Andalusi subjects, the fact that they adopted such customs acknowledges the cultural prestige such traditions held for Hispano-Roman Christians.
19. On Andalusi culture as the culture of prestige not just in Castile but also among the intellectuals of Western Europe, see Menocal, *Ornament of the World*, 176–190.
20. Payne, *History of Spain*, 1: 137.
21. The Castilian vernacular term *mozárabe* was used to distinguish Arabized Iberian Christians from the Hispano-Roman Christians of northern Iberia who did not live under Muslim rule. Although the term *mozárabe* derives from the Arabic, *musta'rib*, "Arabized," it is only found in Christian sources after the tenth century referring pejoratively to Arabized Christians living in Iberia, especially in Toledo. Mikel de Espalza makes a distinction between Mozarabs, Andalusi Christians of Visigothic origin "descended from the Christian inhabitants of the pre-Islamic Iberian Peninsula," and what he defines as "neo-Mozarabs," Christians from the Near East and Europe who settled in al-Andalus before the Reconquest, and "converted Mozarabs," those Andalusi Muslims "who converted to Christianity following the conquest of Toledo." See Espalza, "Mozarabs: An Emblematic Christian Spain," 149–151. Also see Rincón Álvarez, *Mozárabes y mozarabías*, 15–16.

The term itself, though, refers equally to any of these Arabized Christians, and attempts to distinguish certain groups of Mozarabs from others based on ethnic origin, although perhaps important in the discourse of Spanish nationalism, is less important for this study, in which the Arabized Christian community of Toledo and its environs, formed a culturally and socially distinct group from the invading northern Christians of the Reconquest. Though evidence regarding the Mozarabic communities of Iberia is relatively sparse, as Espalza points out, they have been tremendously important in Spanish historiography. The Mozarab community of al-Andalus was a crucial pretext used by both medieval Christian kings and subsequent Spanish historians to establish the political and social legitimacy of the Reconquest. See Espalza, "Mozarabs," 162–163.

22. Criado de Val, "La tierra de Hita," 447–449. The majority of inhabitants of Hita were Muslims, but by the eleventh century the Mozarab nobles were strong enough (or at least were perceived/remembered as being strong enough) to raid the neighboring Muslim town against the wishes of Alfonso VI—an event recorded in Berceo's *Vida de Santo Domingo*. See Criado de Val, "La tierra de Hita," 452. The monastery of Sopetrán, the most important ecclesiastical site in Hita, is emblematic of the region's importance not only as a mixture of religions and ethnic groups, but also as a center of identity (trans)formation. Until the late fourteenth century Sopetrán remained under the control of the see of Toledo and maintained the Mozarab character of the community among the regular clerics who lived there. After passing to the Benedictines the traditional Mozarab images were replaced by Flemish ones. Ibid., 454.
23. Pastor de Togneri, *Del Islam*, 108 and Linehan, *History and the Historians*, 209–221. After the *taifa* kingdom of Toledo was conquered by Alfonso VI in 1085, poorer Mozarabs were gradually disenfranchised by Frankish and Hispano-Roman Christians who bought their lands and took important ecclesiastical and political positions from them.
24. Pastor de Togneri, *Del Islam*, 111.
25. Ibid., 109.
26. Linehan, *History and the Historians*, 219.
27. Pastor de Togneri, *Del Islam*, 116.
28. Linehan, *History and the Historians*, 220.
29. Ibid., 224.
30. Pastor de Togneri, *Del Islam*, 107, and Linehan, *History and the Historians*, 226.
31. See Pastor de Togneri, *Del Islam*, 117 and Rivera Recio, *La Iglesia de Toledo*, 1: 209.
32. Linehan, *History and the Historians*, 227, and Pastor de Togneri, *Del Islam*, 118.
33. Linehan, *History and the Historians*, 251–252.
34. Teófilo Ruiz, *From Heaven to Earth*, 8.
35. Chazan, "Undermining the Jewish Sense of Future," 179.
36. Ibid., 187–190.
37. Tolan, *Saracens*, 171–274. Also see Payne, *History of Spain*, 137.
38. Tolan, *Saracens*, 172–173.

39. This despite the fact that the pluralistic cultural model he cultivated served his own imperialist Christian agenda. Tolan, *Saracens*, 186–187.
40. Burnett, "The Translating Activity in Medieval Spain," 2: 1036–1058, and Glick, *Islamic and Christian Spain*, 257–258.
41. Pastor de Togneri, *Del Islam*, 119. Several of their translations focused on Aristotelian philosophy, including Arab philosophers and exegetes such as al-Fārābī, Ibn Sīnā, and al-Ghazālī, as well as Jewish commentators such as Ibn Gabirol. Books from all over the Arab Empire were brought to Toledo and some of the most important medical and philosophical texts of the Classical and Arab world were made available for the first time in Latin. The Aristotelian material would transform Christianity and Western Europe. See Burnett, "Translating Activity," 2: 1045–1046.
42. Alfonso X clearly respected and emulated Andalusi learning and culture— so much so that his critics eventually disparaged him as being too taken with Arab learning. See Gómez Redondo, *Historia de la prosa*, 1: 860–863. For Toledan cultural activity between these two periods of intense translation activity see Pick, *Conflict and Coexistence*, 110–120.
43. Glick, *Islamic and Christian Spain*, 258. Jews found themselves as true go-betweens mediating between Arabic and Christian European cultures: "The place of Jews in this scheme is obvious: Jewish men were trilingual, knowing Hebrew, Arabic, and a romance language. Jews had indeed been accustomed to translate from Arabic into Hebrew, not a difficult task, given the linguistic and semantic similarities between the two languages, or to write in Judeo-Arabic. In the latter case, they were able to create a flexible medium for scientific and philosophical expression. This fitted them ideally for the work of translation, which involved the creation in the vernacular and in Latin of virtually an entire new scientific language," 258. Also see Márquez Villanueva, "Nueva visión," 125.
44. On translation and the construction of national identities and representations of the Other, see Venuti, *Scandals of Translation*, 67.
45. Alfonso admired and respected Arab learning and in addition to the source material for his encyclopedic histories, he had "texts on magic, the science of the stars, entertaining stories, and games (including chess, draughts, and backgammon)" translated. See Burnett, "Translating Activity," 1047.
46. In their efforts to forge a Castilian cultural identity, Alfonso and his translators exploit what Laurence Venuti has termed the scandalous nature of translation, that is, the domestication of the translated material by shaping it to meet domestic sociopolitical needs. This process entails, among other modifications, the selective translation of only certain works or genres in the original language. See Venuti, *The Scandals of Translation*, 67: "The selection of foreign texts and the development of translation strategies can establish peculiarly domestic canons for foreign literatures, canons that conform to domestic aesthetic values and therefore reveal exclusions and admissions, centers and peripheries that deviate from those current in the foreign language."
47. Translating those (poetic) works in which Muslim Andalusi rulers asserted their political legitimacy would run counter to Alfonso's cultural goal of

establishing that there "can be no legitimate non-Christian polity in Spain." Tolan, *Saracens*, 187.
48. A trend continued by his successors until well after the conquest of the Americas, an event that, like the Reconquest, would once again force Spanish historiography to confront and assimilate the Other.
49. See both Tolan, *Saracens*, 187–190, and Gómez Redondo *Historia de la prosa* 1: 643–795 for detailed studies of the Alfonsine histories and their ideological function.
50. Gómez Redondo, *Historia de la prosa*, 1: 181.
51. Ibid., 1: 182.
52. Ibid., 1: 182–183, 189–192.
53. Ibid., 1: 197–198.
54. Alfonso did establish a school of translators in Toledo, but he preferred the more secularized Arabized city of Seville, where he spent the majority of his time. Linehan, *History and the Historians*, 419–421. Sancho, however, establishes his court in Toledo. Ibid., 447. Clerical criticism of Alfonso X's policies can be found in the courtly literature produced under his estranged son, Sancho IV. O'Callaghan, *Cortes of Castile-León*, 7, mentions a series of late-thirteenth- to early-fourteenth-century courtly treatises that "contain interesting comments on royal policy and the king's relations with his subjects." These include a treatise critical of Alfonso X, the *Liber de preconiis Hispaniae*, written by the courtier-cleric and tutor Gil de Zamora for the young infante Sancho.
55. On the career of Gonzalo Pérez Gudiel, "toledano extraordinario," see Linehan, *History and the Historians*, 448–459. He is given the most important of court offices, *canciller mayor* of Castile and establishes his own ecclesiastical lineage—having his nephews appointed to key clerical positions in Castile in order to further his ideological agenda. Gómez Redondo, *Historia de la prosa*, 1: 860–861; Germán Orduna, "La élite intelectual," 56.
56. Orduna, "La élite intelectual," 56.
57. David Flory discusses how the social use of religious literature focusing especially on Marian tales in thirteenth-century Western Europe corresponds to cultural and political crisis within the church and focuses on the literature as part of a reactionary reform. "Social Uses of Religious Literature," 61–62.
58. On the relationship between Sancho and María de Molina, see Linehan, *History and the Historians*, 447: "Sancho's marriage to her [María de Molina] in 1282 had been incestuous as well as bigamous, in addition to which she was his bastard daughter's godmother: as blatantly uncanonical a union as could be imagined."
59. Gómez Redondo, *Historia de la prosa*, 1: 861–862. The political realities of Sancho's reign paint a very different picture than the cultural model espoused by his court. Despite the image he hoped to convey of himself as loyal Christian knight, divorced from the Andalusi cultural model his father had accommodated to his imperial interests, in the administration of his own realm and in trying to maintain the peace, Sancho did negotiate with the Muslim kings of Iberia—even allying with them if it served his needs,

as, for example, in 1292 when he joined the Nasrid ruler of Granada, Muhammed II, in fighting their mutual enemy, the Merinids of North Africa. Kennedy, *Muslim Spain*, 284. His defeat of Tarifa, taken with the assistance of the Nasrids, was the high point of Sancho's reign, and portrayed as such in the chronicles. See Torres Delgado, *El antiguo reino nazarí*, 207–208. Similarly, as both his father Alfonso X had done, and his son, Fernando IV would do, Sancho IV employed Jews as trusted members of the royal household—personal physicians, secretaries, diplomats, and increasingly as financial administrators. For the Jews in Sancho IV's and Fernando IV's courts see Baer, *History of the Jews*, 130–133, 307–309; and Hillgarth *The Spanish Kingdoms* 1: 296, 346. The Jews in Sancho's court include Abraham el Barchilon, Abraham ibn Shoshan, and Todros ben Judah Halevi.

60. The major literary works of Sancho's reign (four major sapiential treatises, the continuation of his father's chronicles, and a few works difficult to classify, including *Barlaam e Josafat*) subject the Alfonsine cultural model to the conceptual models of the cathedral school of Toledo that clearly stress orthodox Christian faith over philosophical debates. See Gómez Redondo, *Historia de la prosa*, 1: 897–911. The *Libro de los castigos* is less a courtly etiquette guide and more a religious one designed for the safekeeping of Sancho's son, Fernando's soul. In it Sancho is portrayed as a good and legitimate king, one favored by God himself, intent on doing God's work on earth. *Historia de la prosa*, 1: 890–891, 913–923.

61. Gómez Redondo and Linehan both question the identification of the author of this work, Maestre Pedro, with Pedro Gómez Barroso. Gómez Redondo, *Historia de la prosa*, 1: 944–945 and Linehan, *History and the Historians*, 532–533.

62. Gómez Redondo, *Historia de la prosa*, 1: 951–952.

63. Ibid., 1: 958–959. For a discussion of how the Castilian and an earlier Judeo-Iberian Hebrew translation of the go-between *exemplum* of *Calila wa Dimna* offer differing versions of literary acculturation, see Girón-Negrón, "How the Go-Between Cut Her Nose," 231–259.

64. Gómez Redondo, *Historia de la prosa*, 1: 958: "En esta corte se crea la necesidad de contar, pero sobre todo la de oír 'exemplos' para sacar de ellos unas pautas morales de comportamiento."

65. Serés, prologue to *El Conde Lucanor*, l.

66. Romera Castillo, "Presuposiciones." David Flory defines the Marian tale as derived from the *exempla*, but having a different referent, namely the Christian concept of Mary as intercessor. "Social Uses," 65.

67. The literary production of Fernando IV's and Alfonso XI's courts, chiefly in the chronicles and fictional romances, reflect the *molinista* political ideals of putting God before all else, doing good works, and following one's moral compass. Gómez Redondo posits that María de Molina turned to fiction during this period in an attempt to articulate the *molinista* ideology that had previously been expressed in chronicles and wisdom literature because the latter genres had now become the domain of rivals of the crown (the nobles and courtiers like Juan Manuel with their own political agendas). María de

Molina found an alternate mouthpiece for the royal ideology in the nascent Castilian fiction, which was heavily influenced by Christian European Romances of chivalry. *Historia de la prosa*, 2: 1225–1226.

68. Fernando IV assumed the throne at nine years old. An indication of the disorder and turmoil present in the court is the fact that upon becoming king, Fernando was obliged at the *Cortes* de Valladolid in 1295 to "dismiss all the officials of the Royal Household." One of the major architects of the new courtly ideology, however, cannot be dismissed: the Queen Mother María stays on as regent and selects tutors for the young king. Fernando's legitimacy as king is called into question, not only because of his parents' consanguinity, but also because of the claims of Alfonso de la Cerda—Alfonso el Sabio's grandson. Hillgarth, *Spanish Kingdoms*, 1: 312–316. After the twenty-eight-year-old Fernando IV dies, his one-year-old son, Alfonso XI, becomes king in 1312. María served as co-regent first with Sancho's brother Juan, then, after his death, with three men: Sancho's son, Juan, her other son, Felipe, and Alfonso el Sabio's nephew, contemporary of Juan Ruiz and author of the *Conde Lucanor*, Juan Manuel (1282–1348). The sharp divisions between the different royal factions result in a period of turmoil and civil unrest that lasted until after María's death in 1321, after which Castile quickly fell into anarchy. See O'Callaghan, *Cortes*, 93. At fourteen Alfonso XI assumed the throne and began to try and put the kingdom back together. This involved reorganizing his court and killing his former regent, Juan, whom he felt was a potential threat to his authority and legitimacy as king. See Hillgarth, *Spanish Kingdoms*, 1: 338. He thwarted Juan Manuel's royal ambitions through a series of court intrigues. Under Alfonso XI the court contimued to be a potentially treacherous and deadly place for the would-be courtier.

69. Gómez Redondo, *Historia de la prosa*, 2: 1375. For a detailed analysis of how the *Libro del caballero Zifar* corresponds to the historical situation facing Fernando IV see Linehan, *History and the Historians*, 535–548.

70. Gómez Redondo, *Historia de la prosa*, 2: 1439–1457 and Rucquoi and Bizzarri, "Espejos de Príncipes."

71. Moxó, "La promoción política y social de los 'letrados,'" 5–29.

72. Gómez Redondo, *Historia de la prosa*, 1: 1105–1107.

73. Though he may have advocated the Christian agenda of the *molinistas* in his own literary production, Juan Manuel forges his own unique version of the Castilian courtly idea based on his own noble lineage, part of which was the glory of the Andalusi cultural past. He upholds the Christian crusading duty of fighting Muslims in his literary work, but his own practical politics sometimes belied this belief, as, for example, when he allied with Muslim Granada against Alfonso XI. Hillgarth, *Spanish Kingdoms*, 1: 222.

74. In the terminology outlined by Robinson and Rouhi in *Under the Influence*, 3–6, Juan Ruiz uses a "top" form (prose of the *mester de clerecía* and *exempla*) for "bottom" material (fictional love)—thus exploding the nature of each.

75. Vasvári "Non ha mala palabra," 173–174.

NOTES 185

76. "Mester traigo fermoso, non es de joglaría, / mester es sin pecado, ca es de clerezía / fablar curso rimado por la quaderna vía, / a sílabas contadas, ca es grant maestría" *Libro de Alexandre*, stanza 2.
77. Berceo, in fact, in the *Vida de Santo Domingo*, describes his own *mester de clerecía* as prose expressed in the vernacular: "Quiero fer una prosa en roman paladino, / en cual suele el pueblo fablar con so vezino" 2ab. Also see Gómez Redondo, *Poesía española*, 17.
78. Walsh, "Juan Ruiz and the *mester de clerezía*," 62, reads the *LBA* as being a substantial parody of "the *mester de clerecía* and the later cycle of moral poems composed in *quaderna vía*." Juan Ruiz distinguished his *mester de clerecía* from that of other Castilian authors not only in the nature of the thematic material he treats, but also by opening up the very form itself to a variety of meters and elaborate rhymes. Juan Ruiz himself hints at the ways his text differs from others composed in the same meter, using a variety of poetic terms, including even *juglaría* (considered until recently the secular popular verse of Iberian *juglares* that stood in stark contrast to the learned *clerecía*), to designate the work and its meters. See Bayo, "La versificación," 199 and Ekman, "Leçión e muestra de metrificar," 13. For Bayo, the work's *mester de clerecía*, which freely combines hemistiches of seven and eight syllables, can only be understood metrically in the context of the other genres and poetic styles incorporated into the work. See "versificación," 199.
79. Juan Ruiz states that he wants to introduce Castilian Romance-speaking authors to novel forms of poetic composition: "the poem was composed because of many evils and harm / that men and women bring upon each other with their / deceit, and to show extraordinary verse and tales (sinples fablas e versos estraños) to ordinary folk," 1634bcd. These foreign verses may indicate not only the lyric—the *zajal*—but also the use of the *mester de clerecía* as rhymed prose vehicle for the *maqāma*-like narration. Poetry, the traditional vehicle of love in the Andalusi tradition, is relegated to a minor position and used mostly for burlesque satire or formulaic devotional pieces.
80. Recent studies of the *exempla* used in the *LBA* include, Taylor, "*Exempla* and Proverbs," 83–104, which focuses on the original sources; Morreale, "La fábula en la Edad Media," 209–238, which focuses on the scholastic origins of the *exempla*; and Darbord and Valle Videla, "Réflexion sur le technique de l'*exemplum*," 99–113, which focuses on the types of and terminology used to designate the *exempla*. Early studies on the *exempla* in the *LBA* include Lecoy, *Recherches sur le* Libro de buen amor, 113–171; and Michael, "The Function of the Popular Tale," 177–218.
81. For a summary of scholarship on the prose prologue before 1970, see Deyermond, "Some Aspects of Parody," 56–57. For a discussion and summary of recent critical opinions regarding the prose prologue's importance in elucidating the author's intent see Hamilton, "*Libro de buen amor*," 20–25.
82. For a study of the gestures in the *LBA* see Walsh, "Gestures and Voices in the *LBA*," who asserts that the work was written "with performance in mind."

83. The entire episode of the Greeks and the Romans centers on understanding (*entendimiento*) and the mediation of meaning that is at the heart of interpretation. See Gerli, "The Greeks, the Romans, and the Ambiguity of Signs," 411–428, and De Looze, "To Understand Perfectly," 143–145. The author-narrator tells the reader to understand and meditate upon the lessons of the work he/she is reading: "Entiende bien mis dichos e piensa la sentencia; / non me contesca con tigo commo al doctor de Greçia" (46ab). He does not want the *LBA* to be misunderstood the way the Greeks and their knowledge are misunderstood by the Romans. The radical breakdown in communication in the episode of the Greeks and Romans reveals the arbitrariness of all interpretation and points the reader away from the hope of finding universal truths in the text. The episode also particularly points to the unreliability of reconstructing the meaning of inherited authorities—basically the unreliability of the scholastic method.

84. I have adapted Willis's translation of this passage. Willis translates *puntares* as "point," whereas I have given the two meanings Juan Ruiz is playing with here: to play a musical instrument and to punctuate a text.

85. The three surviving manuscripts do not include these poems. Whether the exclusion of the poems originates with the original author or with subsequent copyists does not affect my argument that the *LBA* reflects a moment in which prose sapiential forms like the *exempla* and the proverb had replaced the erotic lyric as the discourse of political legitimacy used both by the royal and ecclesiastical courts. Fourteenth-century copyists could have deemed the poetry unimportant (testifying to its marginalization as a courtly/learned discourse) and deemed it unnecessary, while privileging the prose forms of the *LBA* as those most relevant as discourses of legitimacy. Lawrence, "*Libro de buen amor*: From Script to Print," 46, thinks the poetry, which may have been "inserted in the *registro* on unbound sheets," was accidentally lost. Their loss is, for Lawrence, serious because "[t]hey were the kernel out of which the narrative was created and, as the preserved examples show, they also explained, commented on, or subverted the concomitant episodes." It is difficult for me to believe that the copyists of all three surviving manuscripts would choose to exclude the poetry (or write it on loose folios) if it had survived in the manuscripts they are copying.

86. This is an Aesopic fable, but Juan Ruiz may have known it from the Arab tradition. See Lecoy, *Recherches*, 146–148. Gybbon-Monnypenny, *LBA*, 126, nn82–89, indicates it is not part of the medieval Latin *Phaedrus*. Taylor, "*Exempla* and Proverbs," 101, classifies it as Aesopic but does not identify the source.

87. See Deyermond, "Was It a Vision or a Waking Dream?" 107–122, who interprets the episode of Amor as a dream vision.

88. For Castro, *España en su historia*, 395, the description of the ideal woman corresponds to a combination of Latin and Andalusi poetic models. Alonso, "La bella de Juan Ruiz," 93–94, suggests erotological treatises such as those of the twelfth- and late-thirteenth-century Tunisian authors al-Tīfāshī and al-Tīshānī as the original inspiration for Juan Ruiz. Rico, "Sobre el origen,"

317, and Morros, "Comedia Elegiaca," 85–92, on the other hand, attempt to explain the ideal description of the beautiful woman in light of the pseudo-Ovidian *De Vetula* and other medieval Latin poetic models. For a detailed rebuttal of their arguments see Hamilton, "Rereading the Widow."

89. See Castro, *España en su historia*, 436–445, and Rouhi, *Mediation and Love*.
90. For a study of the sexual discourse in the Pitas Payas story, see Vasvári, "Festive Phallic Discourse," 103–104.
91. In a cynical subversion of the eye-witness testimonial, Amor claims that in the papal court money has the power to make truth into lies and vice-versa (494). Money, like fiction, destabilizes the legitimacy of the church. If even the highest members of the clergy can be ignorant *necios* who have only been given their positions because of money, then their authority as spiritual and intellectual leaders is illegitimate.
92. The pseudo-Ovidian *Pamphilus* was one of the best-read and popular works of the Middle Ages. See Hexter, "Ovid's Body," 327–328, and Burkard, *Archpriest of Hita*, 13.
93. Studies analyzing the similarities and differences in imagery of the *LBA* and *Pamphilus* imagery include Phillips, *The Imagery of the* Libro de buen amor, and Seidenspinner-Núñez, *The Allegory of Good Love*.
94. I have modified Willis's translation of "en uno casados son." He has "joined together [in concubinage]," with his hesitation clearly indicated by the square brackets. I have translated "casados" with its most common and ubiquitous meaning, "married."
95. Debate about the extent to which the Endrina episode follows the *Pamphilus* gravitates between those who assert the episode is a translation with certain emmendations or interpolations to those who claim a more impressionistic adaptation of the pseudo-Ovidian material. Whereas Gybbon-Monypenny advocates the episode is a translation, a review of his verse-by-verse comparison reveals the great number of verses modified, amplified, glossed, added, or interpolated (i.e., that vary from the Latin in significant ways) by Juan Ruiz. See Gybbon-Monypenny, *LBA*, 225, n574–292, n891. Critics such as Francisco Rico and Bienvenido Morros have gone to the *De vetula* in search of another pseudo-Ovidian source for the additional material in the Endrina episode not found in the *Pamphilus*. See Rico, "Sobre el origen," 317–322, and Morros, "La comedia elegiaca," 85–92. As discussed in chapter 4, *De Vetula* itself may derive from the Iberian *maqāmāt* tradition. Despite its possible Andalusi origins, it falls short as an explanation of the development and expanded role of the go-between in the *LBA*. See Hamilton, "Rereading the Widow."
96. Gybbon-Monypenny, *LBA*, 250, n697.
97. Endrina's widowhood has been the object of much critical attention. Louise Vasvári, Louise Mirrer, and Juan Carlos Ramírez Pimienta suggest that Juan Ruiz chose to make Endrina a widow in order to underscore her libidinous nature and social independence; Francisco Rico considers Endrina's marital status as proof of the influence of the pseudo-Ovidian *De Vetula*. Mirrer, "The Widow and the Text," 120–135; Vasvári, "Why Is doña Endrina a

Widow," 259–287; Ramírez Pimienta, "La aventura de doña Endrina y don Melón," 177; Rico, "Sobre el Origin," 320–321. Despite Rico's claim, Endrina's widowhood does not, in my opinion, reflect the influence of *De Vetula*, given that in the *De Vetula* when the protagonist falls in love and woos the beloved she is a young virgin. Only several years later after her husband has died does she return to town and the protagonist again takes up with her, including a discussion of how her body has aged.

98. See Vasvári, "Non ha mala palabra," 181–182.
99. The two proverbs are: "A message that arrives late makes many people impatient" (712c) and "the man who is prepared never grieves so much" (712d).
100. Endrina and Melón's onomastic names, among other things, do serve, though, as a textual memory of the Andalusi poetic tradition of describing lovers as ripe fruit such as pomegranates and melons. John Dagenais offers evidence that Endrina's name may be a euphemism for *mora*. See "Mulberries, Sloe Berries," 398. Louise Vasvári, instead of reading Melón as a fruit, thinks it designates him as a type of weasel or badger, "Vegetal-Genital Onomastics," 9. David Hook, however, favors the vegetal associations of Melón. See "More Melons for Doña Endrina," 196. For a survey of critical opinions and significance on the names in the Endrina episode before 1993, see Vasvári, "Vegetal-Genital Onomastics," 6–8.
101. See Morreale, "La fábula en la Edad Media," 209–238, for a detailed discussion of the mostly scholastic origins of the fables and *exempla* used in the *LBA*.
102. Jayne, "Tales Told by Women," examines the exchange of *exempla* between beloved and go-between in the *LBA*.
103. Gybbon-Monypenny estimates that in the first *lacuna* (between stanzas 765 and 766) some twenty-five lines are missing and in the second *lacuna* (between 781 and 782) some thirty-two stanzas have been lost. Gybbon-Monypenny, *LBA*, 265, 268.
104. Ibid., 289.
105. Ibid., 292. Richard Burkard suggests that Juan Ruiz concludes the episode with the marriage of Endrina and Melón in an attempt to neutralize the immoral seduction of the Ovidian material and make it more palatable for a contemporary clerical audience. See "Courtly Love and Hideous Love," 29.
106. The episode of Endrina and Melón, though full of *exempla* and proverbs, is notably lacking in poetry. Juan Ruiz consciously portrays Endrina and Trotaconventos as masters of sapiential literary forms, but, in contrast to the three previous successful seductions, does not mention the lover's use of poetry. The courtly erotic has been displaced in this episode by the prose of sapiential wisdom literature.
107. This is especially true in the thirteenth-century *Milagros de Nuestra Señora*, in which Gonzalo de Berceo portrays Jews as cruel and bestial to members of their own community (Miracle 16) and who contrive to bring down the Castilian Christian community (Miracle 18).
108. Márquez Villanueva and Monroe, "Nuevos arabismos," 202–207.

109. Many critics, including Deyermond and Gybbon-Monypenny, have read the archpriest's erotic adventures in the Sierras as parodies of the traditional *pastourelle*. Deyermond, "Some Aspects of Parody," 62–64; Gybbon-Monypenny, 305, nn950–2042.
110. Willis translates *probar* as "to prove," whereas I favor and have included in this translation the meaning "to try."
111. Bienvenido Morros analyzes the description of the serranas as an inversion of formulaic *descriptio puellae* in medieval European Latin works. "La comedia elegiaca," 113–117.
112. As discussed within the Arabo- and Judeo-Iberian poetic tradition the poem was identified with jewelry, and the act of composing poetry described as stringing pearls or other jewels into necklaces and bracelets. In this context Juan Ruiz's admission that he is unfamiliar with the type of jewelry used in the Sierra could be a further underscoring of the *pastourelle* as a foreign type of poetic composition.
113. On thirteenth- and fourteenth-century chronicles, see Linehan, *History and the Historians*, 352–419, and Hillgarth, "Spanish Historiography and Iberian Reality," 28.
114. The first extant *serranillas* in Castilian, those of the Marqués de Santillana, postdate the *LBA* by some hundred years.
115. Other literary precedents to the randy nuns of the Carnal and Cuaresma episode include chapter eight of Andreas Capellanus, *Art of Courtly Love*, 142–144, and several French medieval poems. See Lecoy, *Recherches*, 266. Linehan, *The Ladies of Zamora*, provides ample evidence of sexually active nuns in thirteenth-century Iberia.
116. For a detailed study of the medicinal foods and aphrodisiacs (and their Arab origins) attributed to nuns by Trotaconventos, see Pérez Vidal, "Las golosinas de las monjas en el *Libro de buen amor*," 473–478.
117. See Oliver Asín, "Historia y prehistoria del castellano *alaroza*," 389–421 and Willis, introduction to the *Libro de buen amor*, xxix–xxx.
118. Jayne, "Tales Told by Women," 49–55, states that the exchange of *exempla* between beloved and go-between (in both the episode of Endrina and Garoza) illustrates the threat of women's speech, and implicitly their sexuality. Morros, "El episodio de doña Garoza," 417–449, focuses on each woman's agenda and on the origins of the specific *exempla* used in the debate.
119. The *fuero*, or privileges and laws granted to a region, town, or person, date to the early Middle Ages and characterize medieval Iberian society. *Diccionario de la Real Academia Española*, 20th ed., s.v. "Fuero." Heather Ecker includes the *fuero* as one of the most important practices exploited by Castilians in the administration of newly acquired Muslim cities, see "How to Administer a Conquered City," 47.
120. Dunn, "De las figures del arçipreste," 79–93; Hutcheson, "Garoza's Gaze," 261–288.
121. Hutcheson's interpretation explains the inconsistencies and contradictions in the archpriest's physical description, which would make more sense in

the context of the penis than in the description of a man. Hutcheson's assertion is further substantiated by the existence of a similar tale in the Arabic tradition. The ninth-century Baghdadi, al-Jāhiz, tells of a go-between who convinces the beloved to take the lover who has employed her as a husband after describing the enormous size of his penis. See al-Jāhiz, "Pleasures of Girls and Boys," 226. Bienvenido Morros explains the inconsistencies as purposely designed to confuse Garoza about the archpriest's temperament. "El episodio de doña Garoza," 451.
122. Louise Mirrer briefly mentions the *mora* as one of the others represented in the *LBA*, "The Widow and the Text," 120.
123. For a summary of these opinions see Montaner Frutos, "Las *señales non çiertas*," 143–157. Also discussed earlier in this chapter.
124. González Palencia's four-volume study of the archival material of the Mozarabs of Toledo, *Los mozárabes de Toledo en los siglos XII y XIII*, is the best source for original documents. Also see López Gómez, "The Mozarabs," 171–175. See also the section on cultural context earlier in this chapter.
125. The go-between is revived in the *Celestina* (1499). However, instead of being the celebration of Andalusi erotics as we find in the *LBA*, in the *Celestina*, Fernando de Rojas depicts the go-between with the mistrust characteristic of the Judeo-Iberian maqāmāt of Ibn Shabbetai and al-Harīzī.

Conclusion

1. Brague, *Eccentric Culture*, 27.
2. See Costa Fontes, *The Art of Subversion*.
3. González Echevarría, however, does take up the *Celestina* and her Latin American brood in *Celestina's Brood*.

BIBLIOGRAPHY

Ibn 'Abd al-Hakam, 'Abd Allāh. *Futūh Misr.* "Narrative of the Conquest of al-Andalus," trans. David A. Cohen. In *Medieval Iberia: Readings from Christian, Muslim, and Jewish Sources,* ed. Olivia Remie Constable, 32–36. Philadelphia: University of Pennsylvania Press, 1997.

Abrahams, Israel. *Hebrew Ethical Wills.* 1954. Reprint, Philadelphia: Jewish Publication Society of America, 1976.

Albarracín Navarro, Joaquina. "El vestido y adorno hispanoárabes en el *Libro de buen amor.*" In Criado de Val, *Arcipreste de Hita,* 488–494.

Alfonso, Esperanza. "The Uses of Exile in Poetic Discourse: Some Examples from Medieval Hebrew Literature." In *Renewing the Past, Reconfiguring Jewish Culture: From al-Andalus to the Haskalah,* ed. Ross Brann and Adam Sutcliffe, 31–49. Philadelphia: University of Pennsylvania Press, 2004.

Allen, Peter L. *The Art of Love: Amatory Fiction from Ovid to the* Romance of the Rose. Pennsylvania: University of Pennsylvania Press, 1992.

Alonso, Dámaso. "La bella de Juan Ruiz, toda problemas." In *De los siglos oscuros al de oro: Notas y artículos a través de 700 años de letras españolas,* 86–99. Madrid: Gredos, 1958.

Anidjar, Gil. *"Our Place in al-Andalus:" Kabbalah, Philosophy, Literature in Arab Jewish Letters.* Stanford: Stanford University Press, 2002.

Appadurai, Arjun. *Modernity at Large: Cultural Dimensions of Globalization.* Minneapolis: University of Minnesota Press, 1996.

Arberry, A.J., trans. *The Ring of the Dove: A Treatise on the Art and Practice of Arab Love.* London: Luzac Oriental, 1994.

Asín Palacios. Miguel. *Abenházam de Córdoba y su historia crítica de las ideas religiosas.* 5 vols. Madrid: Real Academia de la Historia, 1927–1932. Reprint, Madrid: Turner, 1984.

Assis, Yom Tov. "Sexual Behaviour in Mediaeval Hispano-Jewish Society." In *Jewish History: Essays in Honour of Chimen Abramsky,* 25–59. London: Peter Halban, 1988.

Baer, Yitzhak. *A History of the Jews in Christian Spain.* Vol. 1: *From the Age of Reconquest to the Fourteenth Century,* trans. Louis Schoffman. Philadelphia: Jewish Publication Society of America, 1961.

Bakhtin, Mikhail. *Rabelais and His World,* trans. Helene Iswolsky. Bloomington: Indiana University Press, 1984.

Baldwin, John W. *The Language of Sex: Five Voices from Northern France around 1200*. Chicago: University of Chicago Press, 1994.
Barton, Simon. *A History of Spain*. New York: Palgrave, 2003.
Bayo, Juan Carlos. "La versificación del Arcipreste, toda problemas." In Heusch, El libro de buen amor de Juan Ruiz, 191–216.
Beeston, A.F.L. "Introduction." *The Epistle on Singing-Girls of Jāhiz*, by al-Jāhiz. Approaches to Arabic Literature 2. England: Aris and Phillips, 1980.
Beit-Arié, Malachi. "Collection of Cabbalistic Works. Parma 2784." In *Hebrew Manuscripts in the Biblioteca Palatina in Parma*, ed. Benjamin Richler, palaeographical and codicological descriptions by Malachi Beit-Arié, 314–316. Jerusalem: Jewish National and University Library, 2001.

———. *Supplement of Addenda and Corrigenda to Vol. 1 (A. Neubauer's Catalogue of the Hebrew Manuscripts in the Bodleian Library)*. Oxford: Oxford University Press, 1994.

Berceo, Gonzalo. *Milagros de Nuestra Señora*. Madrid: Cátedra, 1988.

———. *Vida de Santo Domingo*, ed. Teresa Labarta de Chaves. Madrid: Castalia, 1987.

Bhabha, Homi. *The Location of Culture*. London: Routledge, 1994.
Biale, David. *Eros and the Jews from Biblical Israel to Contemporary America*. Berkeley: University California Press, 1997.
Biddick, Kathleen. "Translating the Foreskin." In *Queering the Middle Ages*, ed. Glenn Burger and Steven F. Kruger, 193–212. Medieval Cultures 27. Minneapolis: University of Minnesota, 2001.
Blau, Joseph and Joseph Yahalom. "Poetic Flowers and Beautiful Stories: Early Versions of Passages of al-Harīzī's *Tahkemoni*" (in Hebrew). *Pe'amim* 96 (2003): 5–20.

———. *The Wanderings of Judah al-Harīzī: Five Accounts of His Travels* (in Hebrew). Jerusalem, 2002.

Boswell, John. *Christianity, Social Tolerance, and Homosexuality: Gay People in Western Europe from the Beginning of the Christian Era to the Fourteenth Century*. Chicago: University of Chicago Press, 1980.
Bouhdiba, Abdelwahab. *Sexuality in Islam*. London: Routledge and Kegan Paul, 1985.
Brague, Rémi. *Eccentric Culture: A Theory of Western Civilization*, trans. Samuel Lester. South Bend: St. Augustine's Press, 2002.
Brann, Ross. *The Compunctious Poet: Cultural Ambiguity and Hebrew Poetry in Muslim Spain*. Baltimore: Johns Hopkins University Press, 1991.

———. *Power in the Potrayal: Representations of Jews and Muslims in Eleventh- and Twelfth-Century Islamic Spain*. Princeton, NJ: Princeton University Press, 2002.

Brown, Catherine. "In the Middle." *Journal of Medieval and Early Modern Studies* 30, no. 3 (2002): 547–574.
Brownlee, Marina Scordilis. "Genre as Meaning in the *Libro de buen amor*." In *Poetics of Love in the Middle Ages: Texts and Contexts*, ed. Moshe Lazar and Norris J. Lacy, 53–65. Fairfax, VA: George Mason University Press, 1989.

———. *The Status of the Reading Subject in the* Libro de buen amor. Chapel Hill: University North Carolina Press, 1985.

———."Permutations of the Narrator-Protagonist: The *Serrana* Episodes of the *Libro de buen amor* in Light of the Doña Endrina Sequence." *Romance Notes* 22, no. 1 (1981): 98–101.

Brundage, James A. *Law, Sex, and Christian Society in Medieval Europe.* Chicago: University of Chicago Press, 1987.

Burkard, Richard. *The Archipriest of Hita and the Imitators of Ovid: A Study in the Ovidian Background of the* Libro de buen amor. Newark, DE: Juan de la Cuesta, 1999.

———. "Courtly Love and Hideous Love: Gentility Followed by Rape in the *Libro de buen amor.*" *Journal of the Association for the Interdisciplinary Study of the Arts* 1–2 (1996): 21–31.

Burnett, Charles. "The Translating Activity in Medieval Spain." In Jayyusi, *Legacy of Muslim Spain*, 2: 1036–1058.

Bury, Richard. *The Love of Books: The Philobiblon of Richard de Bury.* Creation of machine-readable version, Charles Keller, University of Virginia. Charlottesville, VA: University of Virginia Library, 1999. http://etext.lib.virginia.edu/modeng/modengB.browse.html (accessed July 9, 2006).

Cadden, Joan. *Meanings of Sex Differences in the Middle Ages: Medicine, Science, and Culture.* Cambridge: Cambridge University Press, 1993.

Calila e Dimna, ed. J.M. Cacho Blecua and María Jesús Lacarra. Madrid: Castalia, 1984.

Cano Ballesta, Juan. "¿Pretende casarse la serrana de Tablada?" *La Corónica* 23 (1994–1995): 3–11.

Capellanus, Andreas. *The Art of Courtly Love*, trans. John Jay Parry. New York: Columbia University Press, 1960.

Carpenter, Dwayne E. *Alfonso X and the Jews: An Edition and Commentary on* Siete Partidas *7.24 "De los judíos."* Berkeley: University of California Press, 1986.

———. " 'Minorities in Medieval Spain' The Legal Status of Jews and Muslims in the *Siete Partidas.*" *Romance Quarterly* 33 (1986): 275–287.

Castro, Américo. *España en su historia: cristianos, moros y judíos.* 2nd. ed. Lectura de Filología. Barcelona: Editorial Crítica, 1983.

———. *La realidad histórica de España.* México: Porrúa, 1954.

Chazan, Robert. "Undermining the Jewish Sense of Future: Alfonso de Valladolid and the New Christian Missionizing." In Meyerson and English, *Christians, Muslims, and Jews*, 179–194.

Cohen, Gerson D. "Esau as Symbol in Early Medieval Thought." In *Jewish Medieval and Renaissance Studies*, ed. Alexander Altmann, 19–48. Studies and Texts 4. Cambridge, MA: Harvard University Press, 1967.

Cohen, Jeffrey Jerome. *Medieval Identity Machines.* Minneapolis: University of Minnesota, 2003.

———. "Introduction." *The Postcolonial Middle Ages.* 1–17. New York: Palgrave Macmillan, 2000.

Cole, Peter. "Introduction." *Selected Poems of Solomon Ibn Gabirol.* 3–37. Princeton, NJ: Princeton University Press, 2001.

Constable, Olivia Remie. "Medieval Spain and Mediterranean Slavery: The Medieval Slave Trade as an Aspect of Muslim-Christian Relations." In *Christendom and Its Discontents: Exclusion, Persecution, and Rebellion, 1000–1500*, ed. Scott L. Waugh and Peter D. Diehl, 264–284. Cambridge: Cambridge University Press, 1996.

Costa Fontes, Manuel. *The Art of Subversion in Inquisitorial Spain: Rojas and Delicado*. Indiana: Purdue University Press, 2004.

Criado de Val, Manuel, ed. *El Arcipreste de Hita El libro, el autor, la tierra, la época*. Actas del I Congreso Internacional sobre el Arcipreste de Hita. Madrid: SERESA, 1973.

———. "La tierra de Hita: El contorno mozárabe del *Libro de buen amor*." In Criado de Val, *Arcipreste de Hita*, 447–455.

Dagenais, John. *The Ethics of Reading in Manuscript Culture: Glossing the* Libro de buen amor. Princeton, NJ: Princeton, 1994.

———. "Mulberries, Sloe Berries; or, Was Doña Endrina a *Mora*?" *Modern Language Notes* 107 (1992): 396–405.

Daly, Saralyn R. trans. *The Book of True Love*, by Juan Ruiz, ed. Anthony N. Zahareas. University Park: Pennsylvania State University Press, 1978.

Darbord, Bernard and Luz Valle Videla. "Réflexion sure le technique de l'*exemplum* dans le *Libro de buen amor: fazañas, fablillas, parlillas, proverbios non mintrosos*." In Heusch, El libro de buen amor *de Juan Ruiz*, 99–113.

Davidson, Israel. *Parody in Jewish Literature*. New York: Columbia University Press, 1907.

Davis, P.J. "The Colonial Subject in Ovid's Exile Poetry." *American Journal of Philology* 123, no. 2 (2002): 257–273.

Decter, Jonathan P. "A Myrtle in the Forest: Landscape and Nostalgia in Andalusian Hebrew." *Prooftexts* 24, no. 2 (2004): 135–166.

De Looze, Laurence. "To Understand Perfectly Is to Misunderstand Completely: 'The Debate in Signs' in France, Iceland, Italy and Spain." *Comparative Literature* 50, no. 2 (1998): 136–154.

Deyermond, Alan. "Some Aspects of Parody in the *Libro de buen amor*." In Gybbon-Monypenny, Libro de buen amor *Studies*, 53–78.

———. "'Was It a Vision or a Waking Dream?': The Anomolous Don Amor and Doña Endrina Episodes Reconsidered." In Haywood and Vasvári, *Companion*, 107–122.

Deyermond, Alan and Roger Walker. "Further Vernacular Source for the *Libro de buen amor*." *Bulletin of Hispanic Studies* 46 (1969): 193–200.

Diamond, Eliezer. *Holy Men and Hunger Artists: Fasting and Asceticism in Rabbinic Culture*. Oxford: Oxford University Press, 2003.

Dishon, Judith. "A Critical Examination of the Literary Work of Judah Ibn Shabbetai" (in Hebrew). Ph.D. diss., Columbia University, 1968.

———. "A Critical Study of 'The Writ of Excommunication' by Judah Ibn Shabbetai" (in Hebrew). *Criticism and Interpretation* 4–5 (1974): 48–52.

———. "The Hebrew *Maqāma* in Spain." In *The Heritage of the Jews in Spain*. Proceedings of the First International Congress, July 1–4, 1991, Tel Aviv.

Ed. Aviva Doron, 65–75. Levinsky College of Education Publishing House, 1994.

———. "The Lost Historical Work of Jonah Ibn Shabbetai" (in Hebrew). *Zion* 36 (1971): 191–199.

———. "The Sources of the *Maqāma* '*Minhat Judah*' by Judah Ibn Shabbetai and Its Influence on the Sixth Maqāma of Judah al-Harīzī" (in Hebrew). *Otzar Yehudei Sefarad* 11–12 (1970): 57–73.

Doniger, Wendy. *The Bedtrick: Tales of Sex and Masquerade.* Chicago: University of Chicago Press, 2000.

Drory, Rina. "Al-Harīzī's *Maqāmat*: A Tricultural Literary Product?" In *The Medieval Translator* 4, ed. Roger Ellis and Ruth Evans, 66–85. Binghamton, NY: Medieval & Renaissance Texts and Studies, 1994.

———. "The *Maqāma*." In Menocal, *Literature of al-Andalus*, 190–210.

———. *Models and Contacts: Arabic Literature and Its Impact on Medieval Jewish Culture.* Leiden: Brill, 2000.

———. "'Words Beautifully Put' Hebrew versus Arabic in Tenth-Century Jewish Literature." In *Genizah Research After Ninety Years: The Case of Judaeo-Arabic*, ed. Joshua Blau and Stefan C. Reif, 53–66. Cambridge: Cambridge Univeristy Press, 1992.

Dunn, Peter N. "De las figures del arçipreste." In Gybbon-Monypenny, *Libro de buen amor Studies*, 79–93.

Ecker, Heather. "How to Administer a Conquered City in al-Andalus." In Robinson and Rouhi, *Under the Influence*, 45–65.

Eisenberg, Daniel. "Juan Ruiz's Heterosexual 'Good Love.'" In *Queer Iberia: Sexualities, Cultures, and Crossings from the Middle Ages to the Renaissance*, ed. Josiah Blackmore and Gregory S. Hutcheson, 250–276. Durham: Duke University Press, 1999.

Ekman, Erik. "'Leçión e muestra de metrificar e rrimar e de trobar': *Trobar* in the *Libro de buen amor*." *Hispanic Journal* 24, nos. 1–2 (2003): 9–21.

Encyclopaedia of Islam. CD-ROM Edition v. 1.0. Leiden: Koninklijke Brill NV, 1999.

Espalza, Mikel. "Mozarabs: An Emblematic Christian Minority in Islamic al-Andalus." In Jayyusi, *Legacy of Muslim Spain*, 149–170.

Fakhry, Majid. *Averroes (Ibn Rushd): His Life, Works and Influence.* Oxford, England: Oneworld, 2001.

Fernández y González, Francisco. "Influencias de las lenguas y letras orientales en la cultura de los pueblos de la península ibérica." *Discursos leídos ante la Real Academia Española.* Madrid: 1894.

Ferroul, Yves. "Abelard's Blissful Castration." In *Becoming Male in the Middle Ages*, ed. Jeffrey Jerome Cohen and Bonnie Wheeler, 129–149. New York: Garland, 1997.

Fishman, Talya. "A Medieval Parody of Misogyny: Judah ibn Shabbetai's *Minhat Yehudah sone hanashim*." *Prooftexts* 8 (1988): 89–111.

Flory, David A. "The Social Uses of Religious Literature: Challenging Authority in the Thirteenth-Century Marian Miracle Tale." *Essays in Medieval Studies* 13 (1996): 61–68.

Foucault, Michel. *The History of Sexuality*, trans. Robert Hurley. Vol. 1. New York: Vintage, 1980.

Fournival, Richard. *La biblionomia de Richard de Fournival du manuscrit 636 de la Bibliothèque de la Sorbonne*, ed. H.J. de Vleeschauwer and transcribed by Léopold Delisle. Pretoria: Mousaion, 1965.

Frank, Daniel, ed. *The Jews of Medieval Islam: Community, Society, and Identity. Proceedings of an International Conference Held by the Institute of Jewish Studies, University College London, 1992.* Études sur le judaisme medieval 16. New York: E.J. Brill, 1995.

Fuery, Patrick. *Theories of Desire*. Melbourne: Melbourne University Press, 1995.

García Gómez, Emilio. "Celestinas en la España musulmana." *Correo erudito* (1940): 190–191.

———, "Introduction." *El collar de la paloma: Tratado sobre el amor y los amantes* by Ibn Hazm de Córdoba. 1st ed. 1952. Madrid: Alianza, 1995.

Gerli, Michael. "Don Amor, the Devil, and the Devil's Brood: Love and the Seven Deadly Sins in the Libro de buen amor." *Revista de Estudios Hispánicos* 16, no. 1 (1982): 67–80.

———. "Recta voluntas est bonus amor: St Augustine and the Didactic Structure of the LBA." *Romance Philology* 35, no. 3 (1982): 500–508.

———. "The Greeks, the Romans, and the Ambiguity of Signs: *De doctrina christiana*, the Fall, and the Hermeneutics of the *Libro de buen amor*." *Bulletin of Spanish Studies* 79 (2002): 411–428.

———. "Vías de la interpretación: sendas, pasadizos, y callejones sin salida en la lectura del *Libro del Arcipreste*." In Heusch, El libro de buen amor *de Juan Ruiz*, 67–80.

Giffen, Lois Anita. "Ibn Hazm and the *Tawq al-hamāma*." In Jayyusi, *Legacy of Muslim Spain*, 420–442.

Girón-Negrón, Luis. "How the Go-Between Cut Her Nose: Two Ibero-Medieval Translations of a *Kalilah wa Dimnah* Story." In Robinson and Rouhi, *Under the Influence*, 231–259.

Glick, Thomas F. *Islamic and Christian Spain in the Early Middle Ages*. Princeton, NJ: Princeton University Press, 1979.

Goitein, S.D. *The Individual: Portrait of a Mediterranean Personality of the High Middle Ages as Reflected in the Cairo Geniza.* Vol. 5: *A Mediterranean Society. The Jewish Communities of the Arab World as Portrayed in the Documents of the Cairo Geniza.* Berkeley: University of California Press, 1988.

———. "The Sexual Mores of the Common People." In al-Sayyid-Marsot, *Society and the Sexes in Medieval Islam*, 43–61.

Gómez Redondo, Fernando. *Historia de la prosa medieval castellana*. 3 vols. Madrid: Cátedra, 1999.

———. *Poesía española. Edad Media: Juglaría, clerecía y romancero*. Vol. 1. Barcelona: Crítica, 1996.

González Echevarría, Roberto. *Celestina's Brood: Continuities of the Baroque in Spanish and Latin American Literature*. Duke: Duke University Press, 1993.

González Palencia, Ángel. *Los mozárabes de Toledo en los siglos XII y XIII*. 4 vols. Madrid, 1926–1930.

Gottheil, Richard and Stephen S. Wise, "Ibn Gabirol." In *The Jewish Encyclopedia*, 526–532. New York: Funk & Wagnalls, 1903–1906.

de la Granja, Fernando. *Maqāmas y risālas andaluzas*. Madrid: Instituto Hispano-Árabe de Cultura, 1976.
Guichard, Pierre. *Al-Andalus: Estructura antropológica de una sociedad islámica en Occidente*. Barcelona: Barral, 1976.
Gybbon-Monypenny, G.B. "Autobiography in the *Libro de buen amor* in Light of Some Literary Comparisons." *Bulletin of Hispanic Studies* 34 (1957): 63–78.
———, introd. and ed. *Libro de buen amor*, by Juan Ruiz. Madrid: Castalia, 1988.
———, ed. *Libro de buen amor Studies*. London: Tamesis, 1970.
———. "The Two Versions of the Libro de buen amor: The Extent and Nature of the Author's Revision." *Bulletin Hispanic Studies* 39 (1962): 205–221.
Haberman, A.M. *Shalosh maqamot 'al ha-nashim: mehen bi-genotan u-mehen be-shivhan, ve-nispah lahen ha-sha'ar ha-shishi mi-sefer* Tahkemoni. Jerusalem: Ben-Uri, 1970–1971.
Halevi, Judah. *Shire ha-Qodesh* (The Liturgical Poetry of Rabbi Yehuda HaLevi), ed. Dov Yarden. 4 vols. Jerusalem: D. Yarden, 1978–1982.
Halkin, A.S. "The Medieval Jewish Attitude toward Hebrew." In *Biblical and Other Studies*, ed. Alexander Altmann, 233–248. Cambridge, MA: Harvard University Press, 1963.
Hamilton, Michelle M. "The *Libro de buen amor*: Work of *Mudejarismo* or Augustinian Autobiography?" *eHumanista: Journal of Iberian Studies* 6 (2006): 19–33. http://www.spanport.ucsb.edu/projects/ehumanista/index.shtml.
———. "Rereading the Widow: A Possible Judeo-Iberian Model for the Pseudo-Ovidian *De Vetula* and the *Libro de Buen amor*." *Speculum* 82 (2007): 97–118.
———. "'Words sweeter than honey:' The Go-Between in Al-Saraqusti's 'Maqāma 9.'" *Journal of Arabic Literature* 34, nos. 1–2 (2003): 206–219.
Al-Harīzī, Judah ben Solomon. *The Tahkemoni*, ed. and trans. Victor E. Reichert, Jerusalem: Raphael Haim Cohen Press, 1965.
———. *The Tahkemoni*, ed. Y. Toporovsky. Tel Aviv: Harav Qoq, 1952.
Harvey, Steven. "The Meaning of Terms Designating Love in Judaeo-Arabic Thought and Some Remarks on the Judaeo-Arabic Interpretation of Maimonides." In *Judaeo-Arabic Studies: Proceedings of the Founding Conference of the Society for Judaeo-Arabic Studies*, ed. Norman Golb, 175–196. Amsterdam, The Netherlands: Harwood, 1997.
Haywood, Louise M. "Juan Ruiz and the *Libro de buen amor*: Contexts and Milieu." In Haywood and Vasvári, *Companion*, 21–38.
Haywood, Louise M. and Louise O. Vasvári, eds. *A Companion to the* Libro de buen amor. Woodbridge, Suffolk: Tamesis, 2004.
Heath, Peter. "Knowledge." In Menocal, *Literature of Al-Andalus*, 96–125.
Hernández, Francisco J. "Juan Ruiz y otros arciprestes, de Hita y aledaños." *La Corónica* 16, no. 2 (1987–1988): 1–31.
———. "The Venerable Juan Ruiz, Archpriest of Hita." *La Corónica* 13 (1984): 10–22.
Heusch, Carlos, ed. *El libro de buen amor de Juan Ruiz, Archiprêtre de Hita*. Paris: Ellipses, 2005.
Hexter, Ralph. "Ovid's Body." In *Constructions of the Classical Body*, ed. James I. Porter, 327–328. Michigan: University of Michigan Press, 1999.

Hexter, Ralph. *Ovid and Medieval Schooling: Studies in Medieval School Commentaries on Ovid's Ars Amatoria, Epistulae ex Ponto, and Epistulae Heroidum*. Munich: Bei-der Arbeo-Gesellschaft, 1986.

———. "Ovid in the Middle Ages: Exile, Mythographer, and Lover." In *Brill's Companion to Ovid*, 413–442. Leiden: E.J. Brill, 2002.

Hillgarth, J.N. *The Spanish Kingdoms 1250–1516*. Vol. 1. Oxford: Clarendon Press, 1976.

———. "Spanish Historiography and Iberian Reality," *History and Theory* 24 (1985): 23–43.

Hook, David. "More Melons for Doña Endrina: Problems of Onomastic Humour in the *Libro de buen amor*." In *Historicist Essays on Hispano-Medieval Narrative In Memory of Roger M. Walker*, ed. Barry Taylor and Geoffrey West, 185–200. London: Maney Publishing for the Modern Humanities Research Association, 2005.

Huss, Matti. "Critical Editions of *Minhat Yehuda, Ezrat Ha-nashim*, and *Ein Mishpat* with Prefaces, Variants, Sources and Annotations" (in Hebrew). 2 vols. PhD diss., Hebrew University, 1991.

Hutcheson, Gregory S. "Garoza's Gaze: Female Sexual Agency in the *Libro de buen amor*." In Robinson and Rouhi, *Under the Influence*, 261–288.

———. "The Sodomitic Moor: Queerness in the Narrative of Reconquista." In *Queering the Middle Ages*, ed. Glenn Burger and Steven F. Kruger, 99–121. Medieval Cultures 27. Minneapolis: University of Minnesota, 2001.

Ibn Adret, Solomon. "The Ban of Solomon Ben Adret." In *The Jew in the Medieval World. A Source Book: 315–1791*, ed and trans. Jacob R. Marcus, 189–192. New York: Atheneum, 1981.

Ibn Buluggīn, 'Abd Allāh. *The Tibyān: Memoirs of 'Abd Allāh ibn Buluggīn, Last Zīrid Amīr of Granada*, trans. Amin T. Tibi. Leiden: E.J. Brill, 1986.

Ibn Ezra, Moses. "Fire Whose Flame No Man Hath Kindled." In *Selected Poems of Moses ibn Ezra*, trans. Solomon Solis-Cohen, 16–22. Philadelphia: Jewish Publication Society of America, 1934.

———. *Kitāb al-Muhādara wal-Mudākara*, ed. Montserrat Abumalham Mas. 2 vols. Madrid: Consejo Superior de Investigaciones Científicas, 1985.

———. "The Poem of Two Exiles." In *Shire ha-Hol*, ed. Hayyim Brody. 1: 24–27. Berlin: Schoken, 1934.

———. *Sefer ha-Anaq*. Hebrew translation of *Kitāb Zahr al-Riyād*. In *Shire ha-Hol*, ed. Hayyim Brody. Berlin: Schoken, 1934. 1: 297–404.

Ibn Gabirol, Solomon. *Poesía Secular*, ed. and trans. Elena Romero. Madrid: Clásicos Alfaguara, 1978.

———. *Shire ha-Hol* (in Hebrew), ed. Heinrich Brody and Jayyim Schirmann. Jerusalem: Shocken, 1974.

———. *Shire ha-Qodesh*, ed. Dov Yarden. Jerusalem, 1973.

Ibn Hazm al-Andalusī, 'Alī ibn Ahmad. *A Book Containing the* Risāla *Known as The Dove's Neck Ring about Love and Lovers*, ed. and trans. A.R. Nykl. Paris: Librarie Orientalise Paul Geuthner, 1931.

———. *Tawq al-hamāma* (The Dove's Neck Ring), ed. Dr. at-Tāhir Ahmad Makkī. Cairo: Dār al-m'ārif bī Misr, 1975.

———. *El Collar de la paloma: Tratado sobre el amor y los amantes de Ibn Hazm de Córdoba*, trans. Emilio García Gómez, prologue José Ortega y Gasset. Madrid: Sociedad de Estudios y Publicaciones, 1952.

———. *The Ring of the Dove: A Treatise on the Art and Practice of Arab Love*, trans. A.J. Arberry. London: Luzac Oriental, 1994.

Ibn Paqūdā, Bahyā ben Joseph. *The Book of Direction to the Duties of the Heart*, ed. and trans. Menahem Mansoor. Routeledge & Kegan Paul, 1973. Reprint, Oxford: Littman Library of Jewish Civilization, 2004.

Ibn al-Qūtiyya. *Kitāb Tarīkh Iftitāh al-Andalus*. Excerpts translated by Bernard Lewis in *Islam from the Prophet Muhammad to the Capture of Constantinople*, 120–123. Vol. 1. New York: Walker and Company, 1974.

Ibn Shabbetai, Judah. *Minhat Yehuda, Ezrat Ha-Nashim*. In Huss, "Critical Editions of *Minhat Yehuda*," 1: 1–35.

Ibn Shuhaid al-Ashja'ī, Abū 'Amir. *Risālat al-tawābi' wa l-zawābi': The Treatise of Familiar Spirits and Demons by Abū 'Amir ibn Shuhaid al-Ashja'ī, al-Andalusī*, ed. James T. Monroe. Publications in Near Eastern Studies 15. Berkeley: University California Press, 1971.

Ibn al-Tabbān, Levi. *Shire Levi al-Tabbān*, ed. Dan Pagis. Jerusalem: Israel Academy of Sciences and Humanities, 1968.

Al-Jāhiz, Abū 'Uthmān 'Amr ibn Bahr. *The Epistle on Singing-Girls of Jāhiz*, trans. A.F.L. Beeston. Approaches to Arabic Literature 2. England: Aris and Phillips, 1980.

———. "The Pleasures of Girls and Boys Compared." In *Sobriety and Mirth: A Selection of the Shorter Writings of al-Jāhiz*, trans. and ed. Jim Colville, 202–230. London: Kegan Paul, 2002.

Jayne, Cynthia Powell. "Tales Told by Women in the *Libro de buen amor*." *Tennessee Philological Bulletin* 36 (1999): 49–55.

Jayyusi, Salma Khadra, ed. *The Legacy of Muslim Spain*. 2 vols. Leiden: Brill, 1994.

Kayser, Wolfgang J. *The Grotesque in Art and Literature*, trans. Ulrich Weisstein. Gloucester, MA: Peter Smith, 1968.

Kelly, Henry Ansgar. *Canon Law and the Archpriest of Hita*. Medieval and Renaissance Text and Studies 27. Binghamton, NY: Medieval and Renaissance Texts and Studies, 1984.

———. "A Juan Ruiz Directory 130–1382." *Mester* 42, no. 2 (1988): 69–93.

———. "Juan Ruiz and Archpriests: Novel Reports." *La Corónica* 16, no. 2 (1987–1988): 32–54.

Kennedy, Hugh. *Muslim Spain and Portugal: A Political History of al-Andalus*. New York: Longman, 1996.

Klopsch, Paul. *Pseudo-Ovidius de Vetula*. Mittelateinische Studien und Texte. Leiden: E.J. Brill, 1967.

Lacan, Jacques. *The Seminar of Jacques Lacan, Book VII: The Ethics of Psychoanalysis*, trans. Dennis Porter. New York: Norton, 1992.

Lacarra, María Jesús. *Pedro Alfonso*. Saragossa: Diputación General de Aragón, 1991.

Lavi, Abraham. "A Comparative Study of al-Harīrī's *Maqāmat* and Their Hebrew Translation by al-Harīzī." Ph.D. diss., University of Michigan, 1979.

Lavin, Audrey A P. "Judah Al-Harīzī: La conexión judío-árabe inesperada." *Romance Notes* 39 (1998): 9–14.

Lawrance, Jeremy. "*Libro de buen amor*: From Script to Print." In Haywood and Vasvári, *Companion*, 39–68.

Lazaroff, Allan. "Bahyā's Asceticism against Its Rabbinic and Islamic Background," *Journal of Jewish Studies* 21 (1970): 11–38.

Lecoy, Félix. *Recherches sur le* Libro de Buen Amor *de Juan Ruiz*. 1938. Reprinted with prologue by Alan Deyermond. Great Britain: Gregg International, 1974.

Levi-Provençal, Évariste. *España musulmana hasta la caída del califato de Córdoba (711–1031 de J.C.)*. Historia de España 5, ed. Ramón Menéndez Pidal. Madrid: Espasa-Calpe, 1957.

Lewis, Bernard. *Islam from the Prophet Muhammad to the Capture of Constantinople*. 2 vols. Oxford: Oxford University Press, 1974.

Libro de Alexandre, ed. Jesús Cañas. Madrid: Cátedra, 1988.

Lida de Malkiel, María Rosa. "Nuevas notas para la interpretación del *Libro de buen amor*." In *Estudios de literatura espaōla y comparada*. Buenos Aires: Editorial Universitaria de Buenos Aires, 1966.

———. *Two Spanish Masterpieces: The* Book of Good Love *and the* Celestina. Urbana: University Illinois Press, 1961.

Linehan, Peter. *History and the Historians of Medieval Spain*. Oxford: Clarendon, 1993.

Linehan, Peter. *The Ladies of Zamora*. University Park: Pennsylvania State University Press, 1992.

Liu, Benjamin M. and James T. Monroe. *Ten Hispano-Arabic Strophic Songs in the Modern Oral Tradition Music and Texts*. University of California Publications in Modern Philology, 125. Berkeley: University California Press, 1989.

Lobel, Diane. *A Sufi-Jewish Dialogue: Philosophy and Mysticism in Bahyā ibn Paqūdā's Duties of the Heart*. Philadelphia: University of Pennyslvania, 2007.

López Gómez, Margarita. "The Mozarabs: Worthy Bearers of Islamic Culture." In Jayyusi, *Legacy of Muslim Spain*, 171–175.

Maimonides. "Translation of an Epistle Addressed by R. Moses Maimonides to R. Samuel ibn Tibbon," trans. H.G. Adler. In *Miscellany of Hebrew Literature*, 1872. 1: 219–228. Reprint, Westport, CT: Greenwood Press, 1975.

Makkī, Mahmoud. "The Political History of al-Andalus (92/711–897/1492)." In Jayyusi, *Legacy of Muslim Spain*, 1: 3–87.

Mansoor, Menahem. "Introduction." *The Book of Direction to the Duties of the Heart* by Bahyā ben Joseph ibn Paqūdā. Routeledge & Kegan Paul, 1973. Reprint, Littman Library of Jewish Civilization. Oxford, 2004.

Manzalaoui, Mahmoud, A. "'I follow the religion of love': The Erotic Surrogate in the Arabic Tradition." In *Poetics of Love in the Middle Ages. Texts and Contexts*, ed. Moshe Lazar and Norris J. Lacy, 119–136. Virginia: George Mason University Press, 1989.

Marcus, Jacob R., ed. *The Jew in the Medieval World. A Source Book: 315–1791*. New York: Atheneum, 1981.

Márquez Villanueva, Francisco. "La nueva biografía de Juan Ruiz." In *Morada de la palabra: Homenaje a Luce y Mercedes López-Baralt*, ed. William Mejías López, 1: 33–51. Puerto Rico: Editorial de la Universidad de Puerto Rico, 2002.

———. "Nueva visión de la escuela de traductores toledanos," In *The Culture of Spanish Jewry*, ed. A. Doron, 123–145. Proceedings of the First International Congress. Tel Aviv, 1994.

———. *Orígenes y sociología del tema celestinesco*. Barcelona: Anthropos, 1993.

Márquez Villanueva, Francisco and James T. Monroe. "Nuevos arabismos en un pasaje del *Libro de Buen Amor* (941 ab)." In Criado de Val, *Arcipreste de Hita*, 202–207.

Martínez Ruiz, Juan "La tradición hispano-árabe en el *Libro de buen amor*." In Criado de Val, *Arcipreste de Hita*, 187–201.

McCoskey, Denise Eileen. "Diaspora in the Reading of Jewish History, Identity, and Difference." *Diaspora* 12, no. 3 (2003): 387–418.

Menéndez Pidal, Ramón. "Título que el Arcipreste de Hita dio al libro de sus poesías," In *Poesía árabe y poesía europea*, 139–145. Madrid: Espasa, 1963.

Menocal, María Rosa. *The Ornament of the World: How Muslims, Jews, and Christians Created a Culture of Tolerance in Medieval Spain*. Boston: Little Brown, 2002.

Menocal, María Rosa, Raymond P. Scheindlin, and Michael Sells, eds. *The Literature of al-Andalus*. Cambridge: Cambridge University Press, 2000.

Meyerson, Mark. D. "Introduction." *Christians, Muslims, and Jews*, eds. Meyerson and English, xi–xxi.

Meyerson, Mark. D. and Edward D. English, eds. *Christians, Muslims, and Jews in Medieval and Early Modern Spain: Interaction and Cultural Change*. Notre Dame Conferences in Medieval Studies 8. Notre Dame: University of Notre Dame Press, 2000.

Michael, Ian. "The Function of the Popular Tale in the *Libro de buen amor*." In Gybbon-Monypenny, Libro de buen amor *Studies*, 177–218.

Michalski, André Stanislaw. "Description in Medieval Spanish Poetry." Ph.D. diss., Princeton University, 1964.

———. "La parodia hagiográfica y el dualismo Eros-Thanatos en el *Libro de buen amor*." In Criado de Val, *Arcipreste de Hita*, 57–77.

Millás Vallicrosa, J.M. *Literatura hebraicoespañola*. Barcelona: Labor, 1968.

Miller, Elaine. *Jewish Multiglossia Hebrew, Arabic and Castilian in Medieval Spain*. Newark, Delaware: Juan de la Cuesta, 2000.

Mirrer, Louise. "The Widow and the Text: Ambivalent Signs in the *Libro de buen amor*." In *Women, Jews and Muslims in the Texts of Reconquest Castile*, 119–135. Ann Arbor, MI: University of Michigan Press, 1996.

Monroe, James T. *The Art of Badī' az-Zamān al-Hamadhānī as Picaresque Narrative*. Beirut: American University Beirut, 1983.

———. "Introduction." *Hispano-Arabic Poetry A Student Anthology*. Berkeley: University California Press, 1974.

———. "Introduction." *Risālat al-tawābi' wa l-zawābi': The Treatise of Familiar Spirits and Demons by Abū 'Amir ibn Shuhaid al-Ashja'ī, al-Andalusī*, by Abū 'Amir ibn Shuhaid al-Ashja'ī. 1–53. Near Eastern Studies 15. Berkeley: University California Press, 1971.

———, ed. and trans. *Al-Maqāmāt al-luzūmīyah*, by Abū l-Tāhir Muhammad ibn Yūsuf al-Tamīmī al-Saraqustī, al-Andalusī, ibn al-Ashtarkūwī. Leiden: Brill, 2001.

———. "Preliminary study." *Maqāmāt al-luzūmīyah*, by Abū l-Tāhir Muhammad ibn Yūsuf al-Tamīmī al-Saraqustī, al-Andalusī, ibn al-Ashtarkūwī, 1–110. Leiden: Brill, 2001.

Monroe, James T. "Al-Saraqustī ibn al-Ashtarkūwī: Andalusi Lexicographer, Poet, and Author of *Al- Maqāmāt al-luzūmīyah.*" *Journal of Arabic Literature* 28 (1997): 1–7.

Monroe, James T. *The Shu'ūbiyya in Al-Andalus: The Risāla of Ibn García and Five Refutations.* Near Eastern Studies 13. Berkeley: University of California Press, 1970.

Montaner Frutos, Alberto. "Las *señales non çiertas* de los arabismos de Juan Ruiz." In Heusch, *El libro de buen amor de Juan Ruiz*, 143–157.

Moran, Bruce T. *Distilling Knowledge: Alchemy, Chemistry, and the Scientific Revolution.* Cambridge, MA: Harvard University Press, 2005.

Moreh, Shmuel. *Live Theatre and Dramatic Literature in the Medieval Arab World.* New York: New York University Press, 1992.

Morreale, Margharita. "La fábula en la Edad Media: El *Libro* de Juan Ruiz como representante castellano del *Isopete.*" In "*Y así dijo la zorra.*" *La tradición fabulística en los pueblos del Mediterráneo*, ed. A. Pérez Jiménez and G. Cruz Andreotti, 209–238. Madrid: Ediciones Clásicas y Charta Antiqua, 2002.

Morros, Bienvenido. "La comedia elegiaca y el *Libro de buen amor.*" *Troianalexandrina* 3 (2003): 77–121.

Morros, Bienvenido. "El episodio de doña Garoza a través de sus fábulas (*Libro de buen amor*, 1332–1507)." *Nueva Revista de Filología Española.* 51, no. 2 (2003): 4127–4464.

Moxó, Salvador. "La promoción política y social de los 'letrados' en la Corte de Alfonso VI." *Hispania* (Madrid) 35 (1975): 5–29.

Al-Nafzawī, Sheikh Abū 'Abdullāh Muhammed ibn 'Umar. *The Glory of the Perfumed Garden. The Missing Flowers*, trans. H.E.J. London: Neville Spearman, 1975.

Navarro Peiro, Ángeles. "Moshe ibn Ezra: El poem de los dos exilios." *Sefarad* 61, no. 2 (2001): 381–393.

———. *Narrativa hispanohebrea (Siglos XII-XV).* Córdoba: Ediciones el Almendro, 1988.

Nemah, H. "Andalusian *Maqāmat.*" *Journal of Arabic Literature* 5 (1974): 83–92.

Neubauer, M.A. *Catalogue of the Hebrew Manuscripts in the Bodleian Library.* 1868. Reprint, Oxford: Clarendon, 1994.

Nirenberg, David. *Communities of Violence: Persecution of Minorities in the Middle Ages.* Princeton, NJ: Princeton University Press, 1996.

———. "Religious and Sexual Boundaries in the Medieval Crown of Aragon." In Meyerson and English, *Christians, Muslims, and Jews*, 141–160.

Nykl, A.R., trans. *A Book Containing the* Risāla *Known as* The Dove's Neck Ring *about Love and Lovers* by 'Alī ibn Ahmad Ibn Hazm al-Andalusī. Paris: Librarie Orientaliste Paul Geuthner, 1931.

———. *Hispano-Arabic Poetry and Its Relations with the Old Provençal Troubadours.* Baltimore: Hispanic Society of America, 1946.

O'Callaghan, Joseph. *The Cortes of Castile-León 1188–1350.* Philadelphia: University of Pennsylvania Press, 1989.

———. *Reconquest and Crusade in Medieval Spain.* Philadelphia: University of Pennsylvania, 2003.

Oliver Asín, Jaime. "Historia y prehistoria del castellano 'alaroza.'" *Boletín de la Real Academia Española* 81 (1950): 389–421.

Orduna, Germán. "La élite intellectual de la escuela catedralicia de Toledo y la literatura en época de Sancho IV." In *La literatura en la época de Sancho IV*, ed. Carlos Alvar and José Manuel Lucía Megías, 53–62. Actas del Congreso Internacional "La Literatura en la Epoca de Sancho IV," Alcalá de Henares, 21–24 de febrero de 1994. Alcalá, Spain: Universidad de Alcalá, 1996.
Ormsby, Eric. "Ibn Hazm." In Menocal, *Literature of al-Andalus*, 237–251.
Pagis, Dan. "Introduction." *Poesía secular* by Selomo ibn Gabirol, ed. Elena Romero, xvii–lxvi. Madrid: Alfaguara, 1978.
———. *Kitāb Al-Hidāya 'ilā Fara'id al-Qulūb*, ed. A.S. Yahuda. Leiden: E.J. Brill, 1912.
Pastor de Togneri, Reyna. *Del Islam al Cristianismo en las fronteras de dos formaciones económico-sociales: Toledo, siglos XI-XIII*. Barcelona: Ediciones Península, 1975.
Patai, Raphael. *The Jewish Alchemists: A History and Source Book*. Princeton, NJ: Princeton University Press, 1994.
Payne, Stanley G. *A History of Spain and Portugal*. Vol. 1. Madison, WI: University of Wisconsin Press, 1973.
Pérez Vidal, José. "Las golosinas de las monjas en el *Libro de buen amor*." In Criado de Val, *Arcipreste de Hita*, 473–478.
Phillips, Gail. *The Imagery of the "Libro de buen amor."* Spanish Series 9. Madison, WI: Hispanic Seminary of Medieval Studies, 1983.
Pick, Lucy K. *Conflict and Coexistence: Archbishop Rodrigo and the Muslims and Jews of Medieval Spain*. Ann Arbor, MI: University of Michigan Press, 2004.
Rabin, C. "Hebrew and Arabic in Medieval Jewish Philosophy." In *Studies in Jewish Religious and Intellectual History*, eds. Siegfired Stein and Raphael Lowe, 235–245. Alabama: University of Alabama Press, 1979.
Ramírez Pimienta, Juan Carlos. "La aventura de doña Endrina y don Melón de la Uerta: El matrimonio de la viuda como control social." *Hispanic Journal* 19, no. 1 (1998): 169–181.
Rashi (Rabbi Shlomo Itzhaki). *The Torah: With Rashi's Commentary Translated, Annotated, and Elucidated*, by Rabbi Yisrael Isser Zvi Herczeg, in collaboration with Rabbi Yaakov Petroff et al. Saperstein Edition. Vols. 4–5. Brooklyn, NY: Mesorah Publications, 2003.
Ray, Jonathan. *The Sephardic Frontier: The Reconquista and the Jewish Community in Medieval Iberia*. Ithaca, NY: Cornell Univeristy Press, 2006.
Reichert, Victor E., trans. *The Tahkemoni*, by Judah al-Harīzī. Jerusalem: Raphael Haim Cohen Press, 1965.
Reilly, Bernard F. *The Medieval Spains*. 1993. Reprint, Cambridge Medieval Textbooks. Cambridge: Cambridge University Press, 2000.
Reynolds, Susan. "The Emergence of Professional Law in the Long Twelfth Century." *Law and History Review* 21, no. 2 (2003): 347–366. http://www.historycooperative.org/journals/lhr/21.2/forum_reynolds.html.
Rico, Francisco. "Sobre el origen de la autobiografía en el *Libro de buen amor*." *Anuario de estudios medievales* 4 (1967): 301–325.
Rincón Álvarez, Manuel. *Mozárabes y mozarabías*. Acta Salmanticensia. Estudios históricos y geográficos 123. Salamanca: Ediciones Universidad de Salamanca, 2003.

Rivera Recio, Juan Francisco. *La Iglesia de Toledo en el siglo XII (1086–1208)*. 2 vols. Roma: Iglesia Nacional Española, 1966–1976.
Robathan, Dorothy M. "Introduction." *The Pseudo-Ovidian De Vetula*. Amsterdam: Adolf M. Hakkert, 1968.
Robinson, Cynthia. *In Praise of Song: The Making of Courtly Culture in al-Andalus and Provence, 1005–1134 A.D.* Leiden: Brill, 2002.
Robinson, Cynthia and Leyla Rouhi, eds. *Under the Influence: Questioning the Comparative in Medieval Castile*. Leiden: Brill, 2005.
Romera Castillo, José. "Presuposiciones en los *Milagros de Nuestra Señora*." In Actas de las III Jornadas de Estudios Berceanos, ed. Claudio García Turzo, Emilio Alarcos Llorach, et al., 149–159. Logroño y Monasterio de Cañas 3–5 diciembre 1979. Logroño: Instituto de Estudios Riojanos, 1981.
Rosen, Tova. "On Tongues Being Bound and Let Loose: Women in Medieval Hebrew Literature." *Prooftexts* 8 (1988): 67–87.
———. "Sexual Politics in a Medieval Hebrew Marriage Debate." *Exemplaria* 12, no. 1 (2000): 157–184.
———. *Unveiling Eve: Reading Gender in Medieval Hebrew Literature*. Philadelphia: University of Pennsylvania Press, 2003.
Rosenblatt, Samuel. Introd. and trans. of *The Book of Beliefs and Opinions* by Saadia Gaon. Yale Judaica Series 1. New Haven, CT: Yale University Press, 1976.
Roth, Norman. "The Care and Feeding of Gazelles: Medieval Arabic and Hebrew Love Poetry." In *Poetics of Love in the Middle Ages. Texts and Contexts*, ed. Moshe Lazar and Norris J. Lacy, 96–118. Virginia: George Mason University Press, 1989.
———. "'Deal Gently with the Young Man': Love of Boys in Medieval Hebrew Poetry of Spain." *Speculum* 57, no. 1 (1982): 20–51.
———. *Jews, Visigoths and Muslims in Medieval Spain: Cooperation and Conflict*. Leiden: E.J. Brill, 1994.
———. "Polemic in Hebrew Religious Poetry of Medieval Spain." *Journal of Semitic Studies* no. 34 (1989): 153–177.
Rouhi, Leyla. *Mediation and Love: A Study of the Go-Between in Key Romance and Near Eastern Texts*. Leiden: Brill, 1999.
Roy, Louis. "Medieval Latin Scholasticism: Some Comparative Features." In *Scholasticism: Cross Cultural and Comparative Perspectives*, ed. José Ignacio Cabezón, 19–34. Albany, NY: State University of New York Press, 1998.
Rubiera Mata, María Jesús. *Literatura hispanoárabe*. Madrid: Editorial MAPFRE, 1992.
Rucquoi, Adeline y Bizzarri, Hugo O. "Los Espejos de Príncipes en Castilla: entre Oriente y Occidente." *Cuaderno histórico de España* 79, no. 1 (2005): 7–30.
Ruggles, D. Fairchild. "Mothers of a Hybrid Dynasty: Race, Geneaology, and Acculturation in al-Andalus." *Journal of Medieval and Early Modern Studies* 34, no. 1 (2004): 65–94.
Ruiz, Juan, Arcipreste de Hita. *Libro de buen amor*, ed. G. B. Gybbon-Monypenny. Madrid: Castalia, 1988.
———. *Libro de buen amor*, trans. and ed. Raymond S. Willis. Princeton: Princeton University Press, 1972.
Ruiz, Teófilo F. *From Heaven to Earth: The Reordering of Castilian Society, 1150–1350*. Princeton, NJ: Princeton University Press, 2004.

Russo, Mary. *The Female Grotesque: Risk, Excess, and Modernity.* New York: Routledge, 1994.

Sáez, Emilio and José Trenchs. "Juan Ruiz de Cisneros (1295/1296–1351/1352) autor del *Buen amor*." In Criado de Val, *Arcipreste de Hita*, 365–368.

Safran, Bezalel. "Bahyā ibn Paqūdā's Attitude toward the Courtier Class." In *Studies in Medieval Jewish History and Literature,* ed. Isadore Twersky, 154–196. Cambridge, MA: Harvard University Press, 1979.

Said, Edward W. *Orientalism.* New York: Vintage, 1979.

Sánchez Albornoz, Claudio. *España: Un enigma histórico.* 2 vols. Buenos Aires: Editorial Sudamericana, 1956.

Al-Saraqustī, Abū l-Tāhir Muhammad ibn Yūsuf al-Tamīmī ibn al-Ashtarkūwī. *Al-Maqāmāt al-luzūmīyah,* ed. Hasan al-Warāglī. Rabat: Matābi' Manshūrāt 'Ukaz, 1995.

———. *Al-Maqāmāt al-luzūmīyah,* trans. James T. Monroe. Leiden: Brill, 2001.

al-Sayyid-Marsot, Afaf Lutfi, ed. *Society and the Sexes in Medieval Islam.* Giorgio Levi Della Vida Conferences. Malibu, CA: Undena Publications, 1979.

Scales, Peter C. *The Fall of the Caliphate of Córdoba: Berbers and Andalusis in Conflict.* Ledien: Brill, 1994.

Scheindlin, Raymond P. *The Gazelle: Medieval Hebrew Poems on God, Israel, and the Soul.* Philadelphia: Jewish Publication Society, 1991.

———. "Merchants and Intellectuals, Rabbis and Poets." In *Cultures of the Jews: A New History,* ed. David Biale, 305–386. New York: Schoken, 2002.

———."The Misogynist." In *Rabbinic Fantasies: Imaginative Narratives from Classical Hebrew Literature,* ed. David Stern and Mark J. Mirsky, 275–294. Yale Judaica Series 29. New Haven: Yale University Press, 1990.

———. *Wine, Women and Death: Medieval Hebrew Poems on the Good Life.* Philadelphia: Jewish Publication Society, 1986.

Schippers, Arie. *Spanish Hebrew Poetry and the Arabic Literary Tradition: Arabic Themes in Hebrew Andalusian Poetry.* Leiden: Brill, 1994.

Schirmann, Hayyim. "The Ephebe in Medieval Hebrew Poetry." *Sefarad* 15 (1955): 55–68.

Schorsch, Jonathan. *Jews and Blacks in the Early Modern World.* New York: Cambridge University Press, 2004.

Segal, David Semha. "Analysis of the Introduction." In *The Book of Tahkemoni,* by Judah al-Harīzī. 417–427. Oregon: Littman, 2001.

———.trans. and ed. *The Book of Tahkemoni,* by Judah al-Harīzī. Oregon: Littman, 2001.

Seidenspinner-Núñez, Dayle. *The Allegory of Good Love: Parodic Perspectivism in the Libro de Buen Amor.* Berkeley: University California Press, 1981.

Sells, Michael. "Love." In Menocal, *Literature of al-Andalus,* 126–158.

Septimus, Bernard. *Hispano-Jewish Culture in Transition. The Career and Controversies of Ramah.* Cambridge, MA: Harvard University Press, 1982.

Serés, Guillermo. Prologue to *El Conde Lucanor,* by Juan Manuel, xxxiii–cx. Barcelona: Crítica, 1994.

———."The Misogynist," trans. Raymond Scheindlin. In Stern and Mirsky, *Rabbinic Fantasies,* 275–294.

Stamm, James R. "The *Loca demanda* of Juan Ruiz: The *Serrana* Sequence in the *Libro de buen amor*." *Journal of Hispanic Philology* 5, no. 3 (1981): 185–197.

Stroumsa, Guy. "Tertullian on Idolatry and the Limits of Tolerance." In *Tolerance and Intolerance in Early Judaism and Christianity*, ed. Graham N. Stanton and Guy G. Stroumsa, 173–184. Cambridge: Cambridge University Press, 1998.

Taylor, Barry. "*Exempla* and Proverbs." In Haywood and Vasvári, *Companion*, 83–104.

Thomas, E.C. Preface to *Philobiblon, The Love of Books* by Richard de Bury, ix–xvi. London: Chatto and Windus, 1909.

Tolan, John V. *Saracens: Islam in the Medieval European Imagination*. New York: Columbia University Press, 2002.

Toporovsky, Y., ed. *Tahkemoni* (in Hebrew), by Judah al-Harīzī. Tel Aviv: Harav Qoq, 1952.

Torres Delgado, Cristobál. *El antiguo reino nazarí de Granada (1232–1340)*. Granada: Ediciones Anel, 1974.

Valle Rodríguez, Carlos. Prologue to *Las asambleas de los sabios (Tahkemoni)*, by Judah al-Harīzī, 9–31. Murcia: Universidad de Murcia, 1988.

Vasvári, Louise O. "Festive Phallic Discourse in the *Libro del arcipreste*." *La Córonica* 22, no. 2 (1993–1994): 89–117.

———. "'Non ha mala palabra si non es a mal tenida:' The Perverted Proverb in the *Libro de buen amor*." In Robinson and Rouhi, *Under the Influence*, 173–198.

———. "Juan Ruiz, Arcipreste de Hita: Fictive Author and Onomastic Pun." *La Corónica* 15, no. 1 (1986–1987): 87–88.

———. "Why Is Doña Endrina a Widow? Traditional Culture and Textuality in the *Libro de buen amor*." In *Upon my Husband's Death: Widows in the Literature and Histories of Medieval Europe*, ed. Louise Mirrer, 259–287. Ann Arbor, MI: University of Michigan Press, 1992.

———. "Vegetal-Genital Onomastics in the *Libro de Buen Amor*." *Romance Philology* 42 (1988): 1–29.

Venuti, *The Scandals of Translation: Towards an Ethics of Difference*. London: Routeledge, 1998.

Vernet, Juan. *Lo que Europa debe al Islam de España*. Barcelona: El Acantilado, 1999.

Vinsauf, Geoffrey. *Poetria Nova*, trans. Ernest Gallo. The Hague: Mouton, 1971.

Wacks, David. *Framing Iberia: Maqāmāt and Frametale Narratives in Medieval Spain*. Leiden: Brill, 2007.

———. "The Performativity of ibn al-Muqaffa''s *Kalīla wa-Dimna* and *al-Maqāmāt al-luzūmiyya* of al-Saraqustī." *Journal of Arabic Literature* 34, nos. 1–2 (2003): 178–189.

Walsh, John K. "Gestures and Voices in the *LBA*." Photocopy, Department of Spanish and Portuguese, University of California, Berkeley.

———. "Juan Ruiz and the *Mester de clerezía*: Lost Context and Lost Parody in the *Libro de buen amor*." *Romance Philology*, 33 (1979–1980): 62–86.

Wasserstein, David. *The Rise and Fall of the Party Kings: Politics and Scoiety in Islamic Spain 1002–1086*. Princeton, NJ: Princeton University Press, 1985.

White, Peter. "Ovid and the Augustan Milieu." In *Brill's Companion to Ovid*, ed. Barbara Weiden Boyd, 1–25. Leiden: Brill, 2002.

Willis, Raymond S. "Introduction." *Libro de buen amor* by Juan Ruiz, Arcipreste de Hita. Princeton: Princeton University Press, 1972.

Wolfson, Elliot R. "The Body in the Text: A Kabbalistic Theory of Embodiment," *Jewish Quarterly Review* 95, no. 3 (2005): 479–500.

———. "Eunuchs Who Keep the Sabbath: Becoming Male and the Ascetic Ideal in Thirteenth-Century Jewish Myticism." In *Becoming Male in the Middle Ages*, ed. Jeffrey Jerome Cohen and Bonnie Wheeler, 151–185. New York: Garland, 1997.

Young, Douglas. *Rogues and Genres: Generic Transformation in the Spanish Picaresque and the Arabic* Maqāma. Newark, DE: Juan de la Cuesta, 2004.

———. "Preachers and Poets: The Popular Sermon in the Andalusi *Maqāma*." *Journal of Arabic Literature* 34, nos. 1–2 (2003): 190–205.

Zeitlin, S. "The Origin of the Term Edom for Rome and the Roman Church." *Jewish Quarterly Review* 60, no. 3 (1970): 262–263.

Zotenberg, H., ed. *Catalogues des Manuscrits Hébreux et Samaritains de la Bibliothèque Impériale*. Paris: Imprimerie impériale, 1866.

INDEX

'Abbasids, 4, 15, 20, 27, 37, 115,
    155–56
Abū Nūwās, 20
adab, 5–6, 18, 19, 29, 42, 52, 53, 57,
    60, 61, 64, 67, 77, 91, 137, 150,
    154
alcahueta, 104, 126, 133
    see also go-between; Trotaconventos
alchemy, 93, 94, 174
Alfonso VI, 35, 110, 111, 179, 180
Alfonso X, el Sabio, 105, 109, 110,
    112, 113–15, 133, 181, 182
Alfonso XI, 109, 115, 117, 118, 183,
    184
algebra, 101
allegory, 50, 54, 59, 70, 72, 74, 93,
    156, 167
Almoravids, 11, 33, 34–36, 49, 56,
    155, 159
'Amirids, 17–19, 21, 30, 152, 153
Amor, *see under* love
al-Andalus, 4–5, 9, 13, 16, 30, 36,
    48–50, 51, 86–87, 92, 102, 138,
    149–50, 153–55, 159
    ethnic make-up, 5, 7, 16–17, 19,
        162, 179
    nationalism, 10–11, 15, 21, 34, 155
    see also Almoravids; *fitna*; Iberia
al-*'aql*, 25, 58, 59, 60, 76, 165
    see also reason
'arabiyya, 19
Arabic language, 6, 13, 19–20, 28, 36,
    38, 50, 51, 53–54, 57, 73–77, 82,
    83, 91, 93, 94, 101, 102, 108–9,
    110, 111, 113, 134, 140, 144,
    171, 174, 179
    see also Hagar, Hebrew
Aristotle, 90, 95
    rational philosophy, 11, 96, 156,
        175, 181
    one-seed theory, 95, 174–75
asceticism, 59–60, 62, 63, 70, 71, 72,
    95, 99, 166, 167
    see also celibacy
assimilation, 8, 11, 50, 52, 80, 102,
    110, 111, 136, 166
astrology, 62, 101, 167

Baghdad, 5, 16, 20, 36, 40, 50, 150,
    151, 160
beauty, 22, 82, 97
    Andalusi ideal, 8, 11–12, 23, 38–40,
        54, 126, 156, 160–61, 186
    Judeo-Iberian ideal, 64, 65–67, 73,
        80–82, 169, 172
    in Western canon, 97–98, 126, 137,
        143, 176, 186
    see also Neoplatonism
Berbers, 5, 6, 19, 35, 36, 104, 154,
    159, 160
    see also Almoravids
Berceo, Gonzalo, 117, 119, 120, 144,
    185, 188
Bible, 53, 56, 72, 113, 170, 175
    Deuteronomy, 168, 175
    Ecclesiastes, 58–59, 70
    Numbers, 60–61, 66, 96, 164, 166,
        175

Bible—*continued*
 Psalms, 72, 121, 125
 Song of Songs, 64, 66, 168, 171, 172
 see also Edom; Esau; Jacob; Median; Sarah; Torah; Zimri
Calila et Dimna, 114, 115, 117, 183
Castile, 56, 104–5, 109, 110–12, 116, 118, 119, 120, 137–38
Castilian Church, 104, 107, 112, 113, 115–16, 132, 145, 182
Castilian nationalism, 109, 112, 114, 117, 119, 127, 146
Castro, Américo, 107–8, 150, 152, 153, 178, 186
La Celestina, 108, 148, 190
celibacy, 93, 95, 99, 100, 101, 166
 see also asceticism
cleric Christian, 7, 8, 13, 89, 95, 99, 100, 101, 102, 104, 106, 109, 117, 126, 127, 128, 138, 176, 177, 180, 182
convivencia, 150
 see also Castro, Américo
Cordoba, 2, 16–17, 21, 25–26, 29, 30, 36, 40, 43, 154, 157
courtiers and courts, 5–6, 7, 8, 103, 126, 147, 151
 Arabic terms for, 5, 20, 151
 Arabo-Andalusi, 5, 6, 10, 17–20, 22, 30, 35, 38, 39, 45, 64, 101, 150, 151, 154, 159, 160
 Judeo-Andalusi, 6, 11, 49, 50, 52–53, 58, 60, 66, 67, 69–70, 81, 92, 101, 152, 162, 165, 167
 ideal in Christian Spain, 114–18, 124, 125
 see also adab; Christian cleric
cuaderna vía, 119, 120, 185
 see also mester de clerecía

De Fournival, Richard, 92, 174
De Vetula, 12, 89–102, 132, 173, 174, 176, 177, 187, 188
Devil, 22, 83, 85, 95, 140, 172
 see also Satan
dhimma, 49, 162
diaspora, 12, 53, 58, 69, 75–76, 86, 87, 149, 151
 see also exile and exiles
Dove's Neck Ring, 10, 15–31, 33, 39, 40, 48, 107, 153, 156–58

East v. West, 2, 3, 51, 92, 106, 110, 138, 147
Edom, 9, 96, 175
 see also Median
Esau, 96, 175, 176
eunuch, 12, 94–97, 101, 102, 159, 166, 175
 see also spadon
exempla (sing. *exemplum*), 81, 91, 107, 114, 117, 118, 119, 120, 123–24, 125, 126–27, 128, 130–32, 140–42, 165, 185, 186, 188
exile and exiles, 2–3, 6–7, 14, 48–49, 56–59, 61–62, 70, 89, 92–93, 101, 148, 150, 162
 see also diaspora

al-Fārābī, 60, 172, 181
Fernando IV, 109, 115, 117, 118, 183, 184
fitna, 15–16, 17, 153
fuero, 141, 189

gazelle, 41, 42–43, 48, 64, 66, 80, 82, 83, 86, 87, 158, 168, 176
al-Ghazālī, 36, 181
gender, 9, 12, 61, 63, 67, 94–95, 102, 174–75, 177
go-between, 1–3, 6, 7–9, 28–29, 51, 55, 71, 90, 103, 105–6, 108, 126, 133–34, 137, 147–48, 161, 172, 190
 in Arabo-Andalusi literature, 10–11, 16–17, 23–27, 30, 41–46, 103, 130
 in Judeo-Iberian literature, 11–12, 51, 61–64, 67–68, 71, 72, 79, 80, 95, 130, 167

in medieval Latin literature, 12, 89, 91–92, 95, 97–102
nature of, 1, 7–9, 126
others in *Libro de buen amor*, 119–21, 123–25, 128, 133
spaces of, 2–4, 29, 100–101, 139, 145
Trotaconventos, 13, 104, 106, 107, 129–35, 138–46

Hagar, 73–76, 81, 83, 93
Halevi, Judah, 50, 170, 171, 175
Hamadhānī, Badi' al-Zamān, 37, 159–60, 161
see also hubb; 'ishq; love
al-Harīrī, Abū Muhammad, 37, 52, 53, 73–74, 160, 170
al-Harīzī, Judah, 6, 11–12, 49, 50, 51–54, 71–86, 92, 93, 101, 106, 136, 137, 152, 163, 170, 171
hawā, 22, 25, 41, 43, 58, 156, 165
Hebrew language, 6, 10, 12, 13, 49, 50, 51, 53, 57, 66, 71–80, 81, 83, 85, 91, 113, 163, 170, 171, 181
see also Arabic
hubb, 22, 25, 41
hybridity, 3, 8, 12–13, 19, 21, 49, 71, 92, 110, 112, 119, 128, 137, 139, 140, 143

Iberia, 1–8, 13–14, 34–35, 46, 48–49, 53, 58, 61, 101, 103, 147–49
Christian culture of, 51, 52, 87, 104, 109, 117, 179–80
ethnic make-up of, 3, 7, 104–6, 108, 110, 112, 119, 121, 128, 134, 143–44, 146, 150
see also al-Andalus; Castile
Ibn Bullugīn, 'Abd Allāh, 154, 159
Ibn Ezra, Moses, 6, 47–49, 55, 56–57, 64, 69, 76, 81, 85, 86, 87, 89, 92, 168, 171, 172
Ibn al-Fakhkhār, Abraham, 54, 69, 163, 164
Ibn Gabirol, Solomon, 50, 55, 57, 62, 72, 79, 92, 162, 165, 181
Ibn García, 6, 155

Ibn Hazm, 'Ali ibn Ahmad, 2, 10, 15–31, 107, 125, 152, 153, 154, 155–56, 157, 158
Ibn Paqūdā, Bahyā, 6, 50, 55, 57, 58–61, 62, 64, 70–71, 93, 101, 162, 164–65, 166, 167
Ibn Shabbetai, Judah, 11, 49, 50–51, 54–59, 61, 62, 65, 69, 70–71, 72, 86, 92, 163, 164, 166, 167, 170
Ibn Shuhaid, Abū 'Amir, 5, 19, 77, 156, 161
'ishq, 22–23

Jacob, 96
al-Jāhiz, 39, 155, 161, 190
jawāri (sing. *jāriya*), 26–29, 38–39, 157, 158
see also slaves

Kabbalah, 58, 96, 166
Kedar, see Hagar; Arabic language

Latin, 10, 12, 13, 89, 91, 92, 94, 96, 101, 102, 109, 111, 113, 174, 175, 181
Libro de buen amor, 13, 103–46, 152, 177–78, 185
Lida de Malkiel, María Rosa, 108, 178
love, 11, 15, 17, 20, 22–23, 24, 26, 28, 29–31, 41–43, 99, 105, 133, 143, 145, 156, 157, 158, 161, 185
god of, 125–28, 131, 138–39
types of, 22–23, 140, 157, 161, 165, 177
see also hawā, hubb

Maimonides, Moses, 6, 64, 96, 164, 170, 171
majlis, 20, 86, 151, 155
Al-Mansūr, 10, 18–19, 20, 21, 152, 153, 154, 155, 157
see also 'Amirids
Manuel, Don Juan, 118, 184
maqāmāt, 11, 31, 33, 37–46, 105, 107, 108–9, 114, 120, 127, 132, 135, 160, 178–79

maqāmāt—continued
  Arabo-Andalusi, 33–46, 52, 54, 71,
    108, 134, 152, 159
  Judeo-Iberian, 12, 49, 50–87, 99,
    102, 108, 134, 136, 137, 162,
    163, 170
Median and Medianites, 56, 61, 62,
  164
mester de clerecía, 106, 107, 119–20,
  135, 138, 144, 185
Midrash, 52, 53, 75, 96
Molina, María, *see molinismo*
molinismo, 112, 116–18, 119, 127, 182,
  183–84
monstrousness, 8–9, 11, 67–69, 79, 87,
  94–97, 98–101, 177
  literary examples, 67–68, 82–85,
    98–99, 100, 136–37, 161
  theories of, 9, 68
mora, 104, 105, 108, 121, 143–44
Mozarabs, 7, 104, 109, 110, 111–12,
  113, 121, 127, 143, 144, 151,
  179–80, 190
Muʿtazilites, 60, 158
muwalladūn, 5, 16

Neoplatonism, 22, 60, 71, 72, 96, 156,
  165, 166
nuns, 105, 138–140, 141, 143, 189

Ovid, 12, 89–91, 92, 99, 101, 102,
  125, 127, 129, 147, 173

Pamphilus de amore, 128–32, 187
pastourelle, 135–38, 189
Pérez Gudiel, Gonzalo, 115–16, 182
philosophy, 5, 36, 90, 91, 92, 93–94,
  101, 102, 156, 167, 169, 181
  see also Aristotle
poetry, 8, 114, 148
  in Andalusi culture, 5–6, 11, 20–21,
    25, 28, 30, 36, 37, 66, 77, 158,
    189
  in Judeo-Andalusi culture, 49–50,
    64–65, 66, 68, 71, 76–78, 80,
    81, 86, 165, 168, 169, 171–72,
    189
  in *Libro de buen amor*, 123–24,
    135–38, 185, 186
  as lies, 64, 79, 81, 85–86, 168
  in *maqāmāt*, 40, 41–45, 52, 65–67,
    68–69, 72, 74, 82–86, 114
  *see also qasīda; mester de clerecía;
    pastourelle; zajal*
Provence, 11, 52, 55, 90, 92, 163, 164

qasīda, 21, 36, 120
qiyān (sing. *qayna*), 26–29, 65, 67, 142
  see also slaves

Rashi, (Solomon Itzhak), 96, 175
reason, 22, 25, 58, 60, 76, 165
Reconquest, 4, 51, 105, 110, 112, 120,
  144, 179, 180
risāla, 21, 37, 155–56
Romance languages (incl. Castilian), 3,
  4, 13, 53, 75, 87, 103, 109, 113,
  121, 127, 146, 181, 185
Ruiz, Juan, 7, 13, 102, 104, 106–9,
  118, 119–20, 124, 125, 126–29,
  133, 134, 135, 142, 147, 178

saqāliba, *see also* Slavs, 5, 19
sajʾ, 21, 33, 37, 74
Sancho IV, 109, 112, 113, 115,
  116–17, 124, 125, 182–83
Saragossa, 34, 35, 55, 57, 71, 163
  see also taifa kings
Sarah, 75–76
al-Saraqustī, Abū l-Tāhir Muhammad,
  11, 31–36, 50, 53, 80, 81, 86,
  152, 159
Satan, 79, 80, 85, 172
  see also Devil
scholasticism, 91, 101, 102, 104, 109,
  116, 119, 125, 128, 141, 146, 147
slaves, 11, 26–29, 38–39, 55, 64, 65,
  69, 77, 93, 95, 157–58, 159, 161,
  168, 170
  see also qiyān, jawāri

Slavs, 5, 19, 27, 35, 155, 159
  see also saqāliba
  spadon, 12, 94, 96–97, 99, 100, 101, 102, 175, 176
  see also eunuch

Tahkemoni
  literary figure, 56, 57–60, 61, 63, 67, 72, 95
  work of al-Harīzī, 53, 54, 71–87, 152, 163, 170
taifa kings (mulūk at-tawā'if), 6, 20, 30, 33, 34–35, 50, 81, 120, 151, 153, 154, 155, 157
  of Denia, 6, 35, 155
  of Saragossa, 11, 34–35, 57
  of Toledo, 35, 111, 180
Tawq al-hamāma, see Dove's Neck Ring
Tevel, 80, 172
  see also monstrousness
al-Tīfāshī, 28, 39, 65, 158, 186
Toledo, 110, 111, 113, 115, 118, 179, 180, 181
  Cathedral School, 116, 128, 183
  School of Translators, 113–14, 182
Torah, 60, 62, 66, 70, 101, 105, 108, 144, 166
  see also Bible
Tosafists, 11, 166
translation, 7, 12, 36, 52, 73–74, 90–91, 92, 94, 101, 102, 106, 113–15, 128, 167, 170, 175, 181–82
  see also Toledo
Trotoconventos, see go-between

Umayyads, 2, 15, 17–19, 20, 21, 30, 120, 149, 150, 152
  Abd al-Rahman II, 5, 21
  Abd al-Rahman III, 21, 50, 151
  al-Hakam II, 21, 154
  al-Hishām II, 18–19

widow, 107, 130, 131, 187–88

zajal, 36, 106, 159, 185
Zimri, 60–61, 166–67
Ziryāb, 5, 20